A Book by G.R.

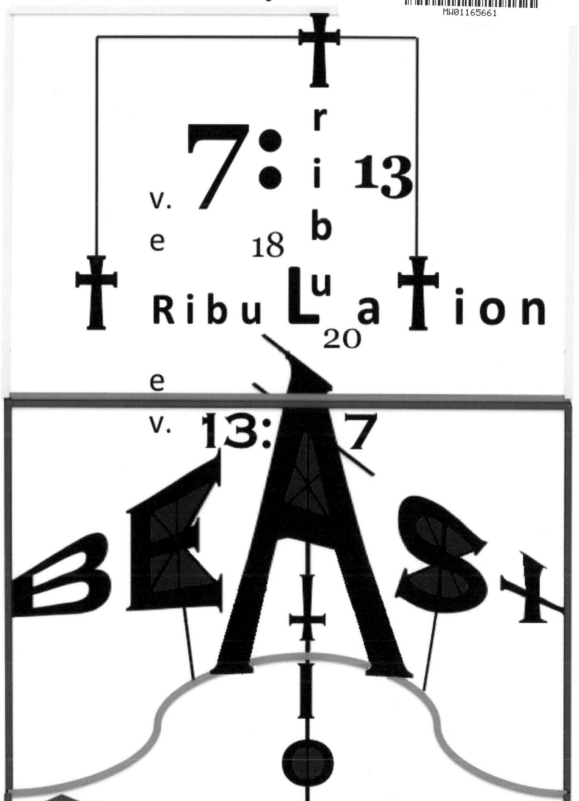

AuthorHouse™
1663 Liberty Drive
Bloomington, IN 47403
www.authorhouse.com
Phone: 1-800-839-8640

Published by AuthorHouse 05/30/2013

ISBN: 978-1-4817-0039-9 (sc)
*   978-1-4817-0040-5 (e)*

Library of Congress Control Number: 2012924127

Any people depicted in stock imagery provided by Thinkstock are models,
and such images are being used for illustrative purposes only.
Certain stock imagery © Thinkstock.

This book is printed on acid-free paper.

Because of the dynamic nature of the Internet, any web addresses or links contained in this book may have changed
since publication and may no longer be valid. The views expressed in this work are solely those of the author and do not
necessarily reflect the views of the publisher, and the publisher hereby disclaims any responsibility for them.

authorHOUSE®

Luke 21:34–36

Exhortation to Be Vigilant.

34"Beware that your hearts do not become drowsy from carousing and drunkenness and the anxieties of daily life, and that day catch you by surprise. [1] 35like a trap. For that day will assault everyone who lives on the face of the earth. 36Be vigilant at all times and pray that you have the strength to escape the tribulations that are imminent and to stand before the Son of Man.[2] "

---

[1] [21:34] 12:45–46; Mt 24:48–50; 1 Thes 5:3, 6–7.
[2] [21:36] Mk 13:33.

When I see the elderly as I walk the streets of New York City, or anywhere for that matter, I say a silent prayer that goes like this: "May God bless the elderly as they blessed us with their kindness, love, patience, and guidance as we were growing up." I say this because the elderly deserve to be blessed, along with their caregivers, and they deserve our respect, more especially in a time when the Tea Party would put them on the budget-cut list.

I have no doubt that my parents are in heaven. As it says in Psalm 7:12, God is a just judge, powerful and patient, not exercising anger every day.

This book is dedicated to my parents, Raymond and Virginia Miller, who blessed me with their kindness, love, patience, and guidance, always.

Contents

Prologue

"I Am a Messenger"

Revelation 1:1-3

1The revelation of Jesus Christ, which God gave to him, to show his servants what must happen soon. He made it known by sending his angel to his servant John,[3] 2who gives witness to the word of God and to the testimony of Jesus Christ by reporting what he saw. 3Blessed is the one[4] who reads aloud and blessed are those who listen to this prophetic message and heed what is written in it, for the appointed time is near.[5]

Throughout the history of Christianity, people have tried to predict the end of days. Even St. Paul the Apostle thought it would occur in his lifetime. The fact is, God continually makes it clear through the Bible (Rev. 3:3, Rev. 16:15, Matt. 24:43, 1 Thess. 5:2, 2 Pet. 3:10, Luke 12:39) that he will come like a thief. Predictions are futile, so focus your energies on repentance and doing good deeds.

From Scripture, two great examples of God's love for us come to mind:

---

[3] [1:1] 22:6–8, 20; Dn 2:28 / 19:10.
[4] [1:3] Blessed is the one: this is the first of seven beatitudes in this book; the others are in Rev 14:13; 16:15; 19:9; 20:6; 22:7, 14. This prophetic message: literally, "the words of the prophecy"; so Rev 22:7, 10, 18, 19 by inclusion. The appointed time: when Jesus will return in glory; cf. Rev 1:7; 3:11; 22:7, 10, 12, 20.
[5] [1:3] 22:7 / Lk 11:28.

John 3:16

16For God so loved the world that he gave[6] his only Son, so that everyone who believes in him might not perish but might have eternal life.[7]

2 Peter 3:8–10

8[8] But do not ignore this one fact, beloved, that with the Lord one day is like a thousand years[9] and a thousand years like one day.[10] 9The Lord does not delay his promise, as some regard "delay," but he is patient with you, not wishing that any should perish but that all should come to repentance.[11] 10But the day of the Lord will come like a thief,[12] and then the heavens will pass away with a mighty roar and the elements will be dissolved by fire, and the earth and everything done on it will be found out.[13]

Scoffers of Religion

Throughout the history of religion, there have been scoffers. THE LETTER OF JUDE, the last letter of the Catholic Letters before the Book of Revelation, is addressed in the most general terms to "those who are called, beloved in

---

[6] [3:16] Gave: as a gift in the incarnation, and also "over to death" in the crucifixion; cf. Rom 8:32.

[7] [3:16] 1 Jn 4:9.

[8] [3:8–10] The scoffers' objection (2 Pt 3:4) is refuted also by showing that delay of the Lord's second coming is not a failure to fulfill his word but rather a sign of his patience: God is giving time for repentance before the final judgment (cf. Wis 11:23–26; Ez 18:23; 33:11).

[9] [3:10] Like a thief: Mt 24:43; 1 Thes 5:2; Rev 3:3. Will be found out: cf. 1 Cor 3:13–15. Some few versions read, as the sense may demand, "will not be found out"; many manuscripts read "will be burned up"; there are further variants in other manuscripts, versions, and Fathers. Total destruction is assumed (2 Pt 3:11).

[10] [3:8] Ps 90:4.

[11] [3:9] Ez 18:23; 1 Tm 2:4.

[12] [3:10] Like a thief: Mt 24:43; 1 Thes 5:2; Rev 3:3. Will be found out: cf. 1 Cor 3:13–15. Some few versions read, as the sense may demand, "will not be found out"; many manuscripts read "will be burned up"; there are further variants in other manuscripts, versions, and Fathers. Total destruction is assumed (2 Pt 3:11).

[13] [3:10] Is 66:15–16; Mt 24:29.

God the Father and kept safe for Jesus Christ" (Jude 1), hence apparently to all Christians. But since its purpose is to warn the addressees against false teachers, the author must have had in mind one or more specific Christian communities located in an unidentified region where the errors in question constituted a danger.

Jude 17–23

17But you, beloved, remember the words spoken beforehand by the apostles of our Lord Jesus Christ,[14] 18for they told you, [15] "In [the] last time there will be scoffers who will live according to their own godless desires."[16] 19These are the ones who cause divisions; they live on the natural plane, devoid of the Spirit.[17] 20But you, beloved, build yourselves up in your most holy faith; pray in the holy Spirit.[18] 21Keep yourselves in the love of God and wait for the mercy of our Lord Jesus Christ that leads to eternal life. [19] [20]22On those who waver, have mercy; 23save others by snatching them out of the fire; on others have mercy with fear, [21]abhorring even the outer garment stained by the flesh.

---

[14] [17] Heb 2:3; 2 Pt 3:2.

[15] [18] 1 Tm 4:1; 2 Tm 3:1–5; 2 Pt 3:3.

[16] [18] This is the substance of much early Christian preaching rather than a direct quotation of any of the various New Testament passages on this theme (see Mk 13:22; Acts 20:30; 1 Tm 4:1–3; 2 Pt 3:3).

[17] [19] 1 Cor 2:14; Jas 3:15.

[18] [20] 2; Eph 6:18; Col 2:7.

[19] [21] Ti 2:13.

[20] [22] Have mercy: some manuscripts read "convince," "confute," or "reprove." Others have "even though you waver" or "doubt" instead of who waver.

[21] [23] With fear: some manuscripts connect the phrase "with fear" with the imperative "save" or with the participle "snatching." Other manuscripts omit the phrase "on others have mercy," so that only two groups are envisioned. Rescue of those led astray and caution in the endeavor are both enjoined. Outer garment stained by the flesh: the imagery may come from Zec 3:3–5, just as that of snatching…out of the fire comes from Zec 3:2; the very garments of the godless are to be abhorred because of their contagion.

Regardless of the meanings of particular saints, bringing as many as possible into repentance before the end of the age may be a desperate case, but it is no lost cause.

The underlying message throughout this book is that all peoples of all nations and all tongues should take advantage of the second chance that God has provided us all.

Who Am I?

__My name is Gary Ray Miller,__ I was born on October 2, 1960, to a father named Raymond, who was a carpenter, and to a beautiful mother named Virginia (nicknamed Gina). The venue of this "blessed event" was the maternity ward of a hospital named after the patron saint of the universal Church, "Prudent Guardian of the Holy Family, and Protector of God's Holy Church," Saint Joseph.

People tend to throw around the name "Antichrist" (or the beast) to literally describe those they hate, like the forty-fourth president of the United States, who is an African American (see Rev. 6:5–6). You need not worry about Barack Hussein Obama being the Antichrist. The fact of the matter is both political parties have serious moral failings that need to be corrected. You do need to worry about the entity described in Revelation 6:7–8. It may not come in the form of a president, but rather a legislative body or political movement that cares not about God nor their fellow man, but rather idolatrous pleasures (see Rom. 1:18–32 and 2 Tim. 3:1–9). However, these symptoms of idolatry are on both sides of the aisle.

I watched a Republican debate during which the crowd laughed and exclaimed, "Yes!" when Rep. Ron Paul was asked if someone without health insurance should be allowed to die. I constantly read of Republican candidates (especially Tea Party candidates) denouncing climate change. I read the speech of the CEO of ExxonMobil saying that we can "adapt" to climate change or we can "engineer our way out of it" (for the sake of ExxonMobil's shareholders?). In all three instances, I see the similarities to Revelation 11:1–14, the story of the two witnesses, the Environmental Protection Agency (FPA) and the Department of Energy (DOE), in which the beast conquered and killed them because of their witnessing to Almighty God. The inhabitants of the earth then celebrated their deaths. We live in troubled times, and the battle lines between good and evil are quickly being drawn.

Each of the letters of the alphabet in Hebrew as well as in Greek has a numerical value. The Greek form of whose name in Hebrew letters gives the required sum (See Rev. 13:18 and associated notes). I take the simple approach of translating my name to Greek letters and applying the Greek numbering system to the letters. As you can see, the result is not the six hundred and sixty-six of the beast.

A	B	Γ	Δ	E	Z	H	Θ
α	β	γ	δ	ε	ζ	η	θ
1	2	3	4	5	7	8	9
I	K	Λ	M	N	Ξ	O	Π
ι	κ	λ	μ	ν	ξ	ο	π
10	20	30	40	50	60	70	80
P	Σ	T	Y	Φ	X	Ψ	Ω
ρ	σ	τ	υ	φ	χ	ψ	ω
100	200	300	400	500	600	700	800

Name	Gary	Ray	Miller
Greek Letters	*Γαρψ*	*Ραψ*	*Μιλλερ*
Number	*804*	*801*	*215*

Total = 1820

Eighteen is the Hebrew life number

(http://en.wikipedia.org/wiki/Chai_(symbol).

Revelation 1:8 says, "I am the Alpha and the Omega," [22] says the Lord God, "the one who is and who was and who is to come, the almighty." [23]

Revelation 18:20 says,

> Rejoice over her, heaven,
>
> > you holy ones, apostles, and
>
> prophets.
>
> For God has judged your case against her."[24]

Assigning English numerical values to my initials

INITIALS	G	R	M
NUMBER	*7*	*18*	*13*

---

[22] [1:8] The Alpha and the Omega: the first and last letters of the Greek alphabet. In Rev 22:13 the same words occur together with the expressions "the First and the Last, the Beginning and the End"; cf. Rev 1:17; 2:8; 21:6; Is 41:4; 44:6.

[23] [1:8] 17; 21:6; 22:13; Is 41:4; 44:6; 48:12.

[24] [18:20] 19:1–2; Dt 32:43.

Seven symbolizes God's totality and perfection. In Genesis 2, God created Heaven and Earth and their entire array in six days and rested from all his work on the seventh day, blessing and making it holy.

Eighteen: See above.

Thirteen: The letter M represents the Virgin Mary on the Miraculous Medal. There were thirteen men at the Passover (Last) Supper: twelve apostles and Jesus Christ.

Revelation 1:3 says, "Blessed is the one[25] who reads aloud and blessed are those who listen to this prophetic message and heed what is written in it, for the appointed time is near.[26] "

I have lived in small towns named Delta, Rome, and Shiloh. My farm was bordered by a church named Maranatha (meaning, "Our Lord, come!" 1 Cor. 16:22). My parents lived in towns named Trinity and Temple. I now live in a town named New Canaan.

I am neither a Republican nor a Democrat. Both parties have their idolatrous moral failings. I strongly believe in a two-party political system and a constitutional republic form of government. My earliest recollection of politics is of a "George Bush for Congress" sign in our Pasadena, Texas front yard. Bush was elected in 1966 to a House of Representatives seat from the Seventh District

---

[25] [1:3] Blessed is the one: this is the first of seven beatitudes in this book; the others are in Rev 14:13; 16:15; 19:9; 20:6; 22:7, 14. This prophetic message: literally, "the words of the prophecy"; so Rev 22:7, 10, 18, 19 by inclusion. The appointed time: when Jesus will return in glory; cf. Rev 1:7; 3:11; 22:7, 10, 12, 20.
[26] [1:3] 22:7 / Lk 11:28.

of Texas. Because of my parents' politics, I was a dyed-in-the-wool Republican from 1966 at age six through Bush versus Gore in 2000 at age forty.

I have a son who has autism. He was given several vaccinations in his early childhood, before he was diagnosed with autism, which contained thimerosal. Thimerosal is a mercury-based vaccine preservative, which is suspected of causing neurodevelopmental delays. Just before President Bush signed the Homeland Security Bill into law, House Majority Leader Dick Armey (R-TX) inserted a provision into the legislation that blocks lawsuits against the maker of thimerosal, Eli Lilley.

Because of the Dick Armey's action, in 2004 I voted for the Kerry-Edwards ticket in the presidential race. After Rep. Joe Barton (R-TX) blocked (held hostage) passage of the Combatting Autism Act, I vowed never to vote Republican again, in any election, until they changed their party platform to one of decency, inclusiveness, and fairness—in other words, back to what once was the party of Lincoln.

In 2006, the Democrats took back control of the House. In 2008, the Democrats took both the legislative and executive branches of government.

In the view of liberals, I am a staunch social conservative who does his very best to live by biblical Scripture. In the view of conservatives, I am a "bleeding-heart" liberal when it comes to protecting the poor, the elderly, the weak, and the environment. In my own view, I am not a politician . . . I am a man of God.

This book covers my life through the aftermath of a failed suicide attempt and two tribulations that occurred between February 2003 and March 2011. I also talk about the period after that, through the present day.

Regardless of what some might say, the Bible is composed of mathematics and science as far back as the books of Genesis and Exodus. Two of the better-known cases were Noah's ark and the Ark of the Covenant. With Noah, God gave him the exact dimensions of the ark and its manifest, based on repopulating the earth. With the Ark of the Covenant, God gave Moses the exact dimensions, materials of construction, and holy contents.

In Genesis 1:26, God said, "Let us make human beings in our image, after our likeness. Let them have dominion over the fish of the sea, the birds of the air, the tame animals, all the wild animals, and all the creatures that crawl on the earth." But through Isaiah's prophecy from God in chapter 24, it was revealed that the world would be become polluted due to the exploitation of the ancient covenant of God's commandments to all humankind.

God then gave us the sciences, so the government departments like the EPA (Environmental Protection Agency) and DOE (Department of Energy) can protect human health and the environment. Even with prophecy from the Book of Isaiah about a polluted earth, Tea Party politicians and their minions declare that the earth is theirs to use as they please, and they claim Departments like the EPA and DOE should be eliminated. Our motivation to keep these departments lies in Scripture: Isaiah 24:5–23.

With God's divine mathematics, conveyed by the Holy Spirit, comes the key of David. It is a series of fourteen crosses (the fourteen stations of the cross) arrayed in four sets of Calvary crosses. The first three sets have repetitive dimensions of thirteen and eighteen inches, between crosses, representing Revelation 1:3 and Revelation 1:8. The fourth set of Calvary crosses in Cypress and Manhattan have varying dimensions between the crosses, which numerically translate into Scripture passages from The Revelation to provide a Holy message. Two additional crosses represent Jesus Christ.

Thank God for the USCCB (United States Conference of Catholic Bishops) and their New American Bible, Revised Edition. I downloaded it to Kindle and have it on all of my electronic devices. Chapter 6, The Scroll, assembles the text, biblical notes, and associated scriptural cross-references from the Book of Revelation, in a spreadsheet format. My intent was twofold: 1) to give the reader an easier-to-read version of Scripture and biblical notes (side by side) along with my commentary, dates, and number of days, where applicable; and 2) to show the reader the significant connection between St. John's prophecy in the Book of Revelation and its connection to the Old Testament prophets, the Gospels, the Epistles, and the Catholic Letters. I wanted to do this to help all people read and understand what the prophets are trying to tell us and how, in many cases, they are telling us the same thing.

All of these visions and prophecies (messages) have been transmitted from God to the prophets through the Holy Spirit. I too am a messenger.

Darkness

February 2003 to June 2003

1 Corinthians 6:15–20

15Do you not know that your bodies are members of Christ? Shall I then take Christ's members and make them the members of a prostitute? [27]Of course not! [28] 16[Or] do you not know that anyone who joins himself to a prostitute becomes one body with her? For "the two," it says, "will become one flesh."[29] 17But whoever is joined to the Lord becomes one spirit with him.[30] 18Avoid immorality. Every other sin a person commits is outside the body, but the immoral person sins against his own body. [31] 19Do you not know that your body is a temple[32] of the holy Spirit within you, whom you have from God, and that you are not your own?[33] 20For you have been purchased at a price. Therefore, glorify God in your body.[34]

---

[27] [6:15b–16] A prostitute: the reference may be specifically to religious prostitution, an accepted part of pagan culture at Corinth and elsewhere; but the prostitute also serves as a symbol for any sexual relationship that conflicts with Christ's claim over us individually. The two…will become one flesh: the text of Gn 2:24 is applied positively to human marriage in Matthew and Mark, and in Eph 5:29–32: love of husband and wife reflect the love of Christ for his church. The application of the text to union with a prostitute is jarring, for such a union is a parody, an antitype of marriage, which does conflict with Christ's claim over us. This explains the horror expressed in 15b.

[28] [6:15] 12:27; Rom 6:12–13; 12:5; Eph 5:30.

[29] [6:16] Gn 2:24; Mt 19:5; Mk 10:8; Eph 5:31.

[30] [6:17] Rom 8:9–10; 2 Cor 3:17.

[31] [6:18] Against his own body: expresses the intimacy and depth of sexual disorder, which violates the very orientation of our bodies

[32] [6:19–20] Paul's vision becomes trinitarian. A temple: sacred by reason of God's gift, his indwelling Spirit. Not your own: but "for the Lord," who acquires ownership by the act of redemption. Glorify God in your body: the argument concludes with a positive imperative to supplement the negative "avoid immorality" of 1 Cor 6:18. Far from being a terrain that is morally indifferent, the area of sexuality is one in which our relationship with God (and his Christ and his Spirit) is very intimately expressed: he is either highly glorified or deeply offended.

[33] [6:19] 3:16–17; Rom 5:5.

[34] [6:20] 3:23; 7:23; Acts 20:28 / Rom 12:1; Phil 1:20.

I tried to destroy myself with a near-full bottle of Zyprexa, prescribed by my then-physician, a childhood friend. Yes, I now know that Zyprexa is for the treatment of schizophrenia and bipolar disorder. I was manic, but not schizophrenic.

I had uncovered possible impropriety at my then-employer, which appeared to have led to the top of the company. I had been outspoken about it. Then the games began, complete with a home break-in in the middle of day.

I finally broke down on a Saturday, and my dad took me to "Dr. Friend's" clinic, where he wrote the aforementioned prescription. He later referred me to a psychiatrist, who casually told me that the prescribed Zyprexa could be used against me in court with regard to my emotional stability.

The scripture quoted above doesn't even begin to measure the damage of my abhorrent actions and the shame that I brought upon my family. This sounds clichéd, but there are no words to justify what I did.

The date was February 22, 2003. It was the day after my wife's birthday. The previous day, I had finally had enough with my employer and resigned after almost twelve years. I gave two weeks' notice and walked out after one week. For many people, being pushed out of something you built, loved, and logged a long tenure in, can equate to a major identity loss and that was my case. My life was my wife, my kids, my parents, and my job. I tried to keep it in that order. However, you see that God wasn't on my list, and the lack of Him led to disorder.

My wife had spent the weekend with her mother and sisters and appeared agitated. I suspected she knew about my infidelity, so I sat her down and admitted that I had not been faithful.

I vaguely remember the rest of the day. It's probably something that I block out. I remember getting the kids to bed. I remember deciding to commit suicide (with absolutely no thought of harming anyone else). I wasn't going to make a mess, and had decided to take the pills and just go to sleep. I was a bit naive about probate matters, so I signed my will, without a witness, and left it on the table. I took the pills, and believe or not, I got in bed, fully clothed, with my wife and went to sleep.

I fell asleep, and approximately one hour later, I became nauseated. I was able vomit out some, but not all of the pills. I know that sounds odd, but I was indifferent about living. I went back to sleep, and that's the last thing I remember for the next three days. My wife told me that I started convulsing. Rather than calling 911, she called my parents, who lived less than two hundred yards from us, on a farm we jointly owned in Liberty County, Texas.

I'll discuss my parents' tragic deaths later in the book, but regardless of those circumstances, I love both my parents and I always will. My dad had a serious heart attack on January 2, 2001. He was defibrillated eighteen times at the hospital in Liberty, Texas and once more on LifeFlight on his way to Memorial Hermann–Texas Medical Center in Houston. He received a stent and recovered with no significant damage to his heart. He did have open-heart surgery approximately seven months later. I'd like to think I helped save his life in January 2001. My dad more than repaid the favor on February 22, 2003.

It's always interesting when you have the opportunity to talk to a veteran who has seen a lot of action in combat. I like to watch Col. Jack Jacobs, who contributes to NBC and MSNBC. He's very mild-mannered and doesn't get excited, nor brag about the fact that he's a Medal of Honor recipient. My dad spent two years in the Korean theater during the Korean War. He saw a lot of combat and was awarded two Bronze Stars with the V device, as well as the Wharang Distinguished Service Medal, which is the highest Korean bravery award. At age seventy, he could do farm work in a stifling one-hundred-degree heat. If he had a project, it was going to get done, regardless if he had to do it all by himself.

My dad didn't brag about his medals, but he did remember how to quickly rescue someone who was dying. My dad was seventy-two at the time of my suicide attempt. He and my mom, who was sixty-eight, rushed to our home. I was on the floor convulsing. My dad grabbed me by my back belt loop and dragged me out of our home, down a sidewalk, and into their waiting car. I always imagined my dad similarly dragging someone out of harm's way in Korea.

They rushed me to the local hospital in Liberty. I was literally knocking on death's door. All I can remember is darkness. I definitely was not knocking on heaven's door.

My stomach was pumped that night, as you would expect. I was in and out of consciousness for two or three days. I remember having my arms tied to a gurney and being intubated. I remember my wife and kids visiting. I remember my aforementioned "childhood friend" visiting. I remember my parents being there for me.

I was transferred to CHRISTUS St. John Hospital in the Houston area, where I regained cognition.

My health insurance had been terminated, coinciding with my last day of service, February 21, 2003. Therefore, I had no health insurance coverage and neither my parents nor I expected the financial impact of an expensive, selfish act.

My father had semiretired at age fifty-nine and a half in 1989, and had logged approximately forty years in the construction business, primarily working in the oil and gas, refining, and petrochemicals business sectors. As of 2003, I had worked approximately twenty-four years in the construction and owner-operator businesses. Nineteen of those years had accrued after graduating for the University of Texas-Austin with a bachelor's degree in civil engineering. I had worked in the same business for five years prior to that, during summers and Christmas holidays, to help pay for my college tuition.

My earliest memory in the business is being a laborer in 1978 at the Exxon (now ExxonMobil) refinery in Baytown, Texas. I was seventeen years old, and I have no idea if any labor laws were violated. It was and is an "inbred" business. If you're really good at something specific (project management, technical subject matter expert, business management, risk management, legal, etc.), you can be a "panacea". If you become a whistleblower, you will also become a "pariah," probably for the rest of your career. Typically, you make lifelong friends with many of the people that you encounter.

I tell you all this because in the 1960s my father worked with several people at what is now a chemical plant along the Houston Ship Channel. I ended up working with some of the same people thirty years later. One of these people was our Senior Vice-President of Engineering, who I ultimately had reported to. His lifelong friendship with my dad got my health insurance reinstated for three months. He didn't do this alone, but sought and received approval from the CEO and chairman of the company. I will always be indebted to this man.

I was transferred from CHRISTUS St. John Hospital to St. Joseph Hospital. As I said in the Prologue, I was born in St. Joseph Hospital, so I assumed that going back there for treatment would be my rebirth. But after I left St. Joseph's, I did not want to live! Everything around me had come crumbling down. I knew how to compartmentalize it, but I had no idea how to rebuild it. My wife had to start working more hours as a flight attendant because of my unemployment and probably because she just didn't want to see me.

Our son had been diagnosed with autism in late September 2002 at Texas Children's Hospital in Houston. Texas Children's Hospital is part of the Baylor College of Medicine. We soon realized that our home county, which was economically depressed, could not offer our son the services he needed. In January 2003, I enrolled him in a private school in West Houston, which specializes in educating autistic children. The drive from our farm in Liberty County, Texas to this school was approximately seventy miles each way.

When my wife went back to work, I was responsible for taking our son to and from school during the periods that she was away. At first, I would drop him at school, and then just stay in my car in the parking lot. I remember that all I ever wanted to do was sleep. Sleeping typically made me forget about everything. I would lean the seat back and just close my eyes for hours.

I was near the bottom without a ladder. I was emaciated. I had gone from a very fit one hundred and fifty pounds to somewhere around one hundred and twenty-five. I remember while I was in St. John's Hospital, someone with a Middle Eastern accent, who said he was a doctor, woke me up in the middle of the night for the sole purpose of telling me that I was very muscular, then asking me if I took steroids. I promptly told him no, and my tone let him know that he was persona non grata in my room.

God Saved Me

In addition to my family, God put people in my life that at least had "sections of a ladder". The first was a former supervisor, who had gone on to work for an engineering contractor. I remember lying in bed one day covered with a sheet, in a state of deep, dark depression. The phone rang and it was he. Given my state of mind at that moment, he probably saved my life. We agreed to meet and talk about me going to work where he was employed.

Shortly after that day, I graduated from leaning the seat back and sleeping, to driving three miles to Einstein Bros. Bagels and slowly adding some weight back on my frame. We met there, and he offered me a job, which I started in June 2003.

The second was a neighbor's family. Our farm was bordered to the north by the farm of one of the top cardiothoracic surgeons in the United States, if not the world. He had trained under and practiced alongside Dr. Michael DeBakey at Baylor College of Medicine and The Methodist Hospital. His daughter and her husband found out that we wanted to sell our farm. The doctor had seen my dad in the pasture, and my dad had discussed it with him. We didn't even have the property listed at the time.

My wife and I knew that we needed to relocate closer to my autistic son's school, because of the drive and because our other two kids needed to be in a better public school system. My wife was suffering from depression as badly as I was. Her world had been turned upside down by my infidelity and now I wanted to sell the farm she loved and relocate to Katy, Texas.

My neighbor's daughter and son-in-law drove up without warning in April 2003, and we immediately started talking about a potential sale. We closed the sale in June 2003. I sold our farm and my parents sold their farm to them. I still keep in touch with the son-in-law. The house that I designed and built sustained heavy damage in Hurricane Ike, and he calls periodically to discuss repairs to the house.

To me, this move appeared to be an opportunity to repair our lives, but in reality, it was the start of the First Tribulation.

The First Tribulation

June 2003 to December 2006

Tobit 4:5-6

5"Through all your days, son, keep the Lord in mind, and do not seek to sin or to transgress the commandments. Perform righteous deeds all the days of your life, and do not tread the paths of wickedness. 6[35] For those who act with fidelity, all who practice righteousness, will prosper in their affairs.[36]

I love stories of good versus evil, the righteous versus the wicked. The Bible is full of them. They started with the Garden of Eden and apocalyptically climax in the Book of Revelation. In an unjust world, it's these stories, which keep our spirits from plunging into darkness.

I have heroes. Everyone should have heroes—someone to look up to and model your life after: Jesus Christ; other righteous characters of the Bible, Torah, and Quran; your parents; your teachers; first responders; people who serve in the military; and public servants, among others. (Public service is a noble occupation, though some of our politics is not. See Rom. 13:1–7 and Luke 20:45—47.) If you get a chance to read the Bible, there is a treasure trove of heroes in the Old and New Testaments. If I'm with one or more of my kids and we start talking theology and how God is very real, I tell these stories to my

---

[35] [4:6] Tb 13:6; Jn 3:21; Eph 4:15.
[36] [4:6] It was commonly thought in the Old Testament that virtue guaranteed earthly prosperity, and sin earthly disaster (Prv 10:2; cf. Dt 28).

kids. I start crying because of the never-ending grace of God and the goodness and the faith we receive from His grace.

The first story is from the Book of Daniel, chapter 3. It involves three devout, God-fearing Hebrews named Shadrach, Meshach, and Abednego. They were enslaved, with many other Hebrews, by Nebuchadnezzar II, king of Babylon. Nebuchadnezzar commanded the Hebrews to build a golden statue dedicated to him, which the Hebrews did. The catch was that when the Hebrews heard the sound of the horn, pipe, zither, dulcimer, harp, double-flute, or any other musical instrument, they had to fall down and worship the golden statue that King Nebuchadnezzar had set up. Whoever does not fall down and worship shall be instantly cast into a white-hot furnace." (Dan. 3:6).

As it happened one day, the music played and these three devout, God-fearing Hebrews refused to kneel and worship.

> 14King Nebuchadnezzar questioned them: "Is it true, Shadrach, Meshach, and Abednego, that you will not serve my god, or worship the golden statue that I set up? ... 16Shadrach, Meshach, and Abednego answered King Nebuchadnezzar II, "There is no need for us to defend ourselves before you in this matter. 17If our God, whom we serve, can save us[37] from the white-hot furnace and from your hands, O king, may he save us! 18But even if he will not, you should know, O king, that we will not serve your god or worship the golden statue which you set up."

---

[37] [3:17] If our God…can save us: the youths do not question the efficacy of the divine power, but whether it will be exercised (v. 18).

19Nebuchadnezzar's face became livid with utter rage against Shadrach, Meshach, and Abednego. He ordered the furnace to be heated seven times more than usual 20and had some of the strongest men in his army bind Shadrach, Meshach, and Abednego and cast them into the white-hot furnace. 21They were bound and cast into the white-hot furnace with their trousers, shirts, hats and other garments, 22for the king's order was urgent. So huge a fire was kindled in the furnace that the flames devoured the men who threw Shadrach, Meshach, and Abednego into it. 23But these three fell, bound, into the midst of the white-hot furnace. (Dan. 3:14, 16–23)

46Now the king's servants who had thrown them in continued to stoke the furnace with naptha, pitch, tow, and brush. 47The flames rose forty-nine cubits above the furnace, 48and spread out, burning the Chaldeans that it caught around the furnace. 49But the angel of the Lord went down into the furnace with Azariah and his companions, drove the fiery flames out of the furnace, 50and made the inside of the furnace as though a dew-laden breeze were blowing through it. The fire in no way touched them or caused them pain or harm. 51Then these three in the furnace with one voice sang, glorifying and blessing God: . . . (Dan. 3:46–51)

90Bless the God of gods, all you who fear the Lord; praise and give thanks, for his mercy endures forever." **Deliverance from**

the Furnace. 91Then King Nebuchadnezzar was startled and rose in haste, asking his counselors, "Did we not cast three men bound into the fire?" "Certainly, O king," they answered. 92"But," he replied, "I see four men unbound and unhurt, walking in the fire, and the fourth looks like a son of God." 93Then Nebuchadnezzar came to the opening of the white-hot furnace and called: "Shadrach, Meshach, and Abednego, servants of the Most High God, come out." Thereupon Shadrach, Meshach, and Abednego came out of the fire. 95Nebuchadnezzar exclaimed, "Blessed be the God of Shadrach, Meshach, and Abednego, who sent his angel to deliver the servants that trusted in him; they disobeyed the royal command and yielded their bodies rather than serve or worship any god except their own God. (Dan. 3: 90–93, 95)

Beginning in 1 Samuel chapter 16, the second story is about King David. Many people know the abbreviated story of David and Goliath, but scripture has all of the characters.

Samuel was a sixth century BC prophet who was a devout servant of God. The king of the Israelites, Saul, had fallen into disfavor with God, and God told Samuel to find a new king.

Samuel Is Sent to Bethlehem. 1³⁸ The LORD said to Samuel: How long will you grieve for Saul, whom I have rejected as

---

³⁸ [16:1] Ru 4:17–22; 1 Kgs 1:39; 1 Chr 11:3; Is 11:1; Mt 2:6; Lk 2:4.

king of Israel? Fill your horn with oil, and be on your way. I am sending you to Jesse of Bethlehem, for from among his sons I have decided on a king. [39] 2But Samuel replied: "How can I go? Saul will hear of it and kill me." To this the LORD answered: Take a heifer along and say, "I have come to sacrifice to the LORD." 3Invite Jesse to the sacrifice, and I myself will tell you what to do; you are to anoint for me the one I point out to you.[40] (1 Sam. 16:1 3)

Jesse had eight sons, seven of whom were at the sacrifice. Samuel began evaluating Jesse's sons.

But the LORD said to Samuel: Do not judge from his appearance or from his lofty stature, because I have rejected him. God does not see as a mortal, who sees the appearance. The LORD looks into the heart.[41] (1 Sam. 16:7)

11Then Samuel asked Jesse, "Are these all the sons you have?" Jesse replied, "There is still the youngest, but he is tending the sheep." Samuel said to Jesse, "Send for him; we will not sit down to eat until he arrives here."[42] 12Jesse had the young man brought to them. He was ruddy, a youth with beautiful eyes, and good looking. The LORD said: There—anoint him, for

---

39 [16:1] David is anointed two more times after Saul's death (2 Sm 2:4; 5:3). In 17:28, his brother Eliab is not aware of David's selection. These repetitions and inconsistencies reflect the final editor's use of multiple sources.

40 [16:3] 1 Sm 9:13, 22, 24

41 [16:7] 1 Sm 10:23–24; 1 Kgs 11:4; 1 Chr 28:9; Prv 15:11; Jer 17:10; 20:12; Lk 16:15; Acts 1:24.

42 [16:11] 1 Sm 17:15, 28, 34; 2 Sm 7:8; Ps 78:70–71.

this is the one![43] 13Then Samuel, with the horn of oil in hand, anointed him in the midst of his brothers, and from that day on, the spirit of the LORD rushed upon David. Then Samuel set out for Ramah.[44] (1 Sam. 16:11–13)

David won Saul's approval and became his armor-bearer.

The Challenge of Goliath. 1The Philistines rallied their forces for battle at Socoh in Judah and camped between Socoh and Azekah at Ephes-dammim. 2Saul and the Israelites rallied and camped in the valley of the Elah, drawing up their battle line to meet the Philistines. 3The Philistines were stationed on one hill and the Israelites on an opposite hill, with a valley between them. 4A champion named Goliath of Gath came out from the Philistine camp; he was six cubits and a span[45] tall. 5He had a bronze helmet on his head and wore a bronze breastplate of scale armor weighing five thousand shekels, 6bronze greaves, and had a bronze scimitar slung from his shoulders. 7The shaft of his javelin was like a weaver's beam, and its iron head weighed six hundred shekels.[46] His shield-bearer went ahead of him.[47] (1 Sam. 17:1–7)

---

43 [16:12] 1 Sm 9:2.
44 [16:13] 1 Sm 10:6; 11:6; Jgs 3:10; 9:9; Sir 46:13.
45 [17:4] Six cubits and a span: about nine feet nine inches (a cubit equals about eighteen inches; a span equals about eight inches). The Greek text and 4QSama read: "four cubits and a span" (six feet nine inches). The description of the Philistine's might and his powerful weapons contrasts with the picture of the youthful David who trusts in God.
46 [17:7] Six hundred shekels: over fifteen pounds.
47 [17:7] 2 Sm 21:19; 1 Chr 11:23; 20:5

David answered him: "You come against me with sword and spear and scimitar, but I come against you in the name of the LORD of hosts, the God of the armies of Israel whom you have insulted. (1 Sam. 17:45). *David killed the giant with nothing more than a sling and a rock and went on to become king of the Israelites.*

In each of these stories, there was a bully or bullies harassing a righteous man or men, and by the grace of Almighty God the righteous man prevailed.

Matthew 5:10

10Blessed are they who are persecuted for the sake of righteousness, [48]for theirs is the kingdom of heaven.[49]

The Unraveling of My Marriage

My wife filed for divorce in May 2004 and I wanted no part of it. I was willing to crawl through shards of glass to salvage the marriage because I still very much loved her and because of the disastrous effects divorce can have on children and we have three.

Texas is a community-property state and the respondent's exposure to financial ruin is typically limited to a 60-40 split. My dad was convinced that I would be left penniless (a 0-100 split) and that he and my mom would be financially exposed as well, so my dad found me an attorney. The guy was probably a

---

[48] [5:10] Righteousness here, as usually in Matthew, means conduct in conformity with God's will.
[49] [5:10] 1 Pt 2:20; 3:14; 4:14.

good family lawyer, but he doubled as an insurance defense attorney who had argued in front of several appeals courts. I politely said no and decided to march forth with my sword and go pro se! When my dad died, I found the name and phone number of the attorney in his wallet.

A Man Who Represents Himself Has a Fool for a Client

Malachi 2:16

For I hate divorce, says the LORD, the God of Israel,

I also hate divorce. Jesus hated divorce. He went against Mosaic Law to change divorce from a mere bill to an act of adultery, so as to prevent it.

Matthew 19:3–12

3[50] Some Pharisees approached him, and tested him,[51] saying, "Is it lawful for a man to divorce his wife for any cause whatever?" 4[52][53] He said in reply, "Have you not read that from the beginning the Creator 'made them male and female' 5[54] and said, 'For this reason a man shall leave his father

---

[50] [19:3–9] Mk 10:2–12.

[51] [19:3] Tested him: the verb is used of attempts of Jesus' opponents to embarrass him by challenging him to do something they think impossible (Mt 16:1; Mk 8:11; Lk 11:16) or by having him say something that they can use against him (Mt 22:18, 35; Mk 10:2; 12:15). For any cause whatever: this is peculiar to Matthew and has been interpreted by some as meaning that Jesus was being asked to take sides in the dispute between the schools of Hillel and Shammai on the reasons for divorce, the latter holding a stricter position than the former. It is unlikely, however, that to ask Jesus' opinion about the differing views of two Jewish schools, both highly respected, could be described as "testing" him, for the reason indicated above.

[52] [19:4–6] Matthew recasts his Marcan source, omitting Jesus' question about Moses' command (Mk 10:3) and having him recall at once two Genesis texts that show the will and purpose of the Creator in making human beings male and female (Gn 1:27), namely, that a man may be joined to his wife in marriage in the intimacy of one flesh (Gn 2:24). What God has thus joined must not be separated by any human being. (The NAB translation of the Hebrew bāśār of Gn 2:24 as "body" rather than "flesh" obscures the reference of Matthew to that text.)

[53] [19:4] Gn 1:27.

[54] [19:5] Gn 2:24; 1 Cor 6:16; Eph 5:31.

and mother and be joined to his wife, and the two shall become one

flesh'? 6So they are no longer two, but one flesh. Therefore, what God

has joined together, no human being must separate." 7 [55] [56] They said to

him, "Then why did Moses command that the man give the woman a bill

of divorce and dismiss [her]?" 8He said to them, "Because of the hardness

of your hearts Moses allowed you to divorce your wives, but from the

beginning it was not so. 9[57] I say to you, [58] whoever divorces his wife

(unless the marriage is unlawful) and marries another commits adultery."

10[His] disciples said to him, "If that is the case of a man with his wife, it is

better not to marry." 11He answered, "Not all can accept [this] word, [59] but

only those to whom that is granted. 12Some are incapable of marriage

because they were born so; some, because they were made so by others;

some, because they have renounced marriage [60] for the sake of the

kingdom of heaven. Whoever can accept this ought to accept it."

---

[55] [19:7] See Dt 24:1–4

[56] [19:7] Dt 24:1–4.

[57] [19:9] 5:32; Lk 16:18; 1 Cor 7:10–11.

[58] [19:9] Moses' concession to human sinfulness (the hardness of your hearts, Mt 19:8) is repudiated by Jesus, and the original will of the Creator is reaffirmed against that concession. (Unless the marriage is unlawful): see note on Mt 5:31–32. There is some evidence suggesting that Jesus' absolute prohibition of divorce was paralleled in the Qumran community (see 11QTemple 57:17–19; CD 4:12b–5:14). Matthew removes Mark's setting of this verse as spoken to the disciples alone "in the house" (Mk 10:10) and also his extension of the divorce prohibition to the case of a woman's divorcing her husband (Mk 10:12), probably because in Palestine, unlike the places where Roman and Greek law prevailed, the woman was not allowed to initiate the divorce.

[59] [19:11] [This] word: probably the disciples' "it is better not to marry" (Mt 19:10). Jesus agrees but says that celibacy is not for all but only for those to whom that is granted by God.

[60] [19:12] Incapable of marriage: literally, "eunuchs." Three classes are mentioned, eunuchs from birth, eunuchs by castration, and those who have voluntarily renounced marriage (literally, "have made themselves eunuchs") for the sake of the kingdom, i.e., to devote themselves entirely to its service. Some scholars take the last class to be those who have been divorced by their spouses and have refused to enter another marriage. But it is more likely that it is rather those who have chosen never to marry, since that suits better the optional nature of the decision: whoever can…ought to accept it.

"Therefore, what God has joined together, no human being must separate"
was my pro se defense to try to save my marriage. My noble effort to save my
marriage with scripture was erased by my "Don Quixote" approach.

My parents finally sent me to a West Houston "acute care facility" in July 2004.
In one of the divorce proceedings while representing myself pro se, the judge, at
the request of my wife's attorney, had ordered to me to see a psychiatrist whom
I had fired when he was treating me for depression. My attending psychiatrist
at the "acute care facility" was coincidentally that very same psychiatrist. Even
though I had exhibited no manic or other psychotic behavior, he gave me an
injection of fluphenazine early in my stay, with the promise that I would soon
be released. I was given the long-acting form, and the side effects I experienced
were almost all documented side affects, including:

Lethargy

Restlessness

Nausea and loss of appetite

Increased salivation or sweating

Dry mouth

Headaches

Constipation

Blurred vision

Difficulty passing urine

Tardive dyskinesia (TD), a disorder involving slow or jerky movements
that one cannot control, often starting in the mouth with tongue rolling or
chewing movements.

When I was released from the hospital after a week, this psychiatrist, with a grin on his face, knew that I had blurred vision and still let me drive my car to a hotel. The side effects became so severe that I finally had to call my parents to come to the hotel and take me to their home in Trinity.

I suspect that this psychiatrist administered the fluphenazine in an attempt to hinder rather than help: possibly to maim or kill. I experienced the side effects for almost a month, and at one point had to visit the emergency room.

Thank goodness for a psychologist named Dr. Steven DeAlmeida, who diagnosed my condition, tested me for psychiatric irregularities at the insistence of opposing counsel, and deemed me quite sane. Dr. DeAlmeida testified on my behalf in the divorce. Physicians like the psychiatrist at "acute care facility" definitely don't practice according to their Hippocratic Oath and should have their medical licenses revoked. I truly believe that health insurance companies tend to steer "troublemakers" toward the doctors who practice such medicine.

After the hospital stay, I realized that I had to hire a lawyer and I did. We trudged through the divorce, and it became final in early 2005. It didn't deter me from trying to reconcile with my ex-wife. I still very much loved her, and I wanted to right my terrible wrong. She finally remarried shortly after I did.

Like I said, I hate divorce. It tears at the fabric of our society. If anyone thinks living together is better, it's not. Marriage is a wonderful institution, but you need to have God in your lives and you must be committed to have a loving marriage. Never go to bed angry with your spouse.

I'm not going to be a hypocrite: I've been divorced twice and I've lived with three different women, two of whom I married. If you find the right person, marry them . . . On Faith.

My Professional Career

Below is my professional resume. Between my employment with Jacobs Field Services and Mustang Engineering, I passed my Series 7 General Securities Representative Exam and my Series 66 Uniform Combined State Law Examination to qualify as a financial advisor. I worked short stints at American Express Financial Advisors and MetLife. I had too many financial commitments and not enough cash flow to succeed as a financial advisor.

I have included my resume so one can see I had a stable work history, employed by only two companies from January 1984 to February 2003. After I left Enterprise Products Co., my work history reflects someone who could not hold a job. My problem was I refused to do anything unethical or possibly unlawful. After blowing the whistle on someone, I was being tested.

Matthew 22:18

Knowing their malice, Jesus said, "Why are you testing me, you hypocrites?

GARY R. MILLER

Senior Project Manager

SUMMARY

Senior Project Manager with more than twenty-five years of industrial and municipal project experience in refining, petrochemical, pipeline, power, pulp and paper, water treatment, and engineering and construction projects. Demonstrated expertise in project engineering and construction management of projects from inception through start-up. Highly motivated self-starter with strong organizational skills. Exceptional communicator accustomed to working efficiently, meeting deadlines, and contributing to high performance management teams.

PROFESSIONAL EXPERIENCE

CHICAGO BRIDGE & IRON, Inc. – Houston, Texas 9/2008 – 6/2009

Senior Project Manager
Responsible for the process automation and safety instrumented systems (DCS/SIS) for the Front End Loading (FEL) 2 and 3 phases of the Cartagena Refinery Project in Cartagena, Colombia.
* Evaluated DCS/SIS proposals on a detailed technical and commercial basis to allow the client to select a supplier. Eliminated $100,000 in redundant and unnecessary equipment on a $30 million supply contract.
* Transitioned design drawings and studies to client's international office ensuring a smooth transition for the client and potential future business for the company.
* Assisted estimating department with Spanish/English language translation on unit rates resulting in estimate refinement and best price.

THE SHAW GROUP, INC. – Houston, Texas 8/2007 – 9/2008

Project Manager
Responsible for refining-sector, proprietary equipment supply and proprietary technology studies (process design packages) for both domestic and international clients. Responsibilities included proposal development, contract development, and project management upon contract approval.
* Developed a pricing system/pricing book for streamlining proprietary equipment estimates reducing costs by an anticipated 70% and further reducing company general and administrative expenses.
* Advised domestic and international clients of proprietary equipment needs for pending and future facility turn-arounds ensuring correct and necessary parts were purchased and avoiding costly facility down time.

MUSTANG ENGINEERING – Houston, Texas 1/2006 – 6/2007

Project Manager
Responsible for project engineering and management of refining clients, including Coffeyville Resources Refining and Marketing, LLC in Coffeyville, Kansas and Valero Texas-Refining, LP in Texas City, Texas.
* Managed design drawing development and review, project schedule development, project labor review and forecasting, and material requisition development for projects ranging in size to $150 million. Completed projects on-time and within budget while maintaining schedule objectives and excellent safety records.
* Managed proposals to debottleneck refineries, distributing proposal documents and leading estimation efforts for bidding process of projects ranging in size to $100 million, resulting

in project deliverability within budget and ensuring client satisfaction. Clients included IAG / Kuwait National Petroleum Company, Holly Corporation / Navajo Refining, IAG / Frontier Refining, Inc., Marathon Petroleum Company, GCRC and ConocoPhillips.

JE MERIT – Houston, Texas 8/2004 – 1/2005

Assistant Alliance Construction Manager
Responsible for the management and construction of an ultra low sulfur diesel facility in Rosemount, Minnesota utilizing UOP hydrocracker technology.
- Managed and participated in the Jacobs Behavioral Based Safety Observation Program (BBSOP) identifying unit safety issues for correction and ensuring a safe working environment.
- Interfaced with the construction manager and client on the construction schedule and progress ensuring clear and concise communication for optimal project results.
- Managed and approved subcontractor work within project scope, monitoring schedules and deadlines resulting in projects being on-time and profitable.

CDI ENGINEERING SOLUTIONS – Houston, Texas 6/2003 – 4/2004

Director – Field Services, Project Manager
Responsible for managing and staffing 20 construction management personnel and executing Engineering Procurement Construction (EPC) and Engineering Procurement Construction Management (EPCm) projects. Served as Primary Regional Center Project Manager for chemical plant projects in DuPont's Old Hickory facility, Old Hickory, Tennessee.

ENTERPRISE PRODUCTS OPERATING LP – Mont Belvieu, Texas 7/1991 – 5/2003

Project Engineering Manager (1996 – 2003)
Responsible for capital projects, in-plant design and pipeline engineering and compliance. Completed in excess of 300 capital projects maintaining budgetary and schedule objectives, without a lost time accident. Projects totaled $600 million.

Project Manager (1991—1996)
Project Engineer (1991 – 1991)

AUSTIN INDUSTRIES – Houston, Texas 1/1984 – 7/1991

Field Engineer (1984—1986)
Superintendent (1987—1987)
Project Engineer (1988—1989)
Project Manager (1989—1991)

EDUCATION

Bachelor of Science Degree in Civil Engineering – University of Texas at Austin – Austin, Texas – 1983

TECHNICAL SKILLS

MS Windows, Apple Macintosh OSX, IWorks, MS Office, LOTUS 1-2-3, WordPerfect, MS Project (Scheduling), Suretrak (Scheduling), Icarus Project Manager (In-Plant Estimating)

ADDITIONAL EDUCATION

HAZOP Methodology – University of Texas at Austin
Hazard Assessment and Risk Analysis Techniques for Process Industries – University of Texas at Austin
Basics of Chemical Engineering – Clemson University Continuing Education

Governor Mitt Romney likes to fire people. I like to put them on probation and try to salvage the relationship. That's why he's where he is (a conservative politician) and I'm where I am (a righteous man).

Throughout the ages, continuity and teamwork have been the keys to success. People are an investment, not a necessary evil. Investing to get the best out of people, creating upwardly mobile opportunities for your employees, and then keeping those employees (continuity) is a recipe for success. Guys like Romney care less about teamwork or continuity and more about headcounts, without objectively evaluating productivity by individual departments.

Low turnover is not only the key to success, but also the key to salvation. Of the twelve original apostles, we only lost one to Satan. Romney's religion goes to his core beliefs in everything he does: That only the subjectively anointed can reach the highest levels in anything.

God is the ultimate recruiter and wants everyone to succeed and to reach the one kingdom of God. The following are two of my favorite Scripture passages in the Bible. I use the first as my e-mail signature.

1 Corinthians 9:19–27

All Things to All. 19[61] Although I am free in regard to all, I have made myself a slave to all so as to win over as many as possible.[62] 20To the Jews I became like a Jew to win over Jews; to those under the law I became like one under the law—though I myself am not under the law—to win over those under the law. 21To those outside the law I became like one outside the law—though I am not outside God's law but within the law of Christ—to win over those outside the law. 22To the weak I became weak, to win over the weak. I have become all things to all, to save at least some.[63] 23All this I do for the sake of the gospel, so that I too may have a share in it. 24[64] Do you not know that the runners in the stadium all run in the race, but only one wins the prize? Run so as to win.[65] 25Every athlete exercises discipline in every way. They do it to win a perishable crown, but we an imperishable one.[66] 26Thus I do not run aimlessly; I do not fight as if I were shadowboxing. 27No, I drive my body and train it, for fear that, after having preached to others, I myself should be disqualified.[67]

---

[61] [9:19–23] In a rhetorically balanced series of statements Paul expands and generalizes the picture of his behavior and explores the paradox of apostolic freedom. It is not essentially freedom from restraint but freedom for service—a possibility of constructive activity.

[62] [9:19] Mt 20:26–27.

[63] [9:22] 10:33; Rom 15:1; 2 Cor 11:29.

[64] [9:24–27] A series of miniparables from sports, appealing to readers familiar with Greek gymnasia and the nearby Isthmian games.

[65] [9:24] Heb 12:1.

[66] [9:25] 2 Tm 2:5 / 2 Tm 4:7–8; Jas 1:12; 1 Pt 5:4.

[67] [9:27] For fear that…I myself should be disqualified: a final paradoxical turn to the argument: what appears at first a free, spontaneous renunciation of rights (1 Cor 9:12–18) seems subsequently to be required for fulfillment of Paul's stewardship (to preach effectively he must reach his hearers wherever they are, 1 Cor 9:19–22), and finally is seen to be necessary for his own salvation (1 Cor 9:23–27). Mention of the possibility of disqualification provides a transition to 1 Cor 10.

2 Peter 3:8–9

8[68] But do not ignore this one fact, beloved, that with the Lord one day is like a thousand years[69] and a thousand years like one day.[70] 9The Lord does not delay his promise, as some regard "delay," but he is patient with you, not wishing that any should perish but that all should come to repentance.[71]

HATE

My dad taught me how to hunt. He taught me how to fish. And two of his greatest life lessons were: 1) Do not hate. It will consume you. 2) Everyone has a bad day and therefore deserves a second chance.

My dad worked in the construction business, with the exception of a stint in Korea, from the time he was eighteen until the time he semiretired in 1990 at age fifty-nine. My dad forgave a man who fired him after twenty-three years of service with that man's company. My dad would hire ex-cons because he knew no one else would, and he knew they needed a second chance in life to stay straight.

1 John 2:11

Whoever hates his brother is in darkness; he walks in darkness and does not know where he is going because the darkness has blinded his eyes.

---

68 [3:8–10] The scoffers' objection (2 Pt 3:4) is refuted also by showing that delay of the Lord's second coming is not a failure to fulfill his word but rather a sign of his patience: God is giving time for repentance before the final judgment (cf. Wis 11:23–26; Ez 18:23; 33:11).

69 [3:8] Cf. Ps 90:4.

70 [3:8] Ps 90:4.

71 [3:9] Ez 18:23; 1 Tm 2:4.

I Hated Dan Duncan!

I worked for a company named Enterprise Products Company for approximately twelve years. I used to watch NFL Films. I remember watching a segment about Dick Butkus in which the narrator said, "He went after you like he hated you from his old neighborhood." . . . Unrelenting tenacity and pride. I hated Dan Duncan like I hated him from the old neighborhood.

One of my subordinates brought me evidence of possible impropriety on large purchase of piping for an interstate pipeline that we were constructing from Texas to Louisiana. The engineering, design, construction, operation, and maintenance of interstate pipelines are regulated by the U.S. Department of Transportation. The appearance of impropriety was the exclusion of one of the line-pipe manufacturers who had been on the bid list. I was livid: Not just because it could have been a violation of the Sherman Anti-Trust Act (a US senator and the FBI quickly put the kibosh on that thought). Not just because it tarnished the department I managed. Because the death, the injury, and the damage to property adjacent to the pipeline, near Beaumont, Texas, could have been significant if the pipeline had not blown out during the hydrostatic test, which was performed prior to operation.

The longitudinal weld seam, which is welded at the pipe mill, was defective due to poorly maintained equipment at the mill. My department had rejected almost sixty percent of the pipe from this mill, yet the mill had no incentive to correct their problems since they would just sell their pipe to someone else. We were extremely lucky to have found this defect. The federal minimum hydrostatic testing duration is eight hours. We tested for twenty-four hours, and the blowout occurred in the twentieth hour.

The Dan Duncans of the world layer themselves with attorneys, and the attorneys layer themselves with private investigators, and the private investigators layer themselves with goons and thugs, who harass the former or current employees who have blown the whistle. The employees have to work for the Dan Duncans of the world until they can find another company to work for. A future employer hopefully doesn't know the employee is a whistle-blower and hopefully has no connection to the former employer. It's quite symbiotic.

Dan Duncan has several claims to fame. He donated $137 million to Baylor College of Medicine (The Baptist Medical School in Houston, Texas, which includes Texas Children's Hospital). He won the Safari Award, for which he killed almost every warm-blooded animal species known to man, including a Russian moose from a helicopter.

His company built the Independence Hub (one of the largest gas production offshore rigs and quite "the beast"), which went into operation on July 23, 2007.

Dan Duncan wanted to make every decision in the company, and would have, if God had granted him the time and the patience. Dan grew up poor in East Texas and came close to shutting down his business in the 1980s. His friends, family, and then-employees helped the company weather the storm. During the nearly twelve years I spent with Enterprise, I saw that Dan was extremely *loyal to those who helped him get into business and periodically would provide favors to them. More often than not, he was good to me, but he sometimes forgot just how much good I had done for him. Even though his "Standards of Business Conduct" (which I was "sworn" to uphold) should have prevented him from doing some of those favors, Dan may have been trying to help a friend, yet restraining trade in the process.*

On March 28, 2010, a little over seven years after I walked out of his facilities for the last time, Dan Duncan died at age seventy-seven. This matter is closed, unless law enforcement chooses to reopen it.

This carries over into the Second Tribulation.

The Second Tribulation

July 2007–March 2011

It's the call you never expect, nor do you want. People say they would never want to outlive their kids. I didn't want to outlive my kids nor my parents. On October 4, 2007, my parents, married for almost fifty-two years, died in a murder-suicide in Bell County, Texas. The call came in to the sheriff's department at 10:47 a.m.

I had taken a job with the Shaw Group in August 2006. I was awaiting comments from a coworker on a proposal that I had completed. It was about 5:30 p.m. when building security called, saying that I had a visitor. I went downstairs. Two men identified themselves to me as Houston Police Department detectives (as I thought to myself, "Who did I make mad now?") and asked me the address of my parents' house. I identified it as 5513 Cliff Lane in Temple, and then things went into slow motion.

The detectives spoke the same words that you hear on Law and Order SVU: "We're-sorry-to-inform-you . . ." Then the numbness set in. I didn't scream, I didn't cry. I began to shake. It was as if the spirits of my parents passed through my heart, saying good-bye.

One of the detectives had me call an investigator with the Bell County Sheriff's Office. The investigator said that my dad had shot and killed my mom. Dad then turned the gun on himself. I told the guy that I didn't believe him. He said, "You can drive here in the morning and we'll meet." I quickly told him that I'd drive there that night. I called my parents' house, still in disbelief. I got their answering machine. I guess that was officially the last time that I heard my mom's voice.

I met with the investigator and got all of gory details. My parents' hands were "bagged" for gunshot residue (GSR) tests, and their bodies were transported to the Dallas County Medical Examiner's office. My first suspicion was that they had been killed and the scene staged to look like a murder-suicide. The investigative details, the autopsy, and finally the confirmation of gunpowder residue, one year and four days after their deaths, did confirm that my dad had fired the pistol that killed my mom and then him.

Belton may be a small town, but the investigator there was thorough and thoughtful. The Dallas County Medical Examiner's Office and the Texas Department of Public Safety (DPS) were another matter. The GSR samples were originally sent to the medical examiner's office. After holding them for approximately five months due to, what they said was, backlog, the medical examiner sent the samples back to the sheriff's department, which sent them to the DPS. The DPS then sent the letter below, refusing to perform the analysis. DPS then returned the samples to the sheriff's department, which sent them back to the medical examiner's office.

At the time of this letter from the DPS, my dad was considered the alleged perpetrator (his body was found at the top of driveway) who killed my mom *(her body was found in the kitchen), but the only way to positively confirm that was by a GSR test.*

I contacted the state representative for the Temple, Texas area and asked for her help in the matter. I received a reply, which basically said that DPS's refusal was their Standard Operating Procedure (SOP), as well as SOP for the Federal Bureau of Investigation (FBI). A lot of acronyms to just say "Get Lost". She was kind enough to provide email attachments from the DPS and FBI.

RCVD APR 8 2008

TEXAS DEPARTMENT OF PUBLIC SAFETY
CRIME LABORATORY SERVICE MSC 0460
PO BOX 4143
AUSTIN, TEXAS 78765-4143
Voice 512-424-2105   Fax 512-424-2869

THOMAS A. DAVIS, JR.
DIRECTOR

DAVID McEATHRON
ASST. DIRECTOR

March 31, 2008

Criminalistics Report

COMMISSION
ALLAN B. POLUNSKY, CHAIR
C. TOM CLOWE, JR.
ELIZABETH ANDERSON
CARIN MARCY BARTH

DPTY LARRY DELHAY
BELL COUNTY SHERIFFS DEPARTMENT
P O BOX 749
BELTON, TEXAS 76513

Laboratory Case Number	Agency Case Number	Offense Date
L-368926	07008295	10/04/07

Suspect(s)
MILLER, RAYMOND DOB: 12-16-30

Victim(s)
MILLER, VIRGINIA DOB: 11-18-34

Offense: Homicide
County of Offense: Bell (014)

Evidence Submitted
On 3/14/08 in person by Larry Delhay
Two gunshot residue kit collected at SWIFS

Requested Analysis
Determine the presence of gunshot primer residue on the samples.

Results of Analysis and Interpretation
The gunshot residue kits are being returned without analysis. It is DPS policy to not perform analysis for gunshot primer residue on samples from shooting victims. In most cases the presence or absence of gunshot primer residue on the hands of victims of shootings can not determine whether or not the subject fired a weapon.

Disposition
The evidence will be returned under separate cover.

Ivan Wilson
Supervising Forensic Scientist
Texas DPS Austin Laboratory

ACCREDITED BY THE AMERICAN SOCIETY OF CRIME LABORATORY DIRECTORS – LAB ACCREDITATION BOARD
COURTESY – SERVICE - PROTECTION

Their deaths, on October 4, 2007, came two days after my forty-seventh birthday. My then-girlfriend and I had celebrated my birthday with my parents the weekend before. My parents looked like two people in their golden years, still very much in love. I had talked to my mom the morning of the fourth. She sounded a little down, but not in fear of her life.

I didn't see this coming. No one did.

The evening after we buried my parents, my girlfriend and I went and bought a lot of fresh flowers at a local store. We put flowers on my parents' grave, as well as every other related Miller grave in the same cemetery. I grieved then, but I didn't really grieve until May 3, 2009.

Death of a loved one takes such an emotional toll on people. It can cause emotional overload, which can lead to things like marital strife and eventual divorce. My girlfriend drove me to Temple that night after my parents' deaths. When I was falling down, she held me up. She and my kids were all I had left.

I began dating my girlfriend the summer before my parents' deaths. We became engaged in January 2008 and began living together. We eloped in June 2008, marrying in the beautiful Sonoma wine country of California. Her two daughters were wise beyond their years, and they were livid about the elopement. It was their mom's third marriage and my second. We had not had the time to truly get to know each other. I left our "new house" on May 1, 2009, and she left me, with the "new house", the following week. We divorced in August 2009.

But my second wife did something that helped my autistic son. She was a special education teacher in the school district where we lived. My son had been attending an autism-specific private school for approximately six years. His level of achievement had been evaluated using non-standard methods and his progress was very difficult to gauge, plus he was not exposed to neuro-typical children. Based on my second wife's recommendation, I enrolled my son in fifth grade at a public school that provided an in-class-support, mainstream teaching environment, and some specialized classes with low teacher-to-student ratios. He attended school in this district through the 6th grade. When not being bullied, he did really well.

I still have the "new house". It was put on the market in May 2011, just before we moved to New York City. I took it off the market in September 2012. Now that the Tribulation has been published, I plan to lease it. It would be nice to donate it to the Church...possibly some day. In the mean time a blessing from the Church will suffice.

Probate

My parents worked hard all their lives. My mom picked cotton in the heat of a Central Texas field to pay for her senior class ring. My mom was "everything-considered-popular" in high school, including valedictorian. Rather than attend college, she chose to attend secretarial school and worked as an administrative assistant for almost forty years. When I cleaned out their house in 2009, I found the Underwood typewriter that she bought from Waco Typewriter Co. in the 1950s. It is sitting a few feet away from me as I peck on this Apple

Bluetooth keyboard. I also found her shorthand guidebook. Does anyone still take shorthand?

As soon as my dad was old enough to drive a nail, he started helping my grandfather and great uncles build houses. That early hard work shaped both my parents. They had grown up during the Great Depression without any luxury. My mom would say that she grew up poor and never wanted to go back. They worked, they saved their money and their net worth at the time of their deaths was over two million dollars. About 40% was lost, almost overnight, when the house of cards on Wall Street came tumbling down in 2008.

Probate is horrible. I hired a probate lawyer within a month of my parents' deaths. Her definition of honesty and my definition greatly differed. She shared offices with a white-collar criminal defense attorney . . . a one-stop shop.

In December 2008, I hired one of the best estate attorneys in the state of Texas, and he's still my lawyer. Four months after my parents died, I became executor of their estate. I had been withdrawing money from my IRA to pay for their funeral and their bills. My parents had wills and codicils that were a bit contradictory and difficult to understand. My lawyer and I waded through the mire of completing probate in April 2009, eighteen months after my parent's deaths. I still don't understand why it took so long. We set up the two trusts and the IRAs. Thank God it's over.

Angels and Demons

There's a whole lot of good in our world, and there's a "hell-full" of bad.

Four significant events, good and evil, occurred between May 2009 and December 2009 that forever changed my life. Without my faith in God, I could not have comprehended nor dealt with them.

Matthew 5:4

Blessed are they who mourn,

for they will be comforted.

I have never been good at grieving. It used to be that I just didn't cry very often, and then coupled with antidepressants, I sometimes walked around emotionally numb. Now, after experiencing the Holy Spirit, I literally sob when I hear Sam Cooke's "Touch the Hem of His Garment" or "Jesus Gave Me Water," or Alan Jackson's "I Love to Tell the Story" or "Blessed Assurance" (my mom's favorite).

First Event

On May 1, 2009, I took my kids to Austin, Texas, for the weekend because my second wife and I had been fighting. It became so bad that I had locked myself in a guest bedroom for three days. I did not want to spend the weekend with her and her parents. That was a "freight-train-derailment" waiting to happen.

I saw both my psychiatrist and therapist that day and both recommended that I not spend the weekend with my in-laws. Our house was on a cul de sac. I rounded the corner, and the truck in our driveway was unmistakably . . . her parents'. My therapist had been adamant: "Don't go there, and definitely don't bring the kids there."

I backed up and turned my car out of the subdivision toward Katy, Texas, where my children lived with their mom. I called ahead to find out if I could forego visitation. My ex-wife refused and said she was going to leave town. I thought she had a new beau. Fact was she'd had a new husband since January 2009. She was under a court order to disclose that fact. Somehow it slipped her mind. She told me in August 2009, when my son came to live with me.

I arrived in Katy and loaded up the kids. Where to go? To a hotel in Houston or to a hotel in Austin? I wanted to get as far away as I could from my second wife, yet stay within a reasonable driving distance from Houston because I was still bound by a return time. My decision was to go west. Our destination became the Marriott Fairfield Inn in south Austin. We arrived and got settled. The kids had suitcases and I had the clothes on my back. I was able to get a toothbrush and toothpaste from the front desk. We ate fast food.

The next morning we went out for breakfast. I noticed a lot of traffic in south Austin, so we headed to northwest Austin and another Marriott Fairfield Inn, where I assumed traffic would be less. The people at the hotel were wonderful. They gave the kids board games to play and we went to the room. We had lunch, and later we went downstairs to get a recommendation for dinner. The staff recommended several good restaurants in the area, with the exception of a Marie Callendar's, which was the closest to our hotel. So it was Marie Callendar's for dinner, because it was the closest to our hotel.

The placed seemed pretty benign. We all ordered, and I had a ham sandwich. I only ate half of it before I began to feel ill. Some guy adorned in Texas A&M clothing, beer in hand, sat at the table nearest to us, and when he sat down, he slammed the beer to the table. I don't know whose attention he wanted or if he just wanted to anger me.

My health was rapidly deteriorating. My knees almost buckled, I was shaking and I assumed something had been put in my food. I felt like I was about to faint, and I needed to use the bathroom. A really ugly Latino guy followed me into the men's room. I was concerned about the welfare of my kids. I was in a stall and my sons were right outside the doors. I was vulnerable. To my knowledge, the Latino was doing nothing but waiting for me.

I used the bathroom, and I coughed harder and louder than I ever have. One cough. It was the same cough that I had when I was quitting chewing tobacco and using Nicorette. I would cough in strings of four. We got out of the restroom alive. I got the kids and signed the tab and I didn't know if I could drive back to the hotel, but we made it.

This was when it got a bit unusual. Back in our room, I used the bathroom again and violently coughed one time. It was like my body was trying to expel something. It felt like I had tachycardia, or a rapid heartbeat. Perhaps that was my body's way of increasing my blood pressure, but that didn't make sense. I have hypertension and hadn't had the opportunity to get my high blood pressure meds before driving to Austin. My blood pressure should have been high.

When I came out of the bathroom, all of a sudden, I said, "I don't know why they want to kill me. I want to teach people not to kill each other." I've never said anything like that before.

John 7:19–20

Did not Moses give you the law? Yet none of you keeps the law. Why are you trying to kill me?" [72] 20The crowd answered, "You are possessed! [73] Who is trying to kill you?" [74]

The kids were watching TV, and I started reading the Bible. I completed Proverbs, one of the Wisdom books of the Old Testament. I gave the Bible to my daughter and told her that Proverbs was a great book in the Bible. It was a good guide to living life: living your life with Wisdom. I read Proverbs when I was going through my first divorce.

The kids eventually went to bed. We were in a suite, so I could stay up and watch TV without disturbing them. I couldn't sleep or get comfortable, and my health was getting worse. I opened the fold out bed, lied down, and felt better. I started watching a boxing match (Ali versus Jürgen Blin) on ESPN Classic.

---

[72] [7:19] Acts 7:53.
[73] [7:20] You are possessed: literally, "You have a demon." The insane were thought to be possessed by a demoniacal spirit.
[74] [7:20] 8:48–49; 10:20.

I finally had to call emergency medical services about an hour later. The EMTs arrived and took my blood pressure. I heard someone say the reading was 90/70, which seemed a bit low. However, he took it again and said it was high. We loaded up the kids and traveled to nearby Seton Medical Center.

The Seton Healthcare Family was founded by the Daughters of Charity of St. Vincent de Paul, a Catholic organization that dates back to seventeenth-century France. Fortunately the hospital was located in close proximity to the hotel. As a Catholic hospital, it had several crucifixes on the walls. I didn't know what to think when the attending physician told me that he had to deliver an abortion and he would be back when that was done.

The two nurses looking after me were husband and wife. They were saying outlandish things and making faces. People have known who I am and what I am before I have. People, in some instances, have tested me. This was one of those times. Was the test to determine if I was the "lawless one"? A false prophet? Or was it a test of my belief in Catholicism?

My kids were in a side room watching children's DVDs. My youngest son came in to the room I was in and asked what that was on the wall. I responded that it was a crucifix and it represented Jesus Christ on the cross. He asked why there were so many. I replied that it was a Catholic hospital and the Catholic Church was the one true church. He looked at me. His eyes started watering, and they looked bloodshot.

My son then told me that their DVD player didn't work very well and they didn't have many DVDs. I told him that we would get them a new DVD player and some new DVDs, through the kindness of our hearts. The male nurse smiled. In his eyes, I was now believable. I followed up and got the hospital a new DVR player and Veggie Tales DVDs.

The ER physician stated that he was ex-army special forces. He had a picture on his cell phone of himself in a full beard and mujahedeen hat. He evidently had done a stint in the Afghan war. Regardless of him testing me, he was a righteous man.

When I arrived at the hospital, my blood pressure was 182/110, and my pulse was in the 140's, and then dropped to 85. They put nitroglycerin ointment on my chest, and I felt much better. I thought the nurse said something about someone tainting my sandwich with Viagra. I don't take Viagra; however, combining that with a nitrate would explain a drop in my blood pressure and the rapid heart beat.

We got a cab back to the hotel at approximately 3:00 a.m. We "crashed" in our beds, but surprisingly didn't sleep very late.

On May 3, 2009, we awoke around nine o'clock. It was like there was no one on the freeways in northwest Austin. I don't know whether to say that I was overwhelmed by grief or by the Holy Spirit, but I was overwhelmed. I can't remember if it was just a thought, or a thought and a remark, but I said that I missed Grandma (the name my kids called my mom). I started sobbing and crumpled on the floor. My youngest son knelt on the floor next to me and asked, "Why are you so poor?"

I said, "For I am rich in love."

2 Corinthians 8:9

For you know the gracious act of our Lord Jesus Christ, that for your sake he became poor although he was rich, so that by his poverty you might become rich.

Granted, I had read Proverbs the night before, but I did not read the Bible on a regular basis. I had never seen that passage from 1 Corinthians.

Then my son asked me, "What is that scratching sound?"

I asked, "Do you mean the cross? The cross dragging across the ground?"

Again, my son's eyes welled with tears and became bloodshot. Then things just stopped.

I had to get the kids fed before 10:00 a.m. to get the hotel's complimentary breakfast. I was preparing waffles downstairs at the breakfast bar, and I asked for a knife. The attendant said that knives were upstairs in our room. I became suspicious immediately, and that was so unfair. I began worrying that something might be wrong with the silverware upstairs. She was Latino, and I was remembering the guy from the night before. My suspicion was prejudiced and was so wrong.

I grabbed two plastic knives. I was able to feed two of my kids waffles, but I still needed to feed my third child. Then guilt set in. I went to the woman, apologized profusely, and asked for forgiveness. I was in tears. The kitchen had closed and she gave me two blueberry bagels. I took the bagels and broke them into eleven or twelve pieces. Why, I don't know. I finally convinced my child to eat the pieces bagel.

I was distraught. I had doubted another human being for her ethnicity. It was literally heart wrenching for me.

Acts 7:54–56

54When they heard this, they were infuriated, and they ground their teeth at him. 55[75] But he, filled with the holy Spirit, looked up intently to heaven and saw the glory of God and Jesus standing at the right hand of God,[76] 56and he said, "Behold, I see the heavens opened and the Son of Man standing at the right hand of God."

Second Event

On June 9, 2009, the kids' mom had summer custody, yet she was driving them to her parents' house in Port Arthur, Texas because she was flying to Spain the

---

[75] [7:55–56] Mt 26:64; Mk 14:62; Lk 22:69; Acts 2:34.
[76] [7:55] He…saw…Jesus standing at the right hand of God: Stephen affirms to the Sanhedrin that the prophecy Jesus made before them has been fulfilled (Mk 14:62).

next day. She told me that her "beau" (who was really her husband) had to go to Spain to deal with probate of his parents' estate.

In my home in Cypress, there is a nook at the end of the foyer leading into the family room. The picture below is a direct view from the family room. You can't see her, Our Lady of Lourdes, from the front door because she is hidden (see Rev. 12:5–6).

I'd been planning to find a Virgin Mary statue to put there, and I found this one online from marianland.com. I bought a thirty-six-inch Our Lady of Lourdes statue at 4:14 p.m. CST on June 9, 2009.

The phone rang at about six o'clock. It was my ex-wife's older sister, and she started telling me a sanitized version of my ex-wife and my kids being in an accident. This woman is a physician's assistant and she was in the ER helping a physician and other assistants, when the kids were brought in. She told me that everything was okay, but then added, "Jesus was in the car with them." I wondered what she meant.

I didn't realize how bad it had been until I got to Port Arthur the next day, where they were staying. Seeing your three small kids beaten up is gut wrenching. I asked whether the children would get additional care. Their mom should have cancelled her trip to Spain, but she said that their grandmother (her mom) would take them to the doctor for follow-up. I was shocked that my ex-wife left them.

My ex-wife had turned in front of an oncoming pickup truck and sustained a broadside impact. She was driving a large SUV, which was very fortunate. The vehicle rolled three times and was upside down when it came to a stop. The kids could not all unbuckle themselves; therefore, people at the scene helped them out of the vehicle.

The bottom line is this: On June 9, 2009, I bought the Our Lady of the Lourdes statute at 4:14 p.m., and 53 minutes later, at 5:07 p.m., the SUV was rolling and Jesus Christ was in the car with them. Never doubt the grace and the goodness of Almighty God. Miracles do happen and this was a miracle.

Third Event

December 15, 2009, was a day before my deceased father's birthday. In 2009, an odd-numbered year, the moms get the kids for Christmas in Texas. My oldest son was going to his mom's on December 18. The Christmas tree in my house was up, but lacking presents. My son was eleven at the time and was midway through his fifth-grade year (I held him back an age-appropriate year before he started public school).

We ate and did homework at the kitchen table . . . family life. A low pass-through wall and the couch separated the kitchen table and the TV, so I almost had to stand to see the TV. A Charlie Brown Christmas was on. I was trying to keep my son focused on homework, but he was up and down trying to watch the TV. I tell him that we had to finish the homework and he asked if we could take a break from homework for five minutes. I said okay. Then I asked how about a break for seven minutes.

My son figuratively exploded! He was up from the table before I could stop him. When he reached the foyer wall, the one with the crosses (a partially built key of David), it was with a shower of obscenities: "YOU B*TCH, YOU F*CK, YOU SON-OF-A-B*TCH!"

As you can probably imagine, I was completely taken aback. At the time, I wore a St. Christopher medal, which I took out to be visible to him. My son was running wildly around the house. He ran up to me and screamed, "I WANT YOU TO BURN THIS F*CKING HOUSE DOWN!" He ran away for a moment, and then ran back to me, screaming, "PUNISH ME! PUNISH ME!"

I was really cool through the whole event. I could not imagine anything other than letting him calm himself. He jumped up and down on the lower bunk of his bed. (The lower and upper beds were perpendicular.) He finally settled down and came back in the living room like nothing had happened.

With the words "PUNISH ME! PUNISH ME!", it became understandable what this episode was.

Matthew 4:10

At this, Jesus said to him, "Get away, Satan! It is written: 'The Lord, your God, shall you worship and him alone shall you serve.'" [77]

Jude 6

6 [78] The angels too, who did not keep to their own domain but deserted their proper dwelling, he has kept in eternal chains, in gloom, for the judgment of the great day.[79]

God's angels know better in their actions. For when these demonic angels sinned, by possessing a young boy in this case, they were looking for redemption ("PUNISH ME! PUNISH ME!"). Yet their ultimate punishment, until and through judgment, is that they and their leader, Satan, will never see redemption; rather, they will see an abyss for one thousand years, then death in a pool of burning sulfur and oil.

---

[77] [4:10] 16:23; Dt 6:13
[78] [6] 2 Pt 2:4, 9
[79] [6] This second example draws on Gn 6:1–4 as elaborated in the apocryphal Book of Enoch (cf. Jude 14): heavenly beings came to earth and had sexual intercourse with women. God punished them by casting them out of heaven into darkness and bondage.

I switched my medal from St. Christopher to St. Michael, leader of the army of God.

Ephesians 6:10–17

Battle against Evil. 10[80] Finally, draw your strength from the Lord and from his mighty power. 11Put on the armor of God so that you may be able to stand firm against the tactics of the devil.[81] 12For our struggle is not with flesh and blood but with the principalities, with the powers, with the world rulers of this present darkness, with the evil spirits in the heavens.[82] 13Therefore, put on the armor of God, that you may be able to resist on the evil day and, having done everything, to hold your ground. [83] 14So stand fast with your loins girded in truth, clothed with righteousness as a breastplate, [84] 15and your feet shod in readiness for the gospel of peace.[85] 16In all circumstances, hold faith as a shield, to quench all [the] flaming arrows of the evil one.[86] 17And take the helmet of salvation and the sword of the Spirit, which is the word of God.[87]

---

[80] [6:10–20] A general exhortation to courage and prayer. Drawing upon the imagery and ideas of Is 11:5; 59:16–17; and Wis 5:17–23, Paul describes the Christian in terms of the dress and equipment of Roman soldiers. He observes, however, that the Christian's readiness for combat is not directed against human beings but against the spiritual powers of evil (Eph 6:10–17; cf. Eph 1:21; 2:2; 3:10). Unique importance is placed upon prayer (Eph 6:18–20).

[81] [6:11] Rom 13:12; 2 Cor 6:7; 10:4; Jas 4:7.

[82] [6:12] 1:21; 2:2; Col 1:13.

[83] [6:13] Rom 13:12.

[84] [6:14] Wis 5:17–20; Is 11:5; Lk 12:35; 1 Thes 5:8

[85] [6:15] Is 52:7.

[86] [6:16] 1 Pt 5:9.

[87] [6:17] Is 59:17; 1 Thes 5:8.

Fourth Event

It was December 18, 2009 and my son had gone to his mom's house for Christmas. After the 3rd event, I had spent three days in Atlanta, Georgia, learning how to set up a franchise to sell flooring products, while my son stayed with a sitter. I'd decided that I wanted to be my own boss, rather than a slave to the energy sector.

With the events that had been occurring for the previous seven months, I felt something very dramatic had happened to me. Something good. Something righteous. Something cleansing. The Christmas tree had been up for a couple of weeks. I believe in simplicity when it came to Christmas. Most of the decorations were from Target. There were a few special ornaments: Some with a picture of each of my kids, and an ornament with a picture of my parents. As far as the inexpensive ball ornaments went, they were red and green, yet I was a bigger fan of green ornaments.

I was a parent experiencing some quiet time, so it was a good opportunity to read the Bible and I decided to read Revelation—not for the first time, but still early in my study of the New Testament.

When putting up the Christmas tree, I had tried to ensure that the ornaments were far enough back on the limb, toward the trunk, that they would not fall. I was reading in my study when I heard something hit the floor in the family room. I quickly went there and discovered two ornaments on the floor. One was the photo of my parents. "It" was trying to tell me that they had fallen from grace and were in hell together. The other was a green ball ornament, which indicated "it" was going to attempt to destroy the earth.

What quickly became obvious was that "it" was the "lawless one" or one of his minions. "It" had been in the house during the previous incident with my son on December 15, and "it" was still in the house.

I pulled out my cross from under my shirt. I put the ornaments back on the tree. I laughed at "it" and asked "it" if that was the best "it" could do. I went back to reading my Bible.

John Mellencamp and India Arie sing a beautiful song called "Peaceful World." John sings the lines, "Until you got to look the Devil in the eye,/you know that bastard is one big lie." So true!

People will probably scrutinize this chapter of the book more than any other. I'm old enough to remember Linda Blair puking up pea-green soup while two priests are exorcising the demons from inside her. I'm still open-minded enough to accept as real, some of the events from the movies The Exorcism of Emily Rose and The Rite. Demonic possession is real and the liberation of people from these demons is the Rite of Exorcism in the Roman Catholic Church. In each of these movies, real priests contributed to the script and production. The book version of The Rite is an excellent read, and I highly recommend it to everyone. Face it; many still think that Satan looks like Hellboy . . . or maybe Hellboy's dad.

I started working on this book in January 2010. I may have been unemployed in the engineering world, but I had been blessed with God's work. We moved to New York City in June 2011, for its proximity to publishing houses, better schools, and to get my son away from some really serious bullying. At the time of our move, Texas did not have anti-bullying laws.

Daniel 12:12–13

12Blessed are they who have patience and persevere for the one thousand three hundred and thirty-five days. 13Go, take your rest, you shall rise for your reward at the end of days."

I came to Manhattan on March 13, 2011, to scout the city for an apartment and a school for my son. As the reader will recall from the First Tribulation, the Independence Hub went into operation on July 23, 2007. That date plus 1,335 days is March 19, 2011. After leasing an apartment on that date, I returned home to Cypress, Texas, to prepare to leave the Houston area where I had been born, raised, and had spent the better part of fifty years. I made the commitment to move to New York City and write this book: My reward from God.

The Key of David

Isaiah 22:22

I will place the key[88] of the House of

    David on his shoulder;

        what he opens, no one will shut,

        what he shuts, no one will open.[89]

Revelation 3:7

To Philadelphia.[90] 7"To the angel of the church in Philadelphia,[91]

write this:

    "'The holy one, the true,

        who holds the key of David,

        who opens and no one shall close,

        who closes and no shall open,[92]

---

[88] [22:22] Key: symbol of authority; cf. Mt 16:19; Rev 3:7.

[89] [22:22] Rev 3:7.

[90] [3:7–13] The letter to Philadelphia praises the Christians there for remaining faithful even with their limited strength (Rev 3:8). Members of the assembly of Satan are again singled out (Rev 3:9; see Rev 2:9). There is no admonition; rather, the letter promises that they will be kept safe at the great trial (Rev 3:10–11) and that the victors will become pillars of the heavenly temple, upon which three names will be inscribed: God, Jerusalem, and Christ (Rev 3:12).

[91] [3:7] Philadelphia: modern Alasehir, ca. thirty miles southeast of Sardis, founded by Attalus II Philadelphus of Pergamum to be an "open door" (Rev 3:8) for Greek culture; it was destroyed by an earthquake in A.D. 17. Rebuilt by money from the Emperor Tiberius, the city was renamed Neo-Caesarea; this may explain the allusions to "name" in Rev 3:12. Key of David: to the heavenly city of David (cf. Is 22:22), "the new Jerusalem" (Rev 3:12), over which Christ has supreme authority.

[92] [3:7] Is 22:22; Mt 16:19.

WHAT IS TRIGONOMETRY?

Trigonometry (from Greek trigōnon "triangle" + metron "measure") is a branch of mathematics that studies triangles and the relationships between their sides and the angles between these sides (http://en.wikipedia.org/wiki/Trigonometry). It's fitting that the Greeks wrote the New Testament, and the ancient Greeks transformed trigonometry into an ordered science, which is used to understand the key of David and decipher a message from God.

St. John was imprisoned on the Greek island of Patmos when he prophesied the Revelation of Jesus Christ.

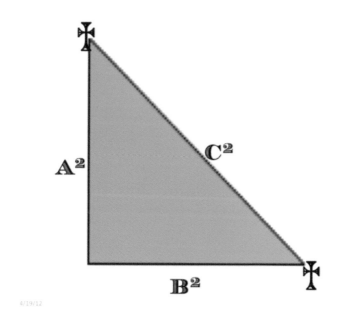

FIGURE 1

$$A^2 + B^2 = C^2$$

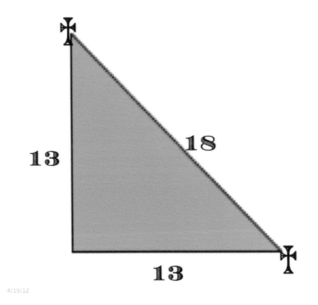

FIGURE 2

A = 13 B = 13

$13^2 + 13^2 = 169 + 169 = 338$

To find C, you take the square root of 338.

$C = \sqrt{338} = 18.38$ (Rounding the number = 18)

With God's divine mathematics, conveyed by the Holy Spirit, comes two keys of David: one for a house I own in Cypress, Texas (Cypress key), and one for the apartment that I was renting in Manhattan (Manhattan key). The keys are a series of fourteen crosses (fourteen stations of the cross, with the twelfth cross in the key matching the twelfth station) arrayed in four sets of Calvary crosses in Cypress and four sets of Calvary crosses in Manhattan.

The first three sets of Calvary crosses have repetitive dimensions between the crosses of thirteen inches and eighteen inches, representing Revelation 1:3 and Revelation 1:8. The fourth sets of Calvary crosses in Cypress and Manhattan have varying dimensions between the crosses, which numerically translate into

64

Scripture passages from The Revelation . . . to provide a Holy message. Two additional crosses (7 and 10) represent Jesus Christ.

In the case of the fourth set of Calvary crosses in Manhattan, the seventh cross is raised from seventy-nine inches to ninety-two inches, symbolizing one or both of the following:

> *The Ascension of Christ.*

> *The Exaltation of the Virgin Mary.*

Revelation 1:3

Blessed is the one[93] who reads aloud and blessed are those who listen to this prophetic message and heed what is written in it, for the appointed time is near.[94]

This dimension of thirteen inches is repeated thirteen times in the Manhattan key and eleven times in the Cypress key. There were thirteen men (twelve apostles plus Christ) at the Passover (Last) Supper. St. John (1) and the three Mary's (Mary, mother of Jesus, Mary of Clopas, and Mary of Magdala) were at the cross when Christ died. The Virgin Mary (1) and the Holy Trinity (3) are another thirteen.

When I was hanging these crosses in the foyer of my home in Cypress, the office that was behind me is thirteen feet by thirteen feet in dimension. The trim

---

[93] [1:3] Blessed is the one: this is the first of seven beatitudes in this book; the others are in Rev 14:13; 16:15; 19:9; 20:6; 22:7, 14. This prophetic message: literally, "the words of the prophecy"; so Rev 22:7, 10, 18, 19 by inclusion. The appointed time: when Jesus will return in glory; cf. Rev 1:7; 3:11; 22:7, 10, 12, 20.
[94] [1:3] 22:7 / Lk 11:28.

pattern of the garage doors on the Cypress house have the same geometric

pattern as the three Calvary crosses (see below).

Revelation 1:8

"I am the Alpha and the Omega,"[95] says the Lord God, "the one who is and who was and who is to come, the almighty."[96]

The 18" dimension is repeated seven times in the Manhattan key and six times in the Cypress key. The Hebrew life number (the "C" dimension or hypotenuse in Figure 1) = 18 (from the heart of the Hebrews to the heart of God).

Psalm 51:12

A clean heart create for me, God; renew within me a steadfast spirit.[97]*According to the system of gematria, the letters of chai add up to eighteen. For this reason, eighteen is a spiritual number in Judaism. Jews often give monetary gifts and donations in multiples of eighteen, which is called "giving chai" (http://en.wikipedia.org/wiki/Chai_(symbol)).*

The "A" and "B" dimensions are the legs of a right triangle, which are both thirteen inches (See Figure 2). Biblically, what this means for Christians is "B" across and "A" up to the bottom of the cross and through the bottom of the cross to its center or heart:

---

[95] [1:8] The Alpha and the Omega: the first and last letters of the Greek alphabet. In Rev 22:13 the same words occur together with the expressions "the First and the Last, the Beginning and the End"; cf. Rev 1:17; 2:8; 21:6; Is 41:4; 44:6.

[96] [1:8] 17; 21:6; 22:13; Is 41:4; 44:6; 48:12.

[97] [51:12] Ez 11:19.

John 14:6

Jesus said to him, "I am the way and the truth[98] and the life. No one comes to the Father except through me.[99]

Below is the diagram that I created to layout the Manhattan key on the west wall of my apartment. The 8, 9, and 11 crosses were on the north wall around the back door.

---

[98] [14:6] The truth: in John, the divinely revealed reality of the Father manifested in the person and works of Jesus. The possession of truth confers knowledge and liberation from sin (Jn 8:32).

[99] [14:6] 8:31–47.

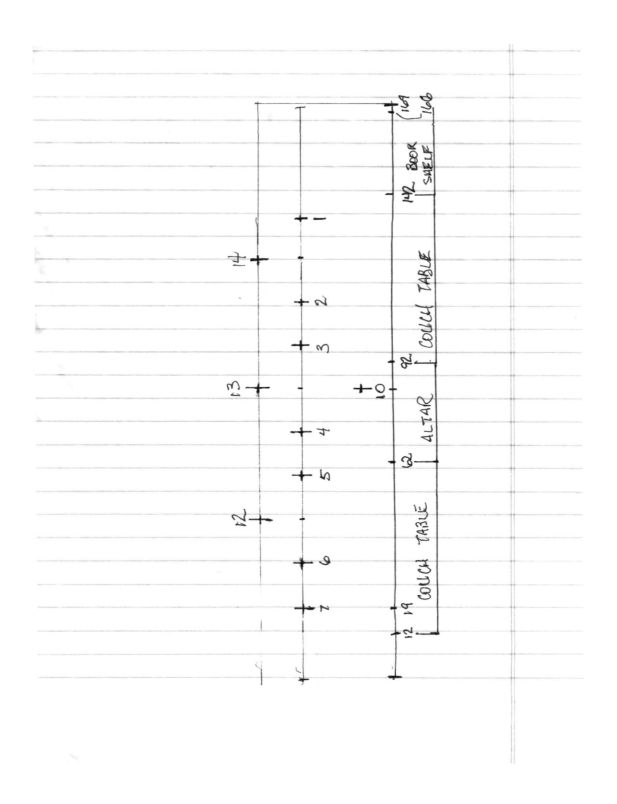

KEY OF DAVID - MANHATTAN

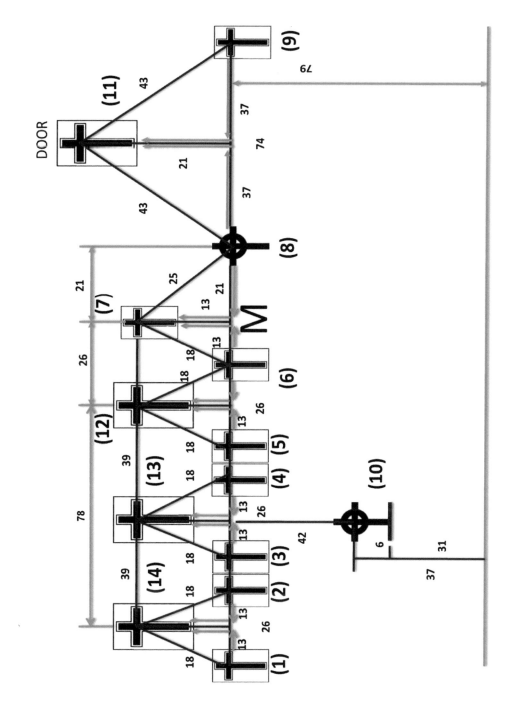

Scripture from the Manhattan Key of David

Revelation 1:3

Blessed is the one[100] who reads aloud and blessed are those who listen to this prophetic message and heed what is written in it, for the appointed time is near.[101]

The 13" dimension is repeated thirteen times.

Revelation 1:8

"I am the Alpha and the Omega,"[102] says the Lord God, "the one who is and who was and who is to come, the almighty."[103]

This 18" dimension is repeated seven times.

When I raised the seventh cross from seventy-nine inches to ninety-two inches, the number of thirteen-inch dimensions went from twelve to thirteen, and the number of eighteen-inch dimensions went from six to seven. This should symbolize the ascension of Christ and the exaltation of the Virgin Mary, which represent the seventh seal and the seven thunders.

---

[100] [1:3] Blessed is the one: this is the first of seven beatitudes in this book; the others are in Rev 14:13; 16:15; 19:9; 20:6; 22:7, 14. This prophetic message: literally, "the words of the prophecy"; so Rev 22:7, 10, 18, 19 by inclusion. The appointed time: when Jesus will return in glory; cf. Rev 1:7; 3:11; 22:7, 10, 12, 20.
[101] [1:3] 22:7 / Lk 11:28.
[102] [1:8] The Alpha and the Omega: the first and last letters of the Greek alphabet. In Rev 22:13 the same words occur together with the expressions "the First and the Last, the Beginning and the End"; cf. Rev 1:17; 2:8; 21:6; Is 41:4; 44:6.
[103] [1:8] 17; 21:6; 22:13; Is 41:4; 44:6; 48:12.

Revelation 2:1

1[104] "To the angel of the church[105] in Ephesus,[106] write this: "'The one who holds the seven stars in his right hand and walks in the midst of the seven gold lampstands says this:

The 21" is repeated twice.

Revelation 2:5

Realize how far you have fallen. Repent, and do the works you did at first. Otherwise, I will come to you and remove your lampstand from its place, unless you repent.

---

[104] [2:1–3:22] Each of the seven letters follows the same pattern: address; description of the exalted Christ; blame and/or praise for the church addressed; threat and/or admonition; final exhortation and promise to all Christians.

[105] [2:1–7] The letter to Ephesus praises the members of the church there for their works and virtues, including discerning false teachers (Rev 2:2–3), but admonishes them to repent and return to their former devotion (Rev 2:4–5). It concludes with a reference to the Nicolaitans (see note on Rev 2:6) and a promise that the victor will have access to eternal life (Rev 2:7).

[106] [2:1] Ephesus: this great ancient city had a population of ca. 250,000; it was the capital of the Roman province of Asia and the commercial, cultural, and religious center of Asia. The other six churches were located in the same province, situated roughly in a circle; they were selected for geographical reasons rather than for the size of their Christian communities. Walks in the midst of the seven gold lampstands: this signifies that Christ is always present in the church; see note on Rev 1:4.

Revelation 2:6

But you have this in your favor: you hate the works of the Nicolaitans,[107] which I also hate.

The 26" dimension repeated four times.

Revelation 3:1

To Sardis.[108] 1 "To the angel of the church in Sardis,[109] write this:

"'The one who has the seven spirits of God and the seven stars says this: "I know your works, that you have the reputation of being alive, but you are dead.

Revelation 3:4

However, you have a few people in Sardis who have not soiled their garments; they will walk with me dressed in white, because they are worthy.[110]

---

[107] [2:6] Nicolaitans: these are perhaps the impostors of Rev 2:2; see note on Rev 2:14–15. There is little evidence for connecting this group with Nicolaus, the proselyte from Antioch, mentioned in Acts 6:5.

[108] [3:1–6] The letter to Sardis does not praise the community but admonishes its members to watchfulness, mutual support, and repentance (Rev 3:2–3). The few who have remained pure and faithful will share Christ's victory and will be inscribed in the book of life (Rev 3:4–5).

[109] [3:1] Sardis: this city, located ca. thirty miles southeast of Thyatira, was once the capital of Lydia, known for its wealth at the time of Croesus (6th century B.C.). Its citadel, reputed to be unassailable, was captured by surprise, first by Cyrus and later by Antiochus. The church is therefore warned to be on guard.

[110] [3:4] 7:13–14.

Revelation 3:7

To Philadelphia.[111] 7"To the angel of the church in Philadelphia,[112]
write this:

> "'The holy one, the true,
>
>> who holds the key of David,
>>
>> who opens and no one shall close,
>>
>> who closes and no one shall open,[113]

says this:

This dimension is repeated three times.

Revelation 3:9

Behold, I will make those of the assembly of Satan who claim to be Jews
and are not, but are lying, behold I will make them come and fall prostrate
at your feet, and they will realize that I love you.[114]

This dimension is repeated twice.

---

[111] [3:7–13] The letter to Philadelphia praises the Christians there for remaining faithful even with their
limited strength (Rev 3:8). Members of the assembly of Satan are again singled out (Rev 3:9; see Rev 2:9).
There is no admonition; rather, the letter promises that they will be kept safe at the great trial (Rev 3:10–11)
and that the victors will become pillars of the heavenly temple, upon which three names will be inscribed:
God, Jerusalem, and Christ (Rev 3:12).

[112] [3:7] Philadelphia: modern Alasehir, ca. thirty miles southeast of Sardis, founded by Attalus II
Philadelphus of Pergamum to be an "open door" (Rev 3:8) for Greek culture; it was destroyed by an
earthquake in A.D. 17. Rebuilt by money from the Emperor Tiberius, the city was renamed Neo-Caesarea;
this may explain the allusions to "name" in Rev 3:12. Key of David: to the heavenly city of David (cf. Is
22:22), "the new Jerusalem" (Rev 3:12), over which Christ has supreme authority.

[113] [3:7] Is 22:22; Mt 16:19.

[114] [3:9] 2:9 / Is 45:14; 60:14.

Revelation 4:2

2 [115]At once I was caught up in spirit.[116] A throne was there in heaven, and

on the throne sat

Revelation 4:3

one whose appearance sparkled like jasper and carnelian. Around the

throne was a halo as brilliant as an emerald.

This dimension is repeated twice.

Revelation 4:7

The first creature resembled a lion, the second was like a calf, the third

had a face like that of a human being, and the fourth looked like an

eagle[117] in flight.

Revelation 7:4

I heard the number of those who had been marked with the seal, one

hundred and forty-four thousand marked[118] from every tribe of the

Israelites:[119]

---

[115] [4:2–8] Much of the imagery here is taken from Ez 1:10.

[116] [4:2–3] Is 6:1 / Ez 1:26–28.

[117] [4:7] Lion…calf…human being…eagle: these symbolize, respectively, what is noblest, strongest, wisest, and swiftest in creation. Calf: traditionally translated "ox," the Greek word refers to a heifer or young bull. Since the second century, these four creatures have been used as symbols of the evangelists Mark, Luke, Matthew, and John, respectively.

[118] [7:4–9] One hundred and forty-four thousand: the square of twelve (the number of Israel's tribes) multiplied by a thousand, symbolic of the new Israel (cf. Rev 14:1–5; Gal 6:16; Jas 1:1) that embraces people from every nation, race, people, and tongue (Rev 7:9).

[119] [7:4] 14:1.

Revelation 7:8

twelve thousand from the tribe of Zebulun, twelve thousand from the tribe of Joseph, and twelve thousand were marked from the tribe of Benjamin.

Revelation 7:9

After this I had a vision of a great multitude, which no one could count, from every nation, race, people, and tongue. They stood before the throne and before the Lamb, wearing white robes and holding palm branches[120] in their hands.

Revelation 9:2

It opened the passage to the abyss,[121] and smoke came up out of the passage like smoke from a huge furnace. The sun and the air were darkened by the smoke from the passage.[122]

Revelation Ch. 10

The Angel with the Small Scroll

---

[120] [7:9] White robes…palm branches: symbols of joy and victory; see note on Rev 3:5.
[121] [9:2] 20:1.
[122] [9:2] Gn 19:28.

Major Schisms of the Catholic Church

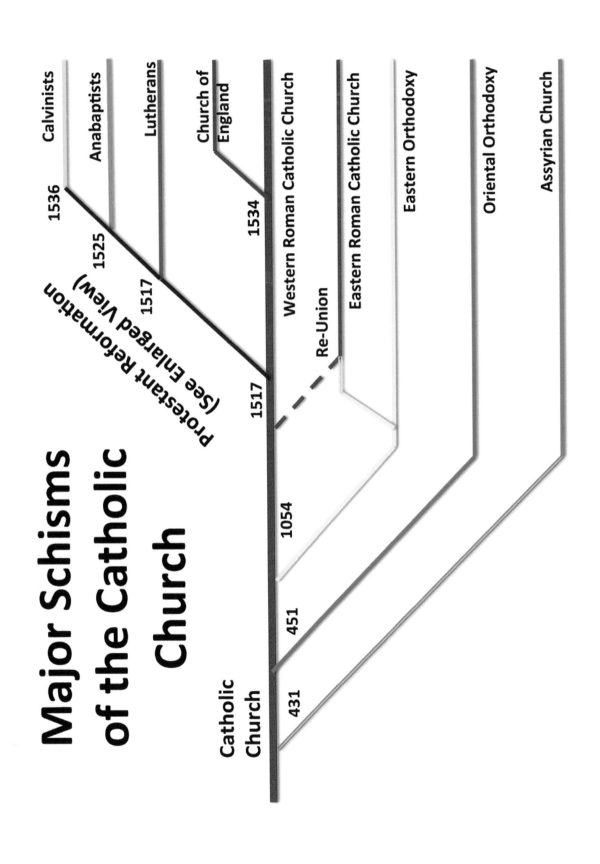

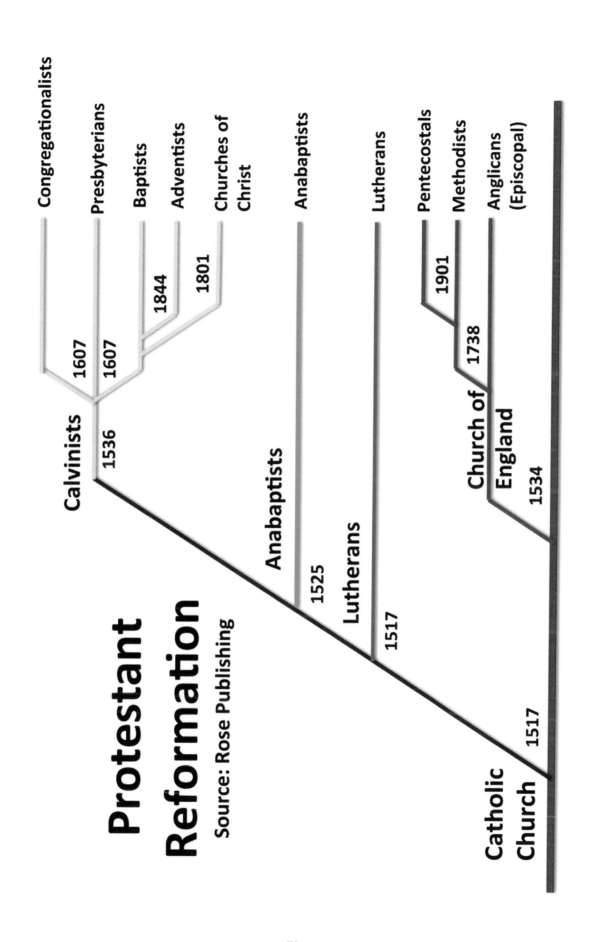

Protestant Reformation

Source: Rose Publishing

Catholic Church

1517

Anabaptists — 1525

Lutherans — 1517

Church of England — 1534

Calvinists — 1536

Anabaptists

Lutherans

Congregationalists — 1607

Presbyterians — 1607

Baptists

Adventists — 1844

Churches of Christ — 1801

Pentecostals — 1901

Methodists — 1738

Anglicans (Episcopal)

Protestant Reformation
"Denominational Offshoot" Churches

Source: Rose Publishing

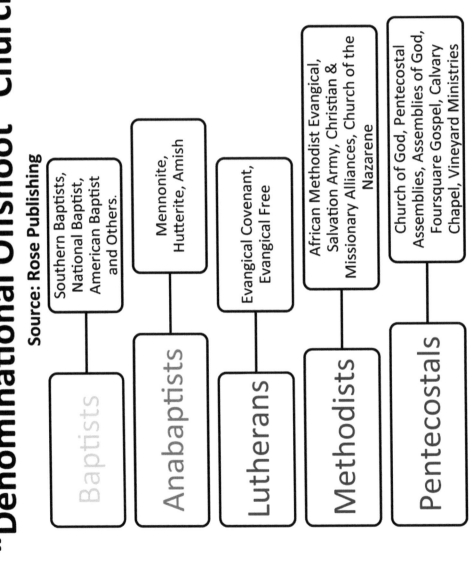

Baptists	Southern Baptists, National Baptist, American Baptist and Others.
Anabaptists	Mennonite, Hutterite, Amish
Lutherans	Evangical Covenant, Evangical Free
Methodists	African Methodist Evangical, Salvation Army, Christian & Missionary Alliances, Church of the Nazarene
Pentecostals	Church of God, Pentecostal Assemblies, Assemblies of God, Foursquare Gospel, Calvary Chapel, Vineyard Ministries

Meaning of the Manhattan Key of David

The Churches

The reader should utilize the three previous diagrams of the Protestant Reformation, the dimensions from the Manhattan key, and the below descriptions of the churches to understand the modern-day church designation and commentary.

Revelation 2:1 The Church of Ephesus

1[123] "To the angel of the church[124] in Ephesus,[125] write this:

"'The one who holds the seven stars in his right hand and walks in the midst of the seven gold lampstands says this:'"

This is repeated twice. The Church in Ephesus is four of the first branches of Protestantism: the Calvinists, the Anglicans, the Lutherans, and the Anabaptists. These four, together with their denominational offshoots, comprise the majority of Protestant churches (see above).

---

[123] [2:1–3:22] Each of the seven letters follows the same pattern: address; description of the exalted Christ; blame and/or praise for the church addressed; threat and/or admonition; final exhortation and promise to all Christians.

[124] [2:1–7] The letter to Ephesus praises the members of the church there for their works and virtues, including discerning false teachers (Rev 2:2–3), but admonishes them to repent and return to their former devotion (Rev 2:4–5). It concludes with a reference to the Nicolaitans (see note on Rev 2:6) and a promise that the victor will have access to eternal life (Rev 2:7).

[125] [2:1] Ephesus: this great ancient city had a population of ca. 250,000; it was the capital of the Roman province of Asia and the commercial, cultural, and religious center of Asia. The other six churches were located in the same province, situated roughly in a circle; they were selected for geographical reasons rather than for the size of their Christian communities. Walks in the midst of the seven gold lampstands: this signifies that Christ is always present in the church; see note on Rev 1:4.

Revelation 2:2 "I know your works, your labor, and your endurance, and that you cannot tolerate the wicked; you have tested those who call themselves apostles but are not, and discovered that they are impostors.[126]"

Revelation 2:3 Moreover, you have endurance and have suffered for my name, and you have not grown weary.

Revelation 2:4 Yet I hold this against you: you have lost the love you had at first.

This could mean their loss of love for the Roman Catholic Church, but more than likely, it refers to their widespread acceptance of divorce, abortion, and homosexuality.

Revelation 2:5 Realize how far you have fallen. Repent, and do the works you did at first. Otherwise, I will come to you and remove your lampstand from its place, unless you repent.

Revelation 2:6 But you have this in your favor: you hate the works of the Nicolaitans,[127] which I also hate.

The 26" dimension is repeated four times. Four signifies the world (in this case meaning throughout the world), from the prologue of the Book of Revelation. Paganism is polytheism—the doctrine of or belief in more than one god or in many gods. Paganism is also the occult.

---

126 [2:2] Who call themselves…impostors: this refers to unauthorized and perverse missionaries; cf. Acts 20:29–30.

127 [2:6] Nicolaitans: these are perhaps the impostors of Rev 2:2; see note on Rev 2:14–15. There is little evidence for connecting this group with Nicolaus, the proselyte from Antioch, mentioned in Acts 6:5.

Revelation 2:24 Notes: The so-called deep secrets of Satan: literally, "the deep things of Satan," a scathing reference to the perverse teaching of the Nicolaitans (Rev. 2:15).

God warns against polytheism in Exodus 20:3–6:

3You shall not have other gods beside me.[128] 4You shall not make for yourself an idol[129] or a likeness of anything[130] in the heavens above or on the earth below or in the waters beneath the earth; 5you shall not bow down before them or serve them.[131] For I, the LORD, your God, am a jealous God, inflicting punishment for their ancestors' wickedness on the children of those who hate me, down to the third and fourth generation[132]; 6but showing love down to the thousandth generation of those who love me and keep my commandments.

The fate of the occult is described in Leviticus 20:6–8.

6Should anyone turn to ghosts and spirits and prostitute oneself with them,[133] I will turn against that person and cut such a one

---

[128] [20:3] Beside me: this commandment is traditionally understood as an outright denial of the existence of other gods except the God of Israel; however, in the context of the more general prohibitions in vv. 4–5, v. 3 is, more precisely, God's demand for Israel's exclusive worship and allegiance.

[129] [20:4] Ex 34:17; Lv 26:1; Dt 4:15–19; 27:15.

[130] [20:4] Or a likeness of anything: compare this formulation to that found in Dt 5:8, which understands this phrase and the following phrases as specifications of the prohibited idol (Hebrew pesel), which usually refers to an image that is carved or hewn rather than cast.

[131] [20:5] Ex 34:7, 14; Nm 14:18; Dt 4:24; 6:15.

[132] [20:5] Jealous: demanding exclusive allegiance. Inflicting punishment…the third and fourth generation: the intended emphasis is on God's mercy by the contrast between punishment and mercy ("to the thousandth generation"—v. 6). Other Old Testament texts repudiate the idea of punishment devolving on later generations (cf. Dt 24:16; Jer 31:29–30; Ez 18:2–4). Yet it is known that later generations may suffer the punishing effects of sins of earlier generations, but not the guilt.

[133] [20:6] Lv 19:31.

off from among the people. 7Sanctify yourselves, then, and be holy; for I, the LORD, your God,[134] am holy. 8Be careful, therefore, to observe my statutes. I, the LORD, make you holy.

Revelation 2:7 """Whoever has ears ought to hear what the Spirit says to the churches. To the victor[135] I will give the right to eat from the tree of life that is in the garden of God."""[136]

Revelation 3:1 The Church of Sardis

To Sardis.[137] 1 "To the angel of the church in Sardis,[138] write this:

"'The one who has the seven spirits of God and the seven stars says this: "I know your works, that you have the reputation of being alive, but you are dead."'

The Church in Sardis are denominational offshoots of the four first branches of the Protestant Reformation. These churches and their further denominational offshoots include, but are not limited to Puritans, Presbyterians, Congregationalists, United Church of Christ, Baptists, Episcopalians, Methodists, Pentecostals, Swiss Brethren, Mennonites, Amish, Hutterites, Quakers, and Moravian Brethren. Several of these churches, at one time or another, have been defined as "Evangelical Christians."

---

[134] [20:7] Lv 11:44.

[135] [2:7] Victor: referring to any Christian individual who holds fast to the faith and does God's will in the face of persecution. The tree of life that is in the garden of God: this is a reference to the tree in the primeval paradise (Gn 2:9); cf. Rev 22:2, 14, 19. The decree excluding humanity from the tree of life has been revoked by Christ.

[136] [2:7] 11, 17, 29; 3:6, 13, 22; 13:9; Mt 11:15.

[137] [3:1–6] The letter to Sardis does not praise the community but admonishes its members to watchfulness, mutual support, and repentance (Rev 3:2–3). The few who have remained pure and faithful will share Christ's victory and will be inscribed in the book of life (Rev 3:4–5).

[138] [3:1] Sardis: this city, located ca. thirty miles southeast of Thyatira, was once the capital of Lydia, known for its wealth at the time of Croesus (6th century B.C.). Its citadel, reputed to be unassailable, was captured by surprise, first by Cyrus and later by Antiochus. The church is therefore warned to be on guard.

"The reputation of being alive, but you are dead": You've gone from your pulpits and your pews being alive with the Word of God, to now dead with the words of politicians, both Republicans and Democrats. You've gone from being revivalists to politicos. You challenge the very laws that prohibit you from endorsing candidates, being political action committees or lobbyists, while maintaining your 501(c)(3) tax-exempt status. As Jesus Christ said in Matthew 22:21, "Then repay to Caesar what belongs to Caesar and to God what belongs to God." *And as St. Paul said in* Romans 13:2,6,7: 2"Therefore, whoever resists authority opposes what God has appointed, and those who oppose it will bring judgment upon themselves" . . . 6This is why you also pay taxes, for the authorities are ministers of God, devoting themselves to this very thing. 7Pay to all their dues, taxes to whom taxes are due, toll to whom toll is due, respect to whom respect is due, honor to whom honor is due.[139]

If I want a political message on the Sabbath, I'll watch the Sunday morning talk shows, but I will not seek it in a House of Prayer. These are the reasons I left the Baptist church. Many have left and have gone on to nondenominational churches to get away from politics and get back to the Word of God.

Revelation 3:2 Be watchful and strengthen what is left, which is going to die, for I have not found your works complete in the sight of my God.

Revelation 3:3 Remember then how you accepted and heard; keep it, and repent. If you are not watchful, I will come like a thief, and you will never know at what hour I will come upon you.[140]

---

[139] [13:7] Mt 22:21; Mk 12:17; Lk 20:25.
[140] [3:3] Mt 24:42–44; Mk 13:33; 1 Thes 5:2; 2 Pt 3:10.

Revelation 3:4 However, you have a few people in Sardis who have not soiled their garments; they will walk with me dressed in white, because they are worthy.[141]

Revelation 3:5 """The victor will thus be dressed in white,[142] and I will never erase his name from the book of life but will acknowledge his name in the presence of my Father and of his angels. [143]

Revelation 3:6 """Whoever has ears ought to hear what the Spirit says to the churches."'

Revelation 3:7 The Church of Philadelphia

This is repeated three times.

To Philadelphia.[144] 7"To the angel of the church in Philadelphia,[145] write this:

---

[141] [3:4] 7:13–14.

[142] [3:5] In white: white is a sign of victory and joy as well as resurrection; see note on Rev 2:17. The book of life: the roll in which the names of the redeemed are kept; cf. Rev 13:8; 17:8; 20:12, 15; 21:27; Phil 4:3; Dn 12:1. They will be acknowledged by Christ in heaven; cf. Mt 10:32.

[143] [3:5] Ps 69:29; Dn 12:1 / Mt 10:32.

[144] [3:7-13] The letter to Philadelphia praises the Christians there for remaining faithful even with their limited strength (Rev 3:8). Members of the assembly of Satan are again singled out (Rev 3:9; see Rev 2:9). There is no admonition; rather, the letter promises that they will be kept safe at the great trial (Rev 3:10-11) and that the victors will become pillars of the heavenly temple, upon which three names will be inscribed: God, Jerusalem, and Christ (Rev 3:12).

[145] [3:7] Philadelphia: modern Alasehir, ca. thirty miles southeast of Sardis, founded by Attalus II Philadelphus of Pergamum to be an "open door" (Rev 3:8) for Greek culture; it was destroyed by an earthquake in A.D. 17. Rebuilt by money from the Emperor Tiberius, the city was renamed Neo-Caesarea; this may explain the allusions to "name" in Rev 3:12. Key of David: to the heavenly city of David (cf. Is 22:22), "the new Jerusalem" (Rev 3:12), over which Christ has supreme authority.

"'The holy one, the true,

who holds the key of David,

who opens and no one shall close,

who closes and no one shall open,[146]

says this:

The Church in Philadelphia is the Roman Catholic Church. It is the "bellwether" of Christianity and it was the first Christian church to be created from the Passover Supper, the crucifixion, and the resurrection of Jesus Christ. St. Peter the Apostle served as the first pope. Their members have kept the Word of God through the centuries, through persecution, through wars, and through scandal. "Little power" means the primary source of income to the church is through charity. They have held fast to the commandments and the canons of the church. I am not a Roman Catholic, but a Protestant by baptism. I do attend Roman Catholic churches.

Revelation 3:8 ""I know your works (behold, I have left an open door[147] before you, which no one can close). You have limited strength, and yet you have kept my word and have not denied my name.

---

146 [3:7] Is 22:22; Mt 16:19
147 [3:8] An open door: opportunities for sharing and proclaiming the faith; cf. Acts 14:27; 1 Cor 16:9; 2 Cor 2:12.

Revelation 3:9 Behold, I will make those of the assembly of Satan who claim to be Jews and are not, but are lying, behold I will make them come and fall prostrate at your feet, and they will realize that I love you.[148]

Revelation 3:10 Because you have kept my message of endurance,[149] I will keep you safe in the time of trial that is going to come to the whole world to test the inhabitants of the earth.

Revelation 3:11 I am coming quickly. Hold fast to what you have, so that no one may take your crown.[150]

Vision of Heavenly Worship

Revelation 4:2 [151]At once I was caught up in spirit.[152] A throne was there in heaven, and on the throne sat.

Revelation 4:3 one whose appearance sparkled like jasper and carnelian. Around the throne was a halo as brilliant as an emerald.

This is repeated twice.

---

[148] [3:9] 2:9 / Is 45:14; 60:14.

[149] [3:10] My message of endurance: this does not refer to a saying of Jesus about patience but to the example of Christ's patient endurance. The inhabitants of the earth: literally, "those who live on the earth." This expression, which also occurs in Rev 6:10; 8:13; 11:10; 13:8, 12, 14; 17:2, 8, always refers to the pagan world.

[150] [3:11] 2:25; 22:7, 20.

[151] [4:2–8] Much of the imagery here is taken from Ez 1:10.

[152] [4:2–3] Is 6:1 / Ez 1:26–28.

Revelation 4:7 The first creature resembled a lion, the second was like a calf, the third had a face like that of a human being, and the fourth looked like an eagle[153] in flight.

Walk the Path of Jesus Christ

Revelation 7:4 I heard the number of those who had been marked with the seal, one hundred and forty-four thousand marked[154] from every tribe of the Israelites:[155]

A thousand in this case is figurative. Per the prologue of Revelation, one thousand means immensity. One hundred and forty-four thousand is the square of twelve (the number of Israel's tribes and also the number of Apostles) multiplied by a thousand, symbolic of the New Israel that embraces people from every nation, race, people, and tongue. The seal is either the impression of a signet ring and/ or the symbol of the Holy Spirit, a dove.

Revelation 7:8 twelve thousand from the tribe of Zebulun, twelve thousand from the tribe of Joseph, and twelve thousand were marked from the tribe of Benjamin.

---

[153] Lion…calf…human being…eagle: these symbolize, respectively, what is noblest, strongest, wisest, and swiftest in creation. Calf: traditionally translated "ox," the Greek word refers to a heifer or young bull. Since the second century, these four creatures have been used as symbols of the evangelists Mark, Luke, Matthew, and John, respectively.

[154] [7:4–9] One hundred and forty-four thousand: the square of twelve (the number of Israel's tribes) multiplied by a thousand, symbolic of the new Israel (cf. Rev 14:1–5; Gal 6:16; Jas 1:1) that embraces people from every nation, race, people, and tongue (Rev 7:9).

[155] [7:4] 14:1.

The key of David has a dimension of seventy-eight inches spanning across three of the upper crosses. The upper crosses are arranged with cross fourteen, the "Love (or Charity) Cross" (1 Cor. 13:13), in the north; cross thirteen, the "Redemption Cross" (Isa. 43:1), in the center; and cross twelve, the crucifix, in the south.

I started looking at the tribes of Zebulun, Joseph, and Benjamin, and at the people within the tribes. Per the map "The Twelve Tribes of Israel" (see Chapter 6, The Scroll), the three tribes were geographically contiguous, with Zebulun to the north, Joseph (consisting of W. Manasseh and Ephraim) in the center, and Benjamin in the south. It is widely accepted that Nazareth was located within the boundary of Zebulun. The map shows that Jerusalem was located within the boundary of Benjamin. These two cities, along with Bethlehem, are referred to as the Holy Lands. Jesus spent his youth and adulthood in Nazareth. (Matt. 2:23; 4:12–16).

The territory of Joseph was thus one of the most valuable parts of the country, and the house of Joseph became the most dominant group in the Kingdom of Israel.
Source: http://en.wikipedia.org/wiki/Tribe_of_Joseph

Jesus traversed a path from Galilee (Zebulun), through Samaria (Joseph) and through Jericho, to Jerusalem (Benjamin). The twelfth and fourteenth crosses match the positions of Benjamin and Zebulun, respectively, on each side of Joseph, which is the thirteenth cross.

In addition, there is the religious representation of the different crosses. The fourteenth cross, Love (and Charity), represents John 3:16. The thirteenth cross, in the center, represents God's redemption of the Jews from their persecution of Jesus and His crucifixion in Jerusalem (Isaiah 43:1). The twelfth cross is the crucifix, representing the death and resurrection of Christ in Jerusalem.

The divine message from Scripture, given to me on June 16, 2012, by the Holy Spirit, is found in John 3:16, Isaiah 43.1, and John 19:17–30.

WALK THE PATH OF JESUS CHRIST: 1) The Love and Charity of Jesus Christ. 2) The redemption of the Jews. 3) Jesus died on the cross for our sins.

14th Cross—John 3:16

13th Cross – Isaiah 43:1

12ᵗʰ Cross—John 19:17–30

Revelation 7:9 After this I had a vision of a great multitude, which no one could count, from every nation, race, people, and tongue. They stood before the throne and before the Lamb, wearing white robes and holding palm branches[156] in their hands.

Symbolic of the New Israel (see Rev. 14:1–5; Gal. 6:16; James 1:1) that embraces people from every nation, race, people, and tongue (Rev. 7:9). "Palm branches," John 12:12–13: This is symbolic of Palm Sunday and the arrival of Jesus in Jerusalem. He who comes in the name of the Lord: referred in Psalm 118:26 to a pilgrim entering the temple gates, but here a title for Jesus (see notes on Matt. 11:3 and John 6:14; 11:27). The New Israel may very well be New York City (residents and visitors from every nation, race, people, and tongue), which is also symbolic of the United Nations. How better to spread the Word of God throughout the World, than through the people of the New Jerusalem.

Revelation 9:2 It opened the passage to the abyss,[157] and smoke came up out of the passage like smoke from a huge furnace. The sun and the air were darkened by the smoke from the passage.[158]

My interpretation of "It" in this Scripture is a Seraph, a type of celestial or heavenly being in the Abrahamic religions. This "burning angel" is traditionally placed in the FIFTH rank of ten in the Jewish angelic hierarchy and the highest rank in the Christian angelic hierarchy. God has sent the Seraph to earth, with the keys to the abyss (See Rev. 20:1), to open the abyss. "Smoke" is air pollution from the abyss.

---

[156] [7:9] White robes…palm branches: symbols of joy and victory; see note on Rev 3:5.
[157] [9:2] 20:1.
[158] [9:2] Gn 19:28.

The Eighth Cross

Revelation Ch. 10 The Angel with the Small Scroll

The eighth cross above is a Celtic cross. The Son of Man is clothed with a white wraparound, and the halo around his head symbolizes eternity. The cross is green, blue, yellow and copper in color. (Rev. 10:1) The "mighty angel come down from heaven wrapped in a cloud, with a halo around his head" refers to the Statue of Liberty. The statue is clothed in a white robe. Seven rays (seven thunders) come from the crown on her head. (Rev. 10:2) "In his hand he held a small scroll." St. John saw the book in Lady Liberty's left hand and proclaimed it the "small scroll"; however, the words of "The New Colossus", by Jewish-American poet Emma Lazarus , on a plaque at the base of the monument, are the contents of the scroll. He (she) placed his (her) right foot on the sea and his (her) left foot on the land (span between Liberty Island and Ellis Island), and then he (she) cried out in a loud voice as a lion roars. When he (she) cried out, the seven thunders raised their voices saying: "Give me your tired, your poor,/ Your huddled masses yearning to breathe free" and swore by the one who lives forever and ever, who created heaven and earth and sea and all that is in them, "There shall be no more delay. At the time when you hear the seventh angel blow his trumpet (this book), the mysterious plan of God shall be fulfilled, as he promised to his servants the prophets" (Rev.10:6-7). The seven thunders are God's voice announcing judgment and doom. (Rev. 1:3: "Blessed is the one who reads aloud and blessed are those who listen to this prophetic message and heed what is written in it, for the appointed time is near." There are thirteen measurements of thirteen inches on the key of David. See Psalm 29:3–9, where thunder, as the voice of Yahweh, is praised seven times. (Rev. 1:8 "'I am the Alpha and the Omega,' says the Lord God, 'the one who is and who was and who is to come, the almighty.'") There are seven measurements of eighteen inches on the Manhattan key of David.

(Rev. 10:11) Then someone said to me, "You must prophesy again about many peoples, nations, tongues, and kings." *This refers to the immigrants going through Ellis Island and the "melting pot" of New York City, where approximately eight million people live. The city hosts the United Nations.*

This angel, the Statue of Liberty, gives people hope. The book she's holding says, "July IV M DCCL XXVI," which in Roman numerals, is the date July 4, 1776 (7–4–1776): The date that the Declaration of Independence was signed. "Take and swallow it" means open, read, and accept the scroll. Words that were once sweet are now sour because of the hypocrisy and sometimes cruelty toward the Mexican immigrants from the south.

All of this represents, by spreading love (loving thy neighbor), spreading the unadulterated Word of God, repentance, and fighting evil and tyranny, we achieve eternal life in the one kingdom of heaven.

The Key of David—Cypress

Jerusalem Cross

Crusaders' Cross

The Jerusalem cross, also known as the Crusaders' cross, is a heraldic cross or Christian symbol consisting of a large Greek cross surrounded by four smaller Greek crosses, one in each quadrant. The simpler form of the cross is known as the Crusaders' Cross" because it was on the papal banner given to the crusaders by Pope Urban II for the First Crusade, and became a symbol of the Latin kingdom of Jerusalem. The Crusader's Cross was first worn by Godfrey of Bouillon, the first leader of the kingdom. The four smaller crosses are said to symbolize either the four books of the Gospel or the four directions in which the Word of Christ spread from Jerusalem. Alternatively, all five crosses can symbolize the five wounds of Christ during the Passion, the Pentateuch, and, presumably, the first five Christian churches.

Its origin may come from Phoenicia, in the shape of a white, sometimes green, eight-pointed cross, known as Maltese cross, each point representing a beatitude, as the Venerable Order of St. John teaches.

The Jerusalem Cross is also used in the flag of Georgia and as a symbol of the Catholic Kairos retreat, where participants are given the pendant at the end of their experience (http://en.wikipedia.org/wiki/Jerusalem_cross).

The first set of crosses that I erected in Cypress, TX was in the form of the Crusaders' or the Jerusalem cross. My second wife and I moved into the Cypress house in mid-March 2009 and were separated by mid-May 2009. She had a few crosses, and we had purchased a few more with the intent of putting them on the foyer wall across from the study. I had no idea what the Crusaders' or Jerusalem crosses were; I just built an array of five crosses. I had one large cross and four smaller crosses, and hung all of them in the same pattern as the Crusaders' cross, directly in front of the study door: My thirteen feet by thirteen feet study. These crosses were the Genesis of building the Cypress key of David in November 2009.

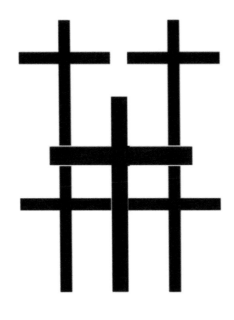

5 CROSSES

I traveled to Atlanta, Georgia, from December 16 through 18, 2009. On the morning of December 18, I awoke sometime around four o'clock in the morning and started writing on the paper reproduced below.

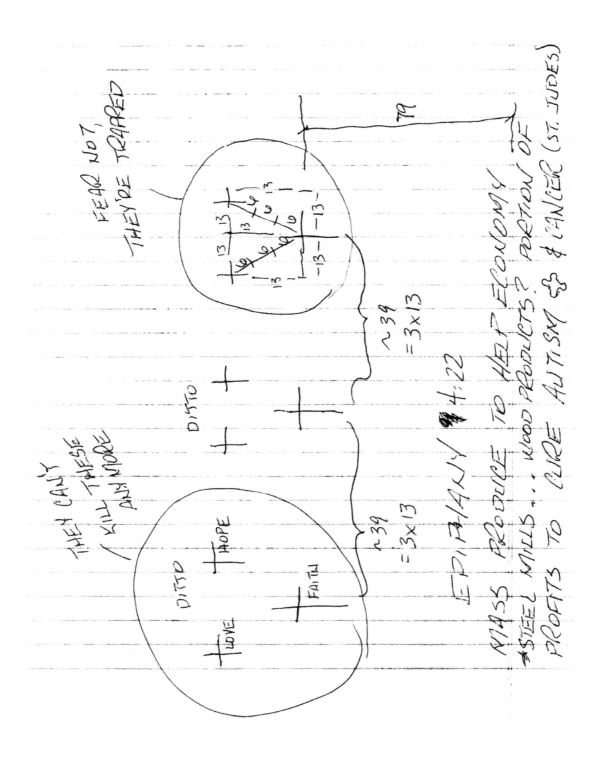

104

Epiphany 4:22

This cross configuration is the same as the one on the Epiphany 4:22 document. When I finished writing the document, I looked at the alarm clock in the hotel room, and the time was 4:22 a.m., EST.

I purchased these three crosses from Hobby Lobby in November 2009. The upper left cross is the wood-layered cross of Love; the upper right cross is the wood-layered cross of Hope; and the center cross, as you can see, is the Faith cross. I had already hung these three crosses in the foyer in the pattern as shown on the Epiphany 4:22 document.

The positive things that resulted from this vision were helping charities, curing disease, and job creation by mass-producing the key. There were; however, a couple of problems with the vision.

Luke 23:33

The Crucifixion

When they came to the place called the Skull, they crucified him and the criminals there, one on his right, the other on his left. [159]

The New Testament places the crucifixion at Golgotha, or place of [the] skull— Κρανίου Τόπος (Kraniou Topos) in Greek, and Calvariae Locus in Latin, from which we get Calvary.

---

[159] [23:33] 22:37; Is 53:12.

The crosses were arranged in an "inverted Calvary" configuration, meaning the crosses on the side (the criminals) were above the cross in the center (Jesus Christ). Not good!

The other thing was determining the eighteen-inch dimension from the thirteen inch by thirteen inch right triangle. However, eighteen inches does not make 6-6-6 in biblical terms. I did find solace knowing that I'm not the first to make this mistake. See "Is 'www' in Hebrew equal to 666?" (**http://www.av1611. org/666/www_666.html**).

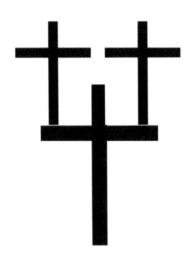

3 INVERTED CROSSES OF CALVARY

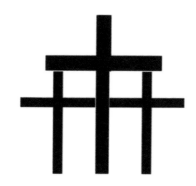

3 CROSSES OF CALVARY

The above diagram of three crosses in Calvary position, shows a true representation, with the cross of Jesus in the center and the crosses of the criminals, below and on both sides, as described in Luke 23:33–34. I'd spent time staring at three sets of three crosses for at least four months, so when I drove right outside my subdivision and past a new church with the crosses of Calvary outside, I quickly realized the my crosses were reversed.

The Cypress key of David was started in November 2009, with the crosses oriented in an inverted Calvary pattern. The last photo that I took of the crosses, when they were still inverted, was in April 2010. The first key of David diagram that I created was started in June 2010, and had the correct Calvary cross orientation. Sometime between April 2010 and June 2010, I found and corrected my mistake.

2 John 7

7 [160] Many deceivers have gone out into the world, those who do not acknowledge Jesus Christ as coming in the flesh; such is the deceitful one and the antichrist.[161]

If he (or it) can deceive me, making the crosses look right and clouding my mind, then he can deceive you.

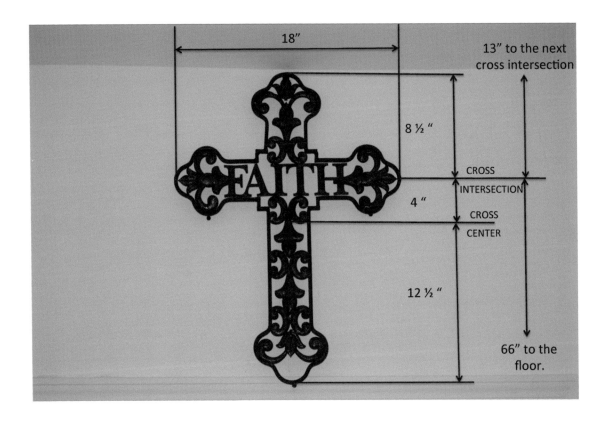

My mom's rule-of-thumb for hanging pictures was to set the vertical center of the frame at eye level. I'm 5' 7" so my eye level, depending on shoes, is typically between 61 inches and 63 inches. I used her rule-of-thumb to set the height for the above "Faith" cross. With the "Cross Intersection" approximately 4 inches above the "Cross Center", the "Cross Intersection" was set 66 inches above the

[160] [7] 1 Jn 2:22; 4:2.
[161] [7] The antichrist: see 1 Jn 2:18–19, 22; 4:3.

floor, in a 5 Cross (Crusader) pattern, directly across from my study. When I started building the Cypress Key, I removed the 2 lower crosses rather than the 2 upper crosses. The Cross Intersection of the 2 upper crosses was 13 inches above the Cross Intersection of the "Faith" cross or at 79 inches above the floor. When I finally realized my mistake, I merely raised the center, or in this case the "Faith" cross, 13 inches above the crosses on each side.

The "Faith" cross and the other 2 crosses were eventually replaced by the below Isaiah 43:1 "Redemption" cross and the 2 "Born Into Eternal Life" crosses.

Cypress Floor Plan

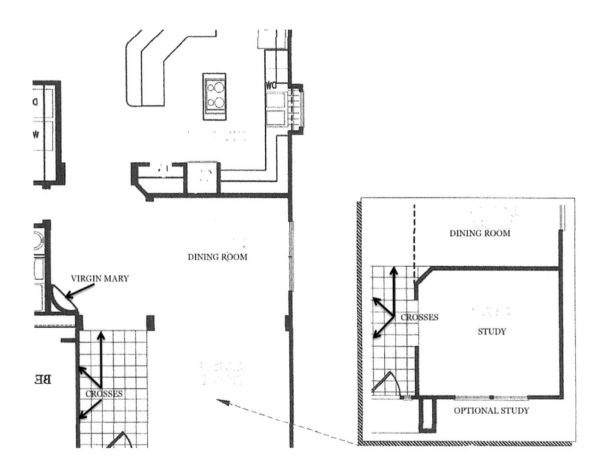

KEY OF DAVID - CYPRESS

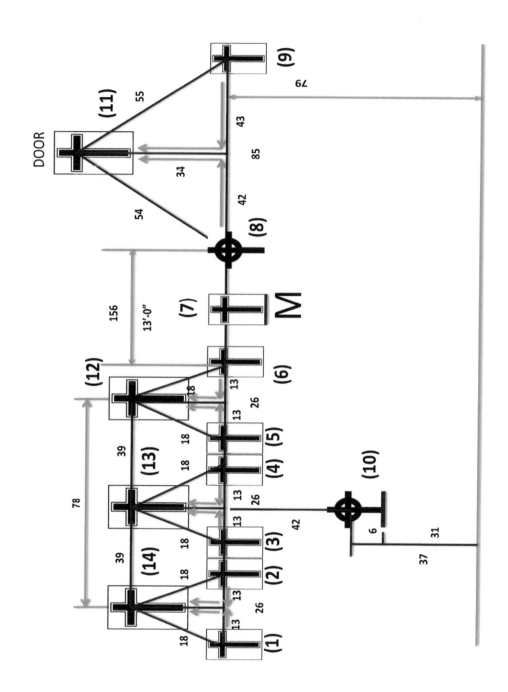

While the Manhattan key points us toward achieving eternal life in the one kingdom of God, the Cypress key points us to separating ourselves from sin with a warning of calamity—a warning due to the sins of the oil and coal companies.

Isaiah 24:5–6

5The earth is polluted because of its

    inhabitants,

        for they have transgressed laws,

    violated statutes,

        broken the ancient covenant.[162] [163]

6Therefore a curse devours the earth,

        and its inhabitants pay for their

    guilt;

Therefore they who dwell on earth have

    dwindled,

        and only a few are left.[164]

---

[162] [24:5] Ancient covenant: God's commandments to all humankind (cf. Gn 9:4–6).

[163] [24:5] Nm 35:33; Hos 4:2–3.

[164] [24:6] Lv 26:15–16.

Scripture from the Cypress Key of David

Revelation 1:3

Blessed is the one[165] who reads aloud and blessed are those who listen to this prophetic message and heed what is written in it, for the appointed time is near.[166]

The 13" dimension is repeated eleven times.

Revelation 1:8

"I am the Alpha and the Omega,"[167] says the Lord God, "the one who is and who was and who is to come, the almighty."[168]

This 18" dimension is repeated six times.

Revelation 2:6

But you have this in your favor: you hate the works of the Nicolaitans,[169] which I also hate.

This 26" dimension is repeated three times.

---

[165] [1:3] Blessed is the one: this is the first of seven beatitudes in this book; the others are in Rev 14:13; 16:15; 19:9; 20:6; 22:7, 14. This prophetic message: literally, "the words of the prophecy"; so Rev 22:7, 10, 18, 19 by inclusion. The appointed time: when Jesus will return in glory; cf. Rev 1:7; 3:11; 22:7, 10, 12, 20.
[166] [1:3] 22:7 / Lk 11:28.
[167] [1:8] The Alpha and the Omega: the first and last letters of the Greek alphabet. In Rev 22:13 the same words occur together with the expressions "the First and the Last, the Beginning and the End"; cf. Rev 1:17; 2:8; 21:6; Is 41:4; 44:6.
[168] [1:8] 17; 21:6; 22:13; Is 41:4; 44:6; 48:12.
[169] [2:6] Nicolaitans: these are perhaps the impostors of Rev 2:2; see note on Rev 2:14–15. There is little evidence for connecting this group with Nicolaus, the proselyte from Antioch, mentioned in Acts 6:5.

Revelation 3:1

To Sardis.[170] 1 "To the angel of the church in Sardis,[171] write this:

"'The one who has the seven spirits of God and the seven stars says this: "I know your works, that you have the reputation of being alive, but you are dead.

Revelation 3:4

However, you have a few people in Sardis who have not soiled their garments; they will walk with me dressed in white, because they are worthy.[172]

Revelation 3:7

To Philadelphia.[173] 7"To the angel of the church in Philadelphia, [174] write this:

"'The holy one, the true,

who holds the key of David,

who opens and no one shall close,

who closes and no one shall open,175

says this:

---

[170] [3:1–6] The letter to Sardis does not praise the community but admonishes its members to watchfulness, mutual support, and repentance (Rev 3:2–3). The few who have remained pure and faithful will share Christ's victory and will be inscribed in the book of life (Rev 3:4–5).

[171] [3:1] Sardis: this city, located ca. thirty miles southeast of Thyatira, was once the capital of Lydia, known for its wealth at the time of Croesus (6th century B.C.). Its citadel, reputed to be unassailable, was captured by surprise, first by Cyrus and later by Antiochus. The church is therefore warned to be on guard.

[172] [3:4] 7:13–14.

[173] [3:7–13] The letter to Philadelphia praises the Christians there for remaining faithful even with their limited strength (Rev 3:8). Members of the assembly of Satan are again singled out (Rev 3:9; see Rev 2:9). There is no admonition; rather, the letter promises that they will be kept safe at the great trial (Rev 3:10–11) and that the victors will become pillars of the heavenly temple, upon which three names will be inscribed: God, Jerusalem, and Christ (Rev 3:12).

[174] [3:7] Philadelphia: modern Alasehir, ca. thirty miles southeast of Sardis, founded by Attalus II Philadelphus of Pergamum to be an "open door" (Rev 3:8) for Greek culture; it was destroyed by an earthquake in A.D. 17. Rebuilt by money from the Emperor Tiberius, the city was renamed Neo-Caesarea; this may explain the allusions to "name" in Rev 3:12. Key of David: to the heavenly city of David (cf. Is 22:22), "the new Jerusalem" (Rev 3:12), over which Christ has supreme authority.

[175] [3:7] Is 22:22; Mt 16:19.

Revelation 4:2

2 [176]At once I was caught up in spirit.[177] A throne was there in heaven, and

on the throne sat

This is repeated twice.

Revelation 4:3

one whose appearance sparkled like jasper and carnelian. Around the

throne was a halo as brilliant as an emerald.

Revelation 5:4

I shed many tears because no one was found worthy to open the scroll or

to examine it.

Revelation 5:5

One of the elders said to me, "Do not weep. The lion of the tribe of Judah,

the root of David,[178] has triumphed, enabling him to open the scroll with

its seven seals."[179]

Revelation 7:8 twelve thousand from the tribe of Zebulun, twelve

thousand from the tribe of Joseph, and twelve thousand were marked

from the tribe of Benjamin.

---

[176] [4:2–8] Much of the imagery here is taken from Ez 1:10.

[177] [4:2–3] Is 6:1 / Ez 1:26–28.

[178] [5:5] The lion of the tribe of Judah, the root of David: these are the messianic titles applied to Christ to symbolize his victory; cf. Rev 22:16; Gn 49:9; Is 11:1, 10; Mt 1:1.

[179] [5:5] Is 11:1, 10; Rom 15:12.

Revelation 7:9

After this I had a vision of a great multitude, which no one could count, from every nation, race, people, and tongue. They stood before the throne and before the Lamb, wearing white robes and holding palm branches[180] in their hands.

Revelation 8:5

Then the angel took the censer, filled it with burning coals from the altar, and hurled it down to the earth. There were peals of thunder, rumblings, flashes of lightning, and an earthquake.[181]

Revelation 9:2

It opened the passage to the abyss,[182] and smoke came up out of the passage like smoke from a huge furnace. The sun and the air were darkened by the smoke from the passage.[183]

---

[180] [7:9] White robes…palm branches: symbols of joy and victory; see note on Rev 3:5.
[181] [8:5] Ez 10:2; Ps 11:6 / 4:5; 11:19; 16:18.
[182] [9:2] 20:1.
[183] [9:2] Gn 19:28.

Revelation 11:3

I will commission my two witnesses[184] to prophesy for those twelve hundred and sixty days, wearing sackcloth.

Revelation 15:6

and the seven angels with the seven plagues came out of the temple. They were dressed in clean white linen, with a gold sash around their chests.[185]

---

[184] [11:3] The two witnesses, wearing sackcloth symbolizing lamentation and repentance, cannot readily be identified. Do they represent Moses and Elijah, or the Law and the Prophets, or Peter and Paul? Most probably they refer to the universal church, especially the Christian martyrs, fulfilling the office of witness (two because of Dt 19:15; cf. Mk 6:7; Jn 8:17).

[185] [15:6] 19:8.

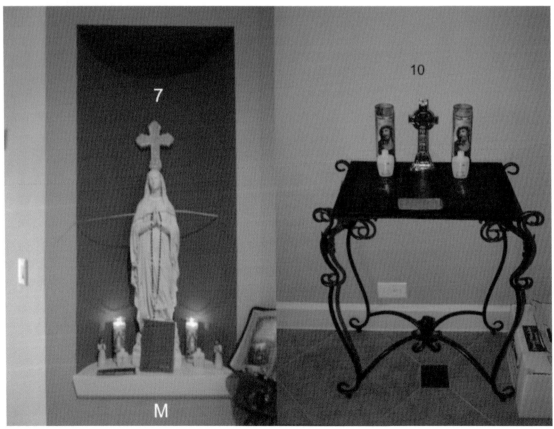

The Meaning of the Cypress Key of David

Revelation 1:3 Blessed is the one[186] who reads aloud and blessed are those who listen to this prophetic message and heed what is written in it, for the appointed time is near.[187]

This is repeated eleven times.

The number thirteen was added twice to the Manhattan key of David, symbolizing the second coming.

Revelation 1:8 "I am the Alpha and the Omega,"[188] says the Lord God, "the one who is and who was and who is to come, the almighty."[189]

This is repeated six times.

The number eighteen was added a seventh time to the Manhattan key of David symbolizing the opening of the seventh seal in Manhattan. Six of the seals had been opened in Cypress. My work could not have been completed in Cypress. The actual second coming occurred in New York City.

---

[186] [1:3] Blessed is the one: this is the first of seven beatitudes in this book; the others are in Rev 14:13; 16:15; 19:9; 20:6; 22:7, 14. This prophetic message: literally, "the words of the prophecy"; so Rev 22:7, 10, 18, 19 by inclusion. The appointed time: when Jesus will return in glory; cf. Rev 1:7; 3:11; 22:7, 10, 12, 20.
[187] [1:3] 22:7 / Lk 11:28.
[188] [1:8] The Alpha and the Omega: the first and last letters of the Greek alphabet. In Rev 22:13 the same words occur together with the expressions "the First and the Last, the Beginning and the End"; cf. Rev 1:17; 2:8; 21:6; Is 41:4; 44:6.
[189] [1:8] 17; 21:6; 22:13; Is 41:4; 44:6; 48:12.

Revelation 2:6 But you have this in your favor: you hate the works of the Nicolaitans,[190] which I also hate.

See the commentary on Revelation 2:6 in the above Manhattan key.

Revelation 3:1 To Sardis.[191] 1 "To the angel of the church in Sardis,[192] write this:

"'The one who has the seven spirits of God and the seven stars says this: "I know your works, that you have the reputation of being alive, but you are dead."'"

See the commentary on Revelation 3:1 in the above Manhattan key.

Revelation 3:4 However, you have a few people in Sardis who have not soiled their garments; they will walk with me dressed in white, because they are worthy.[193]

See the commentary on Revelation 3:4 in the above Manhattan key.

---

[190] [2:6] Nicolaitans: these are perhaps the impostors of Rev 2:2; see note on Rev 2:14–15. There is little evidence for connecting this group with Nicolaus, the proselyte from Antioch, mentioned in Acts 6:5.

[191] [3:1–6] The letter to Sardis does not praise the community but admonishes its members to watchfulness, mutual support, and repentance (Rev 3:2–3). The few who have remained pure and faithful will share Christ's victory and will be inscribed in the book of life (Rev 3:4–5).

[192] [3:1] Sardis: this city, located ca. thirty miles southeast of Thyatira, was once the capital of Lydia, known for its wealth at the time of Croesus (6th century B.C.). Its citadel, reputed to be unassailable, was captured by surprise, first by Cyrus and later by Antiochus. The church is therefore warned to be on guard.

[193] [3:4] 7:13–14.

Revelation 3:7

To Philadelphia.[194] 7"To the angel of the church in Philadelphia, [195] write this:

"'The holy one, the true,

who holds the key of David,

who opens and no one shall close,

who closes and no one shall open,[196]

says this:

See the commentary on Revelation 3:7 in the above Manhattan key.

Vision of Heavenly Worship and Martyrdom

Revelation 4:2 2 [197]At once I was caught up in spirit.[198] A throne was there in heaven, and on the throne sat

This is repeated twice.

---

[194] [3:7–13] The letter to Philadelphia praises the Christians there for remaining faithful even with their limited strength (Rev 3:8). Members of the assembly of Satan are again singled out (Rev 3:9; see Rev 2:9). There is no admonition; rather, the letter promises that they will be kept safe at the great trial (Rev 3:10–11) and that the victors will become pillars of the heavenly temple, upon which three names will be inscribed: God, Jerusalem, and Christ (Rev 3:12).

[195] [3:7] Philadelphia: modern Alasehir, ca. thirty miles southeast of Sardis, founded by Attalus II Philadelphus of Pergamum to be an "open door" (Rev 3:8) for Greek culture; it was destroyed by an earthquake in A.D. 17. Rebuilt by money from the Emperor Tiberius, the city was renamed Neo-Caesarea; this may explain the allusions to "name" in Rev 3:12. Key of David: to the heavenly city of David (cf. Is 22:22), "the new Jerusalem" (Rev 3:12), over which Christ has supreme authority.

[196] [3:7] Is 22:22; Mt 16:19.

[197] [4:2–8] Much of the imagery here is taken from Ez 1:10.

[198] [4:2–3] Is 6:1 / Ez 1:26–28.

Revelation 4:3 one whose appearance sparkled like jasper and carnelian. Around the throne was a halo as brilliant as an emerald.

The Scroll and the Lamb

Revelation 5:4 I shed many tears because no one was found worthy to open the scroll or to examine it.

Revelation 5:5 One of the elders said to me, "Do not weep. The lion of the tribe of Judah, the root of David,[199] has triumphed, enabling him to open the scroll with its seven seals."[200]

See Chapter 6 "The Scroll" for the seven seals.

The 144,000 Sealed

Revelation 7:8 twelve thousand from the tribe of Zebulun, twelve thousand from the tribe of Joseph, and twelve thousand were marked from the tribe of Benjamin.

See the commentary on Revelation 7:8 in the above Manhattan key.

Revelation 7:9 After this I had a vision of a great multitude, which no one could count, from every nation, race, people, and tongue. They stood before

---

[199] [5:5] The lion of the tribe of Judah, the root of David: these are the messianic titles applied to Christ to symbolize his victory; cf. Rev 22:16; Gn 49:9; Is 11:1, 10; Mt 1:1.
[200] [5:5] Is 11:1, 10; Rom 15:12.

the throne and before the Lamb, wearing white robes and holding palm branches[201] in their hands.

Symbolic of the New Jerusalem (see Rev. 14:1–5; Gal. 6:16; James 1:1) that embraces people from every nation, race, people, and tongue (Rev. 7:9). See the commentary on Revelation 7:9 in the above Manhattan key.

Revelation 8:5 Then the angel took the censer, filled it with burning coals from the altar, and hurled it down to the earth. There were peals of thunder, rumblings, flashes of lightning, and an earthquake.[202]

Censers are any type of vessels made for burning incense. These vessels vary greatly in size, form, and material of construction. They may consist of simple earthenware bowls or fire pots on up to intricately carved silver or gold vessels, small tabletop objects a few centimeters tall to as many as several meters high. In many cultures, burning incense has spiritual and religious connotations, and this influences the design and decoration of the censer (http://en.wikipedia.org/wiki/Censer). The censer is used in several Christian churches, particular Roman Catholic and Christian Orthodox.

Revelation 8:5 is the first calamitous event described in this key. It is followed by peals of thunder, rumblings, flashes of lightning, an earthquake and the seven trumpets.

---

[201] [7:9] White robes…palm branches: symbols of joy and victory; see note on Rev 3:5.
[202] [8:5] Ez 10:2; Ps 11:6 / 4:5; 11:19; 16:18.

Revelation 9.2 It opened the passage to the abyss,[203] and smoke came up out of the passage like smoke from a huge furnace. The sun and the air were darkened by the smoke from the passage.[204]

See the commentary on Revelation 9:2 in the above Manhattan key.

The Two Witnesses

Revelation 11:3 I will commission my two witnesses[205] to prophesy for those twelve hundred and sixty days, wearing sackcloth."

The two witnesses are the Environmental Protection Agency (EPA) and the Department of Energy (DOE). Gov. Rick Perry has continually fought the EPA regarding environmental matters in Texas. Because of the lawful environmental restrictions on the oil and coal companies, there is a continuing desire by the Tea Party and their candidates to eliminate the EPA and Department of Energy cabinet positions. The Tea Party will rejoice if they are eliminated.

The Seven Last Plagues

---

[203] [9:2] 20:1.
[204] [9:2] Gn 19:28.
[205] [11:3] The two witnesses, wearing sackcloth symbolizing lamentation and repentance, cannot readily be identified. Do they represent Moses and Elijah, or the Law and the Prophets, or Peter and Paul? Most probably they refer to the universal church, especially the Christian martyrs, fulfilling the office of witness (two because of Dt 19:15; cf. Mk 6:7; Jn 8:17).

Revelation 15:6 and the seven angels with the seven plagues came out of the temple. They were dressed in clean white linen, with a gold sash around their chests.[206]

Revelation 15:7–8 (*Supporting Scripture to Rev. 15:6*) 7One of the four living creatures gave the seven angels seven gold bowls filled with the fury of God, who lives forever and ever. 8Then the temple became so filled with the smoke from God's glory and might that no one could enter it until the seven plagues of the seven angels had been accomplished.[207]

The fury of God, also referred to in Revelation 14:9 and 16:19, is a reference to oil and God's fury in destroying the dinosaurs (dragons) during the Mesozoic Era. (Refer to the seven bowls in Rev. 16:1–21.) If you remember the horrendous oil spill from the Deepwater Horizon disaster, starting in mid-April 2010 and lasting for three months, the oil on the surface of the water looked like blood (See the 3 below photos). See my commentary on Rev. 14:9 and 16:19 in "The Scroll" and the vision of a similar calamitous event in Harris County, Texas.

---

[206] [15:6] 19:8.
[207] [15:8] 1 Kgs 8:10; Is 6:4.

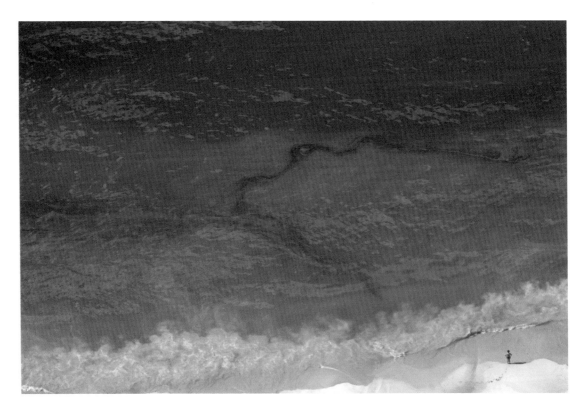

Courtesy of National Geographic / Tyrone Turner

Courtesy of the Associated Press / Patrick Semansky

Courtesy of UPI

I bought a David Weekley home in the Towne Lake subdivision of Cypress, TX in February 2009, and I still own it. Obviously someone in Cypress, Texas, "saw me Coming" (prophecy), because they made several of the garage doors on the Towne Lake David Weekley homes, in this style. They just didn't paint the trim on all of them—it was the homeowner's option.

The Scroll

SCRIPTURE NUMBER	BEGIN DATE	DAYS (END - BEGIN DATES)	END DATE	SCRIPTURE	BIBLICAL NOTES	COMMENTARY
REV.1:1-2				1The revelation of Jesus Christ, which God gave to him, to show his servants what must happen soon. He made it known by sending his angel to his servant John,a 2who gives witness to the word of God and to the testimony of Jesus Christ by reporting what he saw.	* [1:1–3] This prologue describes the source, contents, and audience of the book and forms an inclusion with the epilogue (Rev 22:6–21), with its similar themes and expressions.	
REV. 1:3				3Blessed is the one who reads aloud the words of this prophecy, and blessed are those who hear, and who keep what is written in it, for the time is near.	* [1:3] Blessed is the one: this is the first of seven beatitudes in this book; the others are in Rev 14:13; 16:15; 19:9; 20:6; 22:7, 14. This prophetic message: literally, "the words of the prophecy"; so Rev 22:7, 10, 18, 19 by inclusion. The appointed time: when Jesus will return in glory; cf. Rev 1:7; 3:11; 22:7, 10, 12, 20.	The number 13 on the Key of David (KOD) represents Rev.1:3. There were 13 men at the Passover (Last) Supper ... 12 Apostles and Jesus Christ. Their were 1 man, St. John, and 3 women 1)Mary, the mother of Jesus, 2) Mary of Clopas, 3) Mary of Magdala at the base of the cross. See Jn.19:25-27. The number 13 is called out 13 times on the Manhattan KOD and 11 times on the Cypress KOD.
JN.19-25-27				25* m Standing by the cross of Jesus were his mother and his mother's sister, Mary the wife of Clopas, and Mary of Magdala. 26When Jesus saw his mother* and the disciple there whom he loved, he said to his mother, "Woman, behold, your son."n 27Then he said to the disciple, "Behold, your mother." And from that hour the disciple took her into his home.	* [19:25] It is not clear whether four women are meant, or three (i.e., Mary the wife of Cl[e]opas [cf. Lk 24:18] is in apposition with his mother's sister) or two (his mother and his mother's sister, i.e., Mary of Cl[e]opas and Mary of Magdala). Only John mentions the mother of Jesus here. The synoptics have a group of women looking on from a distance at the cross (Mk 15:40). * [19:26–27] This scene has been interpreted literally, of Jesus' concern for his mother; and symbolically, e.g., in the light of the Cana story in Jn 2 (the presence of the mother of Jesus, the address woman, and the mention of the hour) and of the upper room in Jn 13 (the presence of the beloved disciple; the hour). Now that the hour has come (Jn 19:28), Mary (a symbol of the church?) is given a role as the mother of Christians (personified by the beloved disciple); or, as a representative of those seeking salvation, she is supported by the disciple who interprets Jesus' revelation; or Jewish and Gentile Christianity (or Israel and the Christian community) are reconciled.	

SCRIPTURE NUMBER	BEGIN DATE	DAYS (END - BEGIN DATES)	END DATE	SCRIPTURE	BIBLICAL NOTES	COMMENTARY
JN 14:6				6Jesus said to him, "I am the way, and the truth, and the life; no one comes to the Father but through Me.		
DN.2:28				28But there is a God in heaven who reveals mysteries, and he has shown King Nebuchadnezzar what is to happen in the last days; this was your dream, the visions* you saw as you lay in bed.	* [2:28] The visions: lit., "the visions of your head," a phrasing which distinguishes visionary experiences that are personal from those that are observable by others (see 4:2, 7, 10). That Daniel, unlike the Chaldeans, has access to these visions testifies to his God-given wisdom. Actually, this "dream" is more properly an apocalyptic vision; cf. the very similar message in Daniel's vision of chap. 7.	
LK.11:28				28He replied, "Rather, blessed are those who hear the word of God and observe it."	* [11:27–28] The beatitude in Lk 11:28 should not be interpreted as a rebuke of the mother of Jesus; see note on Lk 8:21. Rather, it emphasizes (like Lk 2:35) that attentiveness to God's word is more important than biological relationship to Jesus.	
REV.1:4-8				Greeting.* 4John, to the seven churches in Asia:* grace to you and peace from him who is and who was and who is to come, and from the seven spirits before his throne,c 5and from Jesus Christ, the faithful witness, the firstborn of the dead and ruler of the kings of the earth. To him who loves us and has freed us* from our sins by his blood,d 6who has made us into a kingdom, priests for his God and Father, to him be glory and power forever [and ever]. Amen.e 7Behold, he is coming amid the clouds, and every eye will see him, even those who pierced him. All the peoples of the earth will lament him. Yes. Amen.f	* [1:4–8] Although Revelation begins and ends (Rev 22:21) with Christian epistolary formulae, there is nothing between Rev 4; 22 resembling a letter. The author here employs the standard word order for greetings in Greek letter writing: "N. to N., greetings…"; see note on Rom 1:1. * [1:4] Seven churches in Asia: Asia refers to the Roman province of that name in western Asia Minor (modern Turkey); these representative churches are mentioned by name in Rev 1:11, and each is the recipient of a message (Rev 2:1–3:22). Seven is the biblical number suggesting fullness and completeness; thus the seer is writing for the whole church.	18 is the Hebrew Life Number. Seven is the biblical number suggesting fullness and completeness; thus the seer is writing for the whole church, or the seven churches being one church. The number 18 is called out 7 times on the Manhattan Key of David (KOD) and 6 (imperfect number) times on the Cypress KOD. * [1:8] The Alpha and the Omega: the first and last letters of the Greek alphabet. 7 represents the 7 stars, lampstands, churches, seals, trumpets, thunders, plagues, and bowls. In Rev 22:13 the same words occur together with the expressions "the First and the Last, the Beginning and the End"; cf. Rev 1:17; 2:8; 21:6; Is 41:4; 44:6. The seer is writing for the whole church which could mean what originated as the Catholic Church. The 13-13-18 right triangle (KOD) was defined in Atlanta, GA. on 12-18-09 business trip. New York City represents the Peoples of the Earth, both residents and United Nations.

SCRIPTURE NUMBER	BEGIN DATE	DAYS (END - BEGIN DATES)	END DATE	SCRIPTURE	BIBLICAL NOTES	COMMENTARY
EX.3:14				14God replied to Moses: I am who I am.* Then he added: This is what you will tell the Israelites: I AM has sent me to you.	I am who I am: Moses asks in v. 13 for the name of the One speaking to him, but God responds with a wordplay which preserves the utterly mysterious character of the divine being even as it appears to suggest something of the inner meaning of God's name: 'ehyeh "I am" or "I will be(come)" for "Yhwh," the personal name of the God of Israel. While the phrase "I am who I am" resists unraveling, it nevertheless suggests an etymological linking between the name "Yhwh" and an earlier form of the Hebrew verbal root h-y-h "to be." On that basis many have interpreted the name "Yhwh" as a third-person form of the verb meaning "He causes to be, creates," itself perhaps a shortened form of a longer liturgical name such as "(God who) creates (the heavenly armies)." Note in this connection the invocation of Israel's God as "LORD (Yhwh) of Hosts" (e.g., 1 Sm 17:45). In any case, out of reverence for God's proper name, the term Adonai, "my Lord," was later used as a substitute. The word LORD (in small capital letters) indicates that the Hebrew text has the sacred name (Yhwh), the tetragrammaton. The word "Jehovah" arose from a false reading of this name as it is written in the current Hebrew text. The Septuagint has egō eimi ho ōn, "I am the One who is" (ōn being the participle of the verb "to be"). This can be taken as an assertion of God's aseity or self-existence, and has been understood as such by the Church, since the time of the Fathers, as a true expression of God's being, even though it is not precisely the meaning of the Hebrew.	
1COR.15:20				20h But now Christ has been raised from the dead, the firstfruits* of those who have fallen asleep.	* [15:20] The firstfruits: the portion of the harvest offered in thanksgiving to God implies the consecration of the entire harvest to come. Christ's resurrection is not an end in itself; its finality lies in the whole harvest, ourselves.	

SCRIPTURE NUMBER	BEGIN DATE	DAYS (END - BEGIN DATES)	END DATE	SCRIPTURE	BIBLICAL NOTES	COMMENTARY
COL.1:18				18He is the head of the body, the church.* He is the beginning, the firstborn from the dead, that in all things he himself might be preeminent.j	* [1:18] Church: such a reference seemingly belongs under "redemption" in the following lines, not under the "creation" section of the hymn. Stoic thought sometimes referred to the world as "the body of Zeus." Pauline usage is to speak of the church as the body of Christ (1 Cor 12:12–27; Rom 12:4–5). Some think that the author of Colossians has inserted the reference to the church here so as to define "head of the body" in Paul's customary way. See Col 1:24. Preeminent: when Christ was raised by God as firstborn fromthe dead (cf. Acts 26:23; Rev 1:5), he was placed over the community, the church, that he had brought into being, but he is also indicated as crown of the whole new creation, over all things. His further role is to reconcile all things (Col 1:20) for God or possibly "to himself."	
HEB.9:14				14how much more will the blood of Christ, who through the eternal spirit* offered himself unblemished to God, cleanse our consciences from dead works to worship the living God.	* [9:14] Through the eternal spirit: this expression does not refer either to the holy Spirit or to the divine nature of Jesus but to the life of the risen Christ, "a life that cannot be destroyed" (Heb 7:16).	
1PT.1:19				19but with the precious blood of Christ as of a spotless unblemished lamb.*	* [1:19] Christians have received the redemption prophesied by Isaiah (Is 52:3), through the blood (Jewish symbol of life) of the spotless lamb (Is 53:7, 10; Jn 1:29; Rom 3:24–25; cf. 1 Cor 6:20).	
1JN.1:7				7But if we walk in the light as he is in the light, then we have fellowship with one another, and the blood of his Son Jesus cleanses us from all sin.f	* [1:5–7] Light is to be understood here as truth and goodness; darkness here is error and depravity (cf. Jn 3:19–21; 17:17; Eph 5:8). To walk in light or darkness is to live according to truth or error, not merely intellectual but moral as well. Fellowship with God and with one another consists in a life according to the truth as found in God and in Christ.	
EX.19:6				6You will be to me a kingdom of priests,* a holy nation.d That is what you must tell the Israelites.	* [19:6] Kingdom of priests: in as much as this phrase is parallel to "holy nation," it most likely means that the whole Israelite nation is set apart from other nations and so consecrated to God, or holy, in the way priests are among the people (cf. Is 61:6; 1 Pt 2:5, 9).	

SCRIPTURE NUMBER	BEGIN DATE	DAYS (END - BEGIN DATES)	END DATE	SCRIPTURE	BIBLICAL NOTES	COMMENTARY
1PT.2:9				9* But you are "a chosen race, a royal priesthood, a holy nation, a people of his own, so that you may announce the praises" of him who called you out of darkness into his wonderful light.h	* [2:9–10] The prerogatives of ancient Israel mentioned here are now more fully and fittingly applied to the Christian people: "a chosen race" (cf. Is 43:20–21) indicates their divine election (Eph 1:4–6); "a royal priesthood" (cf. Ex 19:6) to serve and worship God in Christ, thus continuing the priestly functions of his life, passion, and resurrection; "a holy nation" (Ex 19:6) reserved for God, a people he claims for his own (cf. Mal 3:17) in virtue of their baptism into his death and resurrection. This transcends all natural and national divisions and unites the people into one community to glorify the one who led them from the darkness of paganism to the light of faith in Christ. From being "no people" deprived of all mercy, they have become the very people of God, the chosen recipients of his mercy (cf. Hos 1:9; 2:23).	
DN.7:13				13As the visions during the night continued, I saw coming with the clouds of heavenc One like a son of man.* When he reached the Ancient of Days and was presented before him,	* [7:13–14] One like a son of man: In contrast to the worldly kingdoms opposed to God, which are represented as grotesque beasts, the coming Kingdom of God is represented by a human figure. Scholars disagree as to whether this figure should be taken as a collective symbol for the people of God (cf. 7:27) or identified as a particular individual, e.g., the archangel Michael (cf. 12:1) or the messiah. The phrase "Son of Man" becomes a title for Jesus in the gospels, especially in passages dealing with the Second Coming (Mk 13 and parallels).	
ZEC.12:10				10I will pour out on the house of David and on the inhabitants of Jerusalem a spirit of mercy and supplication, so that when they look on him whom they have thrust through,* f they will mourn for him as one mourns for an only child, and they will grieve for him as one grieves over a firstborn.g	* [12:10] They look on him...thrust through: another possible rendering is "they shall look to me concerning him...thrust through." In either case, the victim is an enigmatic figure, perhaps referring to a Davidic descendant, a priestly leader, or even a true prophet. Some historical event, unknown to us from any surviving source, may underlie this reference. The Gospel of John applies this text to the piercing of Christ's side after his death (19:37).	

SCRIPTURE NUMBER	BEGIN DATE	DAYS (END - BEGIN DATES)	END DATE	SCRIPTURE	BIBLICAL NOTES	COMMENTARY
MT. 24:30	18-Dec-09			30And then the sign of the Son of Man* will appear in heaven, and all the tribes of the earth will mourn, and they will see the Son of Man coming upon the clouds of heaven with power and great glory.	* [24:30] The sign of the Son of Man: perhaps this means the sign that is the glorious appearance of the Son of Man; cf. Mt 12:39–40 where "the sign of Jonah" is Jonah's being in the "belly of the whale." Tribes of the earth will mourn: peculiar to Matthew; cf. Zec 12:12–14. Coming upon the clouds…glory: cf. Dn 7:13 although there the "one like a son of man" comes to God to receive kingship; here the Son of Man comes from heaven for judgment.	
JN19:37				37And again another passage says: "They will look upon him whom they have pierced."v		
IS.41:4				4Who has performed these deeds? Who has called forth the generations from the beginning?a I, the LORD, am the first, and at the last* I am he.	* [41:4] The first…the last: God as the beginning and end encompasses all reality. The same designation is used in 44:6 and 48:12.	
IS.44:6				6Thus says the LORD, Israel's king, its redeemer, the LORD of hosts: I am the first, I am the last; there is no God but me.*	* [44:6] No god but me: with Second Isaiah, Israel's faith is declared to be explicitly monotheistic. However implicit it may have been, earlier formulas did not exclude the existence of other gods, not even that of the first commandment: "You shall not have other gods besides me" (Ex 20:3). Cf. also note on 41:21–29.	God WILL NOT accept polytheistic or pagan faiths.
IS.48:12				12Listen to me, Jacob, Israel, whom I called! I, it is I who am the first, and am I the last.		
REV. 1:9-11				9I, John, your brother, who share with you the distress, the kingdom, and the endurance we have in Jesus, found myself on the island called Patmos* because I proclaimed God's word and gave testimony to Jesus. 10I was caught up in spirit on the Lord's day* and heard behind me a voice as loud as a trumpet, 11which said, "Write on a scroll* what you see and send it to the seven churches: to Ephesus, Smyrna, Pergamum, Thyatira, Sardis, Philadelphia, and Laodicea."	* [1:9–20] In this first vision, the seer is commanded to write what he sees to the seven churches (Rev 1:9–11). He sees Christ in glory, whom he depicts in stock apocalyptic imagery (Rev 1:12–16), and hears him describe himself in terms meant to encourage Christians by emphasizing his victory over death (Rev 1:17–20).	

SCRIPTURE NUMBER	BEGIN DATE	DAYS (END - BEGIN DATES)	END DATE	SCRIPTURE	BIBLICAL NOTES	COMMENTARY
REV. 1:12 - 14				12* Then I turned to see whose voice it was that spoke to me, and when I turned, I saw seven gold lampstands 13and in the midst of the lampstands one like a son of man,* wearing an ankle-length robe, with a gold sash around his chest.h 14The hair of his head was as white as white wool or as snow,* and his eyes were like a fiery flame.	* [1:12–16] A symbolic description of Christ in glory. The metaphorical language is not to be understood literally; cf. Introduction. * [1:13] Son of man: see note on Mk 8:31. Ankle-length robe: Christ is priest; cf. Ex 28:4; 29:5; Wis 18:24; Zec 3:4. Gold sash: Christ is king; cf. Ex 28:4; 1 Mc 10:89; 11:58; Dn 10:5. * [1:14] Hair...as white as white wool or as snow: Christ is eternal, clothed with the dignity that belonged to the "Ancient of Days"; cf. Rev 1:18; Dn 7:9. His eyes were like a fiery flame: Christ is portrayed as * all-knowing; cf. Rev 2:23; Ps 7:10; Jer 17:10; and similar expressions in Rev 2:18; 19:12; cf. Dn 10:6. *	
DN.10:5				5As I looked up, I saw a man* dressed in linen with a belt of fine gold around his waist.a	* [10:5–6] The heavenly person of the vision is probably the angel Gabriel, as in 9:21. Chrysolite: or topaz, a yellowish precious stone. Cf. the visions in Ez 1 and 8.	
REV. 1:15 - 16				15His feet were like polished brass refined in a furnace,* and his voice was like the sound of rushing water. 16In his right hand he held seven stars.* A sharp two-edged sword came out of his mouth, and his face shone like the sun at its brightest.i	[1:15] His feet...furnace: Christ is depicted as unchangeable; cf. Ez 1:27; Dn 10:6. The Greek word translated "refined" is unconnected grammatically with any other word in the sentence. His voice...water: Christ speaks with divine authority; cf. Ez 1:24. * [1:16] Seven stars: in the pagan world, Mithras and the Caesars were represented with seven stars in their right hand, symbolizing their universal dominion. A sharp two-edged sword: this refers to the word of God (cf. Eph 6:17; Heb 4:12) that will destroy unrepentant sinners; cf. Rev 2:16; 19:15; Wis 18:15; Is 11:4; 49:2. His face...brightest: this symbolizes the divine majesty of Christ; cf. Rev 10:1; 21:23; Jgs 5:31; Is 60:19; Mt 17:2.	
JN.4:10				10Jesus answered and said to her,c "If you knew the gift of God and who is saying to you, 'Give me a drink,' you would have asked him and he would have given you living water."		
HEB.4:12				12Indeed, the word of God is living and effective, sharper than any two-edged sword, penetrating even between soul and spirit, joints and marrow, and able to discern reflections and thoughts of the heart.f		

SCRIPTURE NUMBER	BEGIN DATE	DAYS (END - BEGIN DATES)	END DATE	SCRIPTURE	BIBLICAL NOTES	COMMENTARY
REV.1:17-19				17When I caught sight of him, I fell down at his feet as though dead.* He touched me with his right hand and said, "Do not be afraid. I am the first and the last,j 18the one who lives. Once I was dead, but now I am alive forever and ever. I hold the keys to death and the netherworld.* 19Write down, therefore, what you have seen, and what is happening, and what will happen afterwards.*	* [1:17] It was an Old Testament belief that for sinful human beings to see God was to die; cf. Ex 19:21; 33:20; Jgs 6:22–23; Is 6:5. * [1:18] Netherworld: Greek Hades, Hebrew Sheol, the abode of the dead; cf. Rev 20:13–14; Nm 16:33. * [1:19] What you have seen, and what is happening, and what will happen afterwards: the three parts of the Book of Revelation, the vision (Rev 1:10–20), the situation in the seven churches (Rev 2–3), and the events of Rev 6–22.	
DN.8:18				18As he spoke to me, I fell forward unconscious; he touched me and made me stand up.		
REV.1:20				20This is the secret meaning* of the seven stars you saw in my right hand, and of the seven gold lampstands: the seven stars are the angels of the seven churches, and the seven lampstands are the seven churches.	* [1:20] Secret meaning: literally, "mystery." Angels: these are the presiding spirits of the seven churches. Angels were thought to be in charge of the physical world (cf. Rev 7:1; 14:18; 16:5) and of nations (Dn 10:13; 12:1), communities (the seven churches), and individuals (Mt 18:10; Acts 12:15). Some have seen in the "angel" of each of the seven churches its pastor or a personification of the spirit of the congregation.	
REV. 2:1-2				1* "To the angel of the church* in **Ephesus,*** write this: "'The one who holds the seven stars in his right hand and walks in the midst of the seven gold lampstands says this: 2"I know your works, your labor, and your endurance, and that you cannot tolerate the wicked; you have tested those who call themselves apostles but are not, and discovered that they are impostors.*	* [2:1] Ephesus: this great ancient city had a population of ca. 250,000; it was the capital of the Roman province of Asia and the commercial, cultural, and religious center of Asia. The other six churches were located in the same province, situated roughly in a circle; they were selected for geographical reasons rather than for the size of their Christian communities. Walks in the midst of the seven gold lampstands: this signifies that Christ is always present in the church; see note on Rev 1:4. * [2:2] Who call themselves…impostors: this refers to unauthorized and perverse missionaries; cf. Acts 20:29–30. *	

SCRIPTURE NUMBER	BEGIN DATE	DAYS (END - BEGIN DATES)	END DATE	SCRIPTURE	BIBLICAL NOTES	COMMENTARY
REV.2:3-7				3Moreover, you have endurance and have suffered for my name, and you have not grown weary. 4Yet I hold this against you: you have lost the love you had at first. 5Realize how far you have fallen. Repent, and do the works you did at first. Otherwise, I will come to you and remove your lampstand from its place, unless you repent. 6But you have this in your favor: you hate the works of the Nicolaitans,* which I also hate. 7"""Whoever has ears ought to hear what the Spirit says to the churches. To the victor* I will give the right to eat from the tree of life that is in the garden of God."'a	[2:6] Nicolaitans: these are perhaps the impostors of Rev 2:2; see note on Rev 2:14–15. There is little evidence for connecting this group with Nicolaus, the proselyte from Antioch, mentioned in Acts 6:5. * [2:7] Victor: referring to any Christian individual who holds fast to the faith and does God's will in the face of persecution. The tree of life that is in the garden of God: this is a reference to the tree in the primeval paradise (Gn 2:9); cf. Rev 22:2, 14, 19. The decree excluding humanity from the tree of life has been revoked by Christ.	Rev.2:4 The Church in Ephesus are the 4 of the "first branches" of the Protestant Churches: The Calvinists, the Anglicans, the Lutherans, and the Anabaptists. These 4, together with their "denominational offshoots", comprise the Protestants Churches. "The Love They Had At First" was with the Catholic Church. The "loss of love" is: Abortion, homosexuality and divorce. Rev. 2:6 But you have this in your favor: you hate the works of the Nicolaitans (those who accommodated their Christian faith to paganism),* which I also hate.
LEV. 20:6-8, 27				6Should anyone turn to ghosts and spirits and prostitute oneself with them,e I will turn against that person and cut such a one off from among the people. 7Sanctify yourselves, then, and be holy; for I, the LORD, your God,f am holy. 8Be careful, therefore, to observe my statutes. I, the LORD, make you holy. 27A man or a woman who acts as a medium or clairvoyanty shall be put to death. They shall be stoned to death; their bloodguilt is upon them.		
MT.11:15				15Whoever has ears ought to hear.		Hearing it through the spoken word, telepathically or reading it.
REV. 2:8-11				**To Smyrna.** 8"To the angel of the church in Smyrna,* write this: "'The first and the last, who once died but came to life, says this: 9"I know your tribulation and poverty, but you are rich.* I know the slander of those who claim to be Jews and are not, but rather are members of the assembly of Satan.b 10Do not be afraid of anything that you are going to suffer. Indeed, the devil will throw some of you into prison, that you may be tested, and you	* [2:8–11] The letter to Smyrna encourages the Christians in this important commercial center by telling them that although they are impoverished, they are nevertheless rich, and calls those Jews who are slandering them members of the assembly of Satan (Rev 2:9). There is no admonition; rather, the Christians are told that they will suffer much, even death, but the time of tribulation will be short compared to their eternal reward (Rev 2:10), and they will thus	The Church of Smyrna is the Orthodox Christian Church.

SCRIPTURE NUMBER	BEGIN DATE	DAYS (END - BEGIN DATES)	END DATE	SCRIPTURE	BIBLICAL NOTES	COMMENTARY
REV. 2:8-11				will face an ordeal for ten days. Remain faithful until death, and I will give you the crown of life. 11"""Whoever has ears ought to hear what the Spirit says to the churches.c The victor shall not be harmed by the second death.""*	escape final damnation (Rev 2:11).	
JAS.2:5				5Listen, my beloved brothers. Did not God choose those who are poor* in the world to be rich in faith and heirs of the kingdom that he promised to those who love him?a	**[2:5] The poor, "God's poor" of the Old Testament, were seen by Jesus as particularly open to God for belief in and reliance on him alone (Lk 6:20). God's law cannot tolerate their oppression in any way (Jas 2:9).**	"God's law cannot tolerate their oppression in any way (Jas 2:9)." Let this be a prophetic warning to the GOP, particularly the Tea Party.
REV. 2:12-14				**To Pergamum.*** 12"To the angel of the church in Pergamum,* write this: "'The one with the sharp two-edged sword says this: 13"I know that you live where Satan's throne* is, and yet you hold fast to my name and have not denied your faith in me, not even in the days of Antipas, my faithful witness, who was martyred among you, where Satan lives. 14* Yet I have a few things against you. You have some people there who hold to the teaching of Balaam, who instructed Balak to put a stumbling block before the Israelites: to eat food sacrificed to idols and to play the harlot.d	* [2:12] Pergamum: modern Bergama, ca. forty-five miles northeast of Smyrna, a center for various kinds of pagan worship. It also had an outstanding library (the word parchment is derived from its name). * [2:13] Satan's throne: the reference is to emperor worship and other pagan practices that flourished in Pergamum, perhaps specifically to the white marble altar erected and dedicated to Zeus by Eumenes II (197–160 B.C.). * **[2:14–15] Like Balaam, the biblical prototype of the religious compromiser (cf. Nm 25:1–3; 31:16; 2 Pt 2:15; Jude 11), the Nicolaitans in Pergamum and Ephesus (Rev 2:6) accommodated their Christian faith to paganism. They abused the principle of liberty enunciated by Paul (1 Cor 9:19–23).**	
NM.25:1-3				Worship of Baal of Peor. 1While Israel was living at Shittim,* the people profaned themselves by prostituting themselves with the Moabite women.a 2These then invited the people to the sacrifices of their god, and the people ate of the sacrificesb and bowed down to their god. 3Israel thereby attached itself to the Baal of Peor,c and the LORD's anger flared up against Israel.		Again, this is a warning against pagan worship and polytheism.

SCRIPTURE NUMBER	BEGIN DATE	DAYS (END - BEGIN DATES)	END DATE	SCRIPTURE	BIBLICAL NOTES	COMMENTARY
NM.31:16				16"These are the very ones who on Balaam's advice were behind the Israelites' unfaithfulness to the LORD in the affair at Peor,a so that plague struck the LORD's community.		
2PT.2:15				15Abandoning the straight road, they have gone astray, following the road of Balaam, the son of Bosor,* who loved payment for wrongdoing,l	[2:15] Balaam, the son of Bosor: in Nm 22:5, Balaam is said to be the son of Beor, and it is this name that turns up in a few ancient Greek manuscripts by way of "correction" of the text. Balaam is not portrayed in such a bad light in Nm 22. His evil reputation and his madness (2 Pt 2:16), and possibly his surname Bosor, may have come from a Jewish tradition about him in the first/second century, of which we no longer have any knowledge.	
JUDE11				11Woe to them!j They followed the way of Cain, abandoned themselves to Balaam's error for the sake of gain, and perished in the rebellion of Korah.*	* [11] Cain...Balaam...Korah: examples of rebellious men and of the punishment their conduct incurred; cf. Gn 4:8–16; Nm 16:1–35; 31:16. See note on 2 Pt 2:15.	
REV. 2:15-17				Revelation 2:15 So hast thou also them that hold the doctrine of the Nicolaitans, which thing I hate. Revelation 2:16 Repent; or else I will come unto thee quickly, and will fight against them with the sword of my mouth. Revelation 2:17 He that hath an ear, let him hear what the Spirit saith unto the churches; To him that overcometh will I give to eat of the hidden manna, and will give him a white stone, and in the stone a new name written, which no man knoweth saving he that receiveth it.	* [2:14–15] Like Balaam, the biblical prototype of the religious compromiser (cf. Nm 25:1–3; 31:16; 2 Pt 2:15; Jude 11), the Nicolaitans in Pergamum and Ephesus (Rev 2:6) accommodated their Christian faith to paganism. They abused the principle of liberty enunciated by Paul (1 Cor 9:19–23). * [2:17] The hidden manna: this is the food of life; cf. Ps 78:24–25. White amulet: literally, "white stone," on which was written a magical name, whose power could be tapped by one who knew the secret name. It is used here as a symbol of victory and joy; cf. Rev 3:4–5. New name: this is a reference to the Christian's rebirth in Christ; cf. Rev 3:12; 19:12; Is 62:2; 65:15.	
IS.62:2				2Nations shall behold your vindication, and all kings your glory; You shall be called by a new name bestowed by the mouth of the LORD.b		
IS.65:15				15You will leave your name for a curse to my chosen ones when the Lord GOD slays you, and calls his servants by another name.		

TRIBULATION - CHAPTER 6 - THE SCROLL

SCRIPTURE NUMBER	BEGIN DATE	DAYS (END - BEGIN DATES)	END DATE	SCRIPTURE	BIBLICAL NOTES	COMMENTARY
REV. 2:18-22				**To Thyatira.*** 18"To the angel of the church in Thyatira,* write this: "'The Son of God, whose eyes are like a fiery flame and whose feet are like polished brass, says this: 19"I know your works, your love, faith, service, and endurance, and that your last works are greater than the first. 20Yet I hold this against you, that you tolerate the woman Jezebel, who calls herself a prophetess, who teaches and misleads my servants to play the harlot and to eat food sacrificed to idols.* 21I have given her time to repent, but she refuses to repent of her harlotry. 22So I will cast her on a sickbed and plunge those who commit adultery with her into intense suffering unless they repent of her works.	* [2:18–29] The letter to Thyatira praises the progress in virtue of this small Christian community (Rev 2:19) but admonishes them for tolerating a false prophet who leads them astray (Rev 2:20). Her fate is sealed, but there is hope of repentance for her followers (Rev 2:21–22). Otherwise, they too shall die (Rev 2:23). They are warned against Satanic power or knowledge (Rev 2:24–25). Those who remain faithful will share in the messianic reign, having authority over nations (Rev 2:26–27), and will in fact possess Christ himself (Rev 2:8). * [2:18] Thyatira: modern Akhisar, ca. forty miles southeast of Pergamum, a frontier town famous for its workers' guilds (cf. Acts 16:14), membership in which may have involved festal meals in pagan temples. * [2:20] The scheming and treacherous Jezebel of old (cf. 1 Kgs 19:1–2; 21:1–14; 2 Kgs 9:22, 30–34) introduced pagan customs into the religion of Israel; this new Jezebel was doing the same to Christianity.	
REV. 2:23-29				23I will also put her children* to death. Thus shall all the churches come to know that I am the searcher of hearts and minds and that I will give each of you what your works deserve.f 24But I say to the rest of you in Thyatira, who do not uphold this teaching and know nothing of the so-called deep secrets of Satan:* on you I will place no further burden, 25except that you must hold fast to what you have until I come. 26"'To the victor,* who keeps to my ways* until the end, I will give authority over the nations.g 27He will rule them with an iron rod. Like clay vessels will they be smashed, 28just as I received authority from my Father. And to him I will give the morning star. 29"'Whoever has ears ought to hear what the Spirit says to the churches.'"	* [2:23] Children: spiritual descendants. * [2:24] The so-called deep secrets of Satan: literally, "the deep things of Satan," a scathing reference to the perverse teaching of the Nicolaitans (Rev 2:15). * [2:26–28] The Christian who perseveres in faith will share in Christ's messianic authority (cf. Ps 2:8–9) and resurrection victory over death, symbolized by the morning star; cf. Rev 22:16. f. [2:23] 1 Sm 16:7; Jer 11:20; 17:10. g. [2:26] 12:5; Ps 2:8–9.	See Commentary Rev.2:3-7. It's a recurring theme of God's scathing disdain for pagan religions.

SCRIPTURE NUMBER	BEGIN DATE	DAYS (END - BEGIN DATES)	END DATE	SCRIPTURE	BIBLICAL NOTES	COMMENTARY
1SM.16:7				7But the LORD said to Samuel: Do not judge from his appearance or from his lofty stature, because I have rejected him. God does not see as a mortal, who sees the appearance. **The LORD looks into the heart.d**		1SM17:45 "David answered him: "You come against me with sword and spear and scimitar, but I come against you in the name of the LORD of hosts, the God of the armies of Israel whom you have insulted." Through the Faith in God in David's heart, David slayed the Philistine giant.
JER.11:20				20But, you, LORD of hosts, just Judge, searcher of mind and heart, Let me witness the vengeance you take on them, for to you I have entrusted my cause!k		
JER.17:10				10I, the LORD, explore the mind and test the heart, Giving to all according to their ways, according to the fruit of their deeds.f		Repent per 2Pt.3:8-10 and do good deeds like every day is Judgment Day.
PS:2:8-9				8Ask it of me, and I will give you the nations as your inheritance, and, as your possession, the ends of the earth. 9With an iron rod you will shepherd them, like a potter's vessel you will shatter them."f		
REV. 3-1-6				To Sardis.* 1"To the angel of the church in Sardis,* write this: "'The one who has the seven spirits of God and the seven stars says this: "I know your works, that you have the reputation of being alive, but you are dead. 2Be watchful and strengthen what is left, which is going to die, for I have not found your works complete in the sight of my God. 3Remember then how you accepted and heard; keep it, and repent. If you are not watchful, I will come like a thief, and you will never know at what hour I will come upon you.a 4However, you have a few people in Sardis who have not soiled their garments; they will walk with me dressed in white, because they are worthy.b5"""The victor will thus be dressed in white,* and I will never erase his name from the book of life but will acknowledge his name in the presence of my Father and of his angels.c 6"""Whoever has ears ought to hear what the Spirit says to the churches."'	* [3:1–6] The letter to Sardis does not praise the community but admonishes its members to watchfulness, mutual support, and repentance (Rev 3:2–3). The few who have remained pure and faithful will share Christ's victory and will be inscribed in the book of life (Rev 3:4–5). * [3:5] In white: white is a sign of victory and joy as well as resurrection; see note on Rev 2:17. The book of life: the roll in which the names of the redeemed are kept; cf. Rev 13:8; 17:8; 20:12, 15; 21:27; Phil 4:3; Dn 12:1. They will be acknowledged by Christ in heaven; cf. Mt 10:32.	"I know your works, that you have the reputation of being alive, but you are dead. The Church in Sardis are "denominational offshoots" of the 4 "first branches" of the Protestant Reformation (See the Church of Ephesus). These Churches (and their further "denominational offshoots") include, but are not limited to: Presbyterians, Congregationalists, Churches of Christ, Baptists, Episcopal, Methodists, Pentecostals, Adventists. Many of these Churches defined the term "Evangelical Christians". "The reputation of being alive, but you are dead". You've gone from your Pulpits and your Pews being alive with the Word of God, to now dead, with the words of politicians and right-wing groups. This is the reason I left the Baptist Church. Many have left and have gone to non-denominational churches to get away from politics and get back to the Word of God. Sardis needs a revival of faith.

SCRIPTURE NUMBER	BEGIN DATE	DAYS (END - BEGIN DATES)	END DATE	SCRIPTURE	BIBLICAL NOTES	COMMENTARY
MT.24:36				The Unknown Day and Hour.* 36p "But of that day and hour no one knows, neither the angels of heaven, nor the Son,* but the Father alone.	* [24:36] Many textual witnesses omit nor the Son, which follows Mk 13:32. Since its omission can be explained by reluctance to attribute this ignorance to the Son, the reading that includes it is probably original.	
MT.24:42-44				42* s Therefore, stay awake! For you do not know on which day your Lord will come. 43t Be sure of this: if the master of the house had known the hour of night when the thief was coming, he would have stayed awake and not let his house be broken into. 44So too, you also must be prepared, for at an hour you do not expect, the Son of Man will come.	* [24:42–44] Cf. Lk 12:39–40. The theme of vigilance and readiness is continued with the bold comparison of the Son of Man to a thief who comes to break into a house.	
MK.13:33				33n Be watchful! Be alert! You do not know when the time will come.		
1THES.5:2				2For you yourselves know very well that the day of the Lord will come like a thief at night.b		
2 PT.3:8-10				8* But do not ignore this one fact, beloved, that with the Lord one day is like a thousand years* and a thousand years like one day.g 9The Lord does not delay his promise, as some regard "delay," but he is patient with you, not wishing that any should perish but that all should come to repentance.h 10But the day of the Lord will come like a thief,* and then the heavens will pass away with a mighty roar and the elements will be dissolved by fire, and the earth and everything done on it will be found out.i	* [3:8–10] The scoffers' objection (2 Pt 3:4) is refuted also by showing that delay of the Lord's second coming is not a failure to fulfill his word but rather a sign of his patience: God is giving time for repentance before the final judgment (cf. Wis 11:23–26; Ez 18:23; 33:11).	God has given us lifetimes for repentance and good works. Both Catholic and Protestant Churches have either confession or spiritual renewal (reaffirmation of faith) which facilitate that repentance; however, repentance to me can be as simple as reciting the Lord's Prayer (MT6:1-18). But you should want to recite it daily.
PS.69:29				29May they be blotted from the book of life; not registered among the just!q		
DN.12:1				1"At that time there shall arise Michael,a the great prince, guardian of your people; It shall be a time unsurpassed in distress since the nation began until that time. At that time your people shall escape, everyone who is found written in the book.*		

SCRIPTURE NUMBER	BEGIN DATE	DAYS (END - BEGIN DATES)	END DATE	SCRIPTURE	BIBLICAL NOTES	COMMENTARY
MT.10:32				32* Everyone who acknowledges me before others I will acknowledge before my heavenly Father.	* [10:32–33] In the Q parallel (Lk 12:8–9), the Son of Man will acknowledge those who have acknowledged Jesus, and those who deny him will be denied (by the Son of Man) before the angels of God at the judgment. Here Jesus and the Son of Man are identified, and the acknowledgment or denial will be before his heavenly Father.	
REV. 3:7-9	23-Mar-12	1	24-Mar-12	To Philadelphia.* 7"To the angel of the church in Philadelphia,* write this: "'The holy one, the true, who holds the key of David, who opens and no one shall close, who closes and no one shall open,d says this: 8"''I know your works (behold, I have left an open door* before you, which no one can close). You have limited strength, and yet you have kept my word and have not denied my name. 9Behold, I will make those of the assembly of Satan who claim to be Jews and are not, but are lying, behold I will make them come and fall prostrate at your feet, and they will realize that I love you.e	* [3:7–13] The letter to Philadelphia praises the Christians there for remaining faithful even with their limited strength (Rev 3:8). Members of the assembly of Satan are again singled out (Rev 3:9; see Rev 2:9). * [3:8] An open door: opportunities for sharing and proclaiming the faith; cf. Acts 14:27; 1 Cor 16:9; 2 Cor 2:12. * [3:10] My message of endurance: this does not refer to a saying of Jesus about patience but to the example of Christ's patient endurance. The * [3:8] An open door: opportunities for sharing and proclaiming the faith; cf. Acts 14:27; 1 Cor 16:9; 2 Cor 2:12.	**The Church of Philadelphia** The Church in Philadelphia is the Roman Catholic Church. It was the 1st Christian Church to be created from the Passover Supper, the Crucifixion and Resurrection of Jesus Christ and St. Peter the Apostle served as the first Pope. Their members have kept the Word of God throughout schisms in faith, throughout persecution, throughout wars and throughout scandal. "Little power" meaning the primary source of income to the Church is through charity. They have held fast to the Commandments and the Canons of the Church. I am not a Catholic, but a Protestant by Baptism. I do attend Catholic Churches. "Who holds the Key of David" which is a pattern of 14 Crosses, originally erected in Cypress, TX and then erected in Manhattan, NY with a different meaning, based on their location. "My works" are building the Key in Manhattan, literally and figuratively, the door cannot be shut. The dates are when the Manhattan was built. In Rev.3:9, Christ and all of the Apostles were Galilean Jews; therefore the statement: "I will make those of the assembly of Satan who claim to be Jews and are not, but are lying, behold I will make them come and fall prostrate at your feet, and they will realize that I love you". "Jews in this case was a reference for holiness and was the predominant religion at that time. The Manhattan KOD was build on 3-23-12 and 3-24-12

TRIBULATION - CHAPTER 6 - THE SCROLL

SCRIPTURE NUMBER	BEGIN DATE	DAYS (END - BEGIN DATES)	END DATE	SCRIPTURE	BIBLICAL NOTES	COMMENTARY
IS22:22				22I will place the key* of the House of David on his shoulder; what he opens, no one will shut, what he shuts, no one will open.g	* [22:22] Key: symbol of authority; cf. Mt 16:19; Rev 3:7.	
MT.16:19				19I I will give you the keys to the kingdom of heaven.* Whatever you bind on earth shall be bound in heaven; and whatever you loose on earth shall be loosed in heaven."	* [16:19] The keys to the kingdom of heaven: the image of the keys is probably drawn from Is 22:15–25 where Eliakim, who succeeds Shebnah as master of the palace, is given "the key of the house of David," which he authoritatively "opens" and "shuts" (Mt 22:22). Whatever you bind...loosed in heaven: there are many instances in rabbinic literature of the pleased to reveal his Son to me...."	
IS.45:14				14Thus says the LORD: The earnings of Egypt, the gain of Ethiopia, and the Sabeans,* tall of stature, Shall come over to you and belong to you; they shall follow you, coming in chains. Before you they shall bow down, saying in prayer: "With you alone is God; and there is none other, no other god!e	* [45:14] Egypt...Ethiopia...Sabeans: the Egyptians and their allies who, when conquered by Cyrus, are seen as acknowledging the God of Israel; cf. 43:3.	
IS.60:14				14The children of your oppressors shall come, bowing before you; All those who despised you, shall bow low at your feet. They shall call you "City of the LORD," "Zion of the Holy One of Israel."	* [60:10–18] The glorious promises for the future continue: the wealth of the nations (vv. 5, 10), tribute from kings, glorification of the Temple, peace and justice (cf. Ps 85:11). *	
REV. 3:10-13	18-Jun-03	2831	19-Mar-11	10Because you have kept my message of endurance,* I will keep you safe in the time of trial that is going to come to the whole world to test the inhabitants of the earth. 11I am coming quickly. Hold fast to what you have, so that no one may take your crown.f 12"""The victor I will make into a pillar* in the temple of my God, and he will never leave it again. On him I will inscribe the name of my God and the name of the city of my God, the new Jerusalem, which comes down out of heaven from my God, as well as my new name.g 13"""Whoever has ears ought to hear what the Spirit says to the churches."'	* [3:10] My message of endurance: this does not refer to a saying of Jesus about patience but to the example of Christ's patient endurance. The inhabitants of the earth: literally, "those who live on the earth." This expression, which also occurs in Rev 6:10; 8:13; 11:10; 13:8, 12, 14; 17:2, 8, always refers to the pagan world. * [3:12] Pillar: this may be an allusion to the rebuilding of the city; see note on v 7. New Jerusalem: it is described in Rev 21:10–22:5.	2 Tribulations, each of 3 1/2 years, from the time of my departure from Shiloh.

TRIBULATION - CHAPTER 6 - THE SCROLL

SCRIPTURE NUMBER	BEGIN DATE	DAYS (END - BEGIN DATES)	END DATE	SCRIPTURE	BIBLICAL NOTES	COMMENTARY
EZ.48:35				35The circuit of the city shall be eighteen thousand cubits. From now on the name of the city is "The LORD is there."n		
EZ.19:13				13Now she is planted in a wilderness, in a dry, parched land.g		
MT. 24:22-28				22And if those days had not been shortened, no one would be saved; but for the sake of the elect they will be shortened. 23j If anyone says to you then, 'Look, here isthe Messiah!' or, 'There he is!' do not believe it. 24False messiahs and false prophets will arise, and they will perform signs and wonders so great as to deceive, if that were possible, even the elect. 25Behold, I have told it to you beforehand. 26So if they say to you, 'He is in the desert,' do not go out there; if they say, 'He is in the inner rooms,' do not believe it.* 27k For just as lightning comes from the east and is seen as far as the west, so will the coming of the Son of Man be. 28Wherever the corpse is, there the vultures will gather.		
REV. 3:14-17				**To Laodicea.** 14"To the angel of the church in Laodicea,* write this: "'The Amen, the faithful and true witness, the source of God's creation, says this:h 15"I know your works; I know that you are neither cold nor hot.* I wish you were either cold or hot. 16* So, because you are lukewarm, neither hot nor cold, I will spit you out of my mouth. 17* i For you say, 'I am rich and affluent and have no need of anything,' and yet do not realize that you are wretched, pitiable, poor, blind, and naked.	* [3:14–22] The letter to Laodicea reprimands the community for being lukewarm (Rev 3:15–16), but no particular faults are singled out. Their material prosperity is contrasted with their spiritual poverty, the violet tunics that were the source of their wealth with the white robe of baptism, and their famous eye ointment with true spiritual perception (Rev 3:17–18). But Christ's chastisement is inspired by love and a desire to be allowed to share the messianic banquet with his followers in the heavenly kingdom (Rev 3:9–21).aid after the devastating earthquake of A.D. 60/61. The Amen: this is a divine title (cf. Hebrew text of Is 65:16) applied to Christ; cf. 2 Cor 1:20. Source of God's creation:	I've seen this in both Catholic and Protestant churches, so its not specific to one religion. I've seen it in some towns more than others. 1Tim6:10 For the love of money is the root of all evils, and some people in their desire for it have strayed from the faith and have pierced themselves with many pains. Heb13:5-6 5Let your life be free from love of money but be content with what you have, for he has said, "I will never forsake you or abandon you." 6Thus we may say with confidence: "The Lord is my helper, [and] I will not be afraid. What can anyone do to me?"

147

SCRIPTURE NUMBER	BEGIN DATE	DAYS (END - BEGIN DATES)	END DATE	SCRIPTURE	BIBLICAL NOTES	COMMENTARY
REV. 3:14-17					literally, "the beginning of God's creation," a concept found also in Jn 1:3; Col 1:16–17; Heb 1:2; cf. Prv 8:22–31; Wis 9:1–2. * [3:15–16] Halfhearted commitment to the faith is nauseating to Christ; cf. Rom 12:11. * [3:16] Spit: literally, "vomit." The image is that of a beverage that should be either hot or cold. Perhaps there is an allusion to the hot springs of Hierapolis across the Lycus river from Laodicea, which would have been lukewarm by the time they reached Laodicea. *	
REV. 3:18				18I advise you to buy from me gold refined by fire* so that you may be rich, and white garments to put on so that your shameful nakedness may not be exposed, and buy ointment to smear on your eyes so that you may see.	[3:17] Economic prosperity occasioned spiritual bankruptcy. * [3:18] Gold…fire: God's grace. White garments: symbol of an upright life; the city was noted for its violet/purple cloth. Ointment…eyes: to remove spiritual blindness; one of the city's exports was eye ointment (see note on Rev 3:14).	This is God's warning to all: Economic prosperity, without God in your life, can lead to spiritual bankruptcy.
PRV.13:7				7One acts rich but has nothing; another acts poor but has great wealth.*	* [13:7] Appearances can be deceiving; possessions do not always reveal the true state of a person.	This will be the continued conflict between the haves and the have not's. This is the fundamental issue that I have with former Gov. Mitt Romney, Rep. Paul Ryan and the Tea Party. They care nothing about the poor.
LK.12:21				21Thus will it be for the one who stores up treasure for himself but is not rich in what matters to God."*	* [12:21] Rich in what matters to God: literally, "rich for God."	" "
1TIM.6:17-19				Right Use of Wealth.* 17Tell the rich in the present age not to be proud and not to rely on so uncertain a thing as wealth but rather on God, who richly provides us with all things for our enjoyment.n 18Tell them to do good, to be rich in good works, to be generous, ready to share, 19thus accumulating as treasure a good foundation for the future, so as to win the life that is true life.o	* [6:17–19] Timothy is directed to instruct the rich, advising them to make good use of their wealth by aiding the poor.	" "

SCRIPTURE NUMBER	BEGIN DATE	DAYS (END - BEGIN DATES)	END DATE	SCRIPTURE	BIBLICAL NOTES	COMMENTARY
REV. 3:19-22				19Those whom I love, I reprove and chastise. Be earnest, therefore, and repent.j 20""Behold, I stand at the door and knock. If anyone hears my voice and opens the door, [then] I will enter his house and dine with him, and he with me.* 21I will give the victor the right to sit with me on my throne, as I myself first won the victory and sit with my Father on his throne.k 22""Whoever has ears ought to hear what the Spirit says to the churches.""		
REV. 4:1-4				Vision of Heavenly Worship.* 1After this I had a vision of an open door* to heaven, and I heard the trumpetlike voice that had spoken to me before, saying, "Come up here and I will show you what must happen afterwards." 2* At once I was caught up in spirit.a A throne was there in heaven, and on the throne sat 3one whose appearance sparkled like jasper and carnelian. Around the throne was a halo as brilliant as an emerald. 4Surrounding the throne I saw twenty-four other thrones on which twenty-four elders* sat, dressed in white garments and with gold crowns on their heads.b	* [4:1–11] The seer now describes a vision of the heavenly court in worship of God enthroned. He reverently avoids naming or describing God but pictures twenty-four elders in priestly and regal attire (Rev 4:4) and God's throne and its surroundings made of precious gems and other symbols that traditionally express the majesty of God. * [4:1] The ancients viewed heaven as a solid vault, entered by way of actual doors. * [4:2–8] Much of the imagery here is taken from Ez 1:10. *	24 Elders = 12 tribes of Israel: Judah, Reuben, Gad, Asher, Naphtali, Manasseh, Simeon, Levi, Issachar, Zebulun, Joseph, Benjamin + 12 apostles: Peter, Andrew, James The Greater, James The Lesser, John, Philip, Bartholomew, Matthew, Thomas, Thaddeus, Simon & Matthias.
IS.6:1				1In the year King Uzziah died,* I saw the Lord seated on a high and lofty throne,a with the train of his garment filling the temple.		

SCRIPTURE NUMBER	BEGIN DATE	DAYS (END - BEGIN DATES)	END DATE	SCRIPTURE	BIBLICAL NOTES	COMMENTARY
EZ.1:26-28				26Above the firmament over their heads was the likeness of a throne that looked like sapphire; and upon this likeness of a throne was seated, up above, a figure that looked like a human being.* r 27And I saw something like polished metal, like the appearance of fire enclosed on all sides, from what looked like the waist up; and from what looked like the waist down, I saw something like the appearance of fire and brilliant light surrounding him.s 28Just like the appearance of the rainbow in the clouds on a rainy day so was the appearance of brilliance that surrounded him. Such was the appearance of the likeness of the glory of the LORD. And when I saw it, I fell on my face and heard a voice speak.t	* [1:26] Looked like a human being: the God who transcends the powers of the human imagination is pictured here in the likeness of an enthroned human king.	Scripture continuously describes God as something looking like fire: EX.2:23, EX.14:24, EX.19:18, 1KGS.18:38, DN.7:9, EZ.1:26-27

SCRIPTURE NUMBER	BEGIN DATE	DAYS (END - BEGIN DATES)	END DATE	SCRIPTURE	BIBLICAL NOTES	COMMENTARY
EZ.1:26-28				The foyer wall in Cyress across from the study on February 9, 2010. The sunshine through the entry door glass creates this image.	The same setting, but this photograph was taken on November 13, 2010. The difference in photos is the position of the Sun relative to the axis of the Earth, between the 2 dates. The message here is how different people of the Earth view the Almighty God. At least in the case of Christians, Jews, and Muslims, He is the same God.	
IS.24:23				23Then the moon will blush and the sun be ashamed,r For the LORD of hosts will reign on Mount Zion and in Jerusalem, glorious in the sight of the elders.*		

SCRIPTURE NUMBER	BEGIN DATE	DAYS (END - BEGIN DATES)	END DATE	SCRIPTURE	BIBLICAL NOTES	COMMENTARY
REV. 4:5-7				5From the throne came flashes of lightning, rumblings, and peals of thunder.* Seven flaming torches burned in front of the throne, which are the seven spirits of God. 6c In front of the throne was something that resembled a sea of glass like crystal.* In the center and around the throne, there were four living creatures covered with eyes in front and in back. 7The first creature resembled a lion, the second was like a calf, the third had a face like that of a human being, and the fourth looked like an eagle* in flight.	* [4:5] Flashes of lightning, rumblings, and peals of thunder: as in other descriptions of God's appearance or activity; cf. Rev 8:5; 11:19; 16:18; Ex 19:16; Ez 1:4, 13. The seven spirits of God: the seven "angels of the presence" as in Rev 8:2 and Tb 12:15. * [4:6] A sea of glass like crystal: an image adapted from Ez 1:22-26. Four living creatures: these are symbols taken from Ez 1:5-21; they are identified as cherubim in Ez 10:20. Covered with eyes: these suggest God's knowledge and concern. * [4:7] Lion...calf...human being...eagle: these symbolize, respectively, what is noblest, strongest, wisest, and swiftest in creation. Calf: traditionally translated "ox," the Greek word refers to a heifer or young bull. Since the second century, these four creatures have been used as symbols of the evangelists Mark, Luke, Matthew, and John, respectively.	
EX.24:10				10and they beheld the God of Israel. Under his feet there appeared to be sapphire tilework, as clear as the sky itself.		
REV. 4:8-10				8The four living creatures, each of them with six wings,* were covered with eyes inside and out. Day and night they do not stop exclaiming: "Holy, holy, holy is the Lord God almighty, who was, and who is, and who is to come."d 9Whenever the living creatures give glory and honor and thanks to the one who sits on the throne, who lives forever and ever, 10the twenty-four elders fall down before the one who sits on the throne and worship him, who lives forever and ever. They throw down their crowns before the throne, exclaiming:	* [4:8] Six wings: like the seraphim of Is 6:2. Along with the twenty-four elders, they praise God unceasingly in humble adoration (Rev 4:8-11). [4:6] A sea of glass like crystal: an image adapted from Ez 1:22-26. Four living creatures: these are symbols taken from Ez 1:5-21; they are identified as cherubim in Ez 10:20. Covered with eyes: these suggest God's knowledge and concern. *	

SCRIPTURE NUMBER	BEGIN DATE	DAYS (END - BEGIN DATES)	END DATE	SCRIPTURE	BIBLICAL NOTES	COMMENTARY
IS.6:2-3				2Seraphim* were stationed above; each of them had six wings: with two they covered their faces, with two they covered their feet, and with two they hovered.b 3One cried out to the other: "Holy, holy, holy* is the LORD of hosts! All the earth is filled with his glory!"	* [6:2] Seraphim: the plural of saraph ("to burn"), a term used to designate the "fiery" serpents of the wilderness (Nm 21:8; Dt 8:15), and to refer to "winged" serpents (Is 14:29; 30:6). Here, however, it is used adjectivally of the cherubim, who are not serpent-like, as seen in the fact that they have faces and sexual parts ("feet"). See the adaptation of these figures by Ezekiel (Ez 1:10–12; 10:4–15). * [6:3] Holy, holy, holy: these words have been used in Christian liturgy from the earliest times.	
REV. 4:11				11"Worthy are you, Lord our God, to receive glory and honor and power, for you created all things; because of your will they came to be and were created."e	[4:7] Lion...calf...human being...eagle: these symbolize, respectively, what is noblest, strongest, wisest, and swiftest in creation. Calf: traditionally translated "ox," the Greek word refers to a heifer or young bull. Since the second century, these four creatures have been used as symbols of the evangelists Mark, Luke, Matthew, and John, respectively.	
ROM.4:17				17as it is written, "I have made you father of many nations." He is our father in the sight of God, in whom he believed, who gives life to the dead and calls into being what does not exist.k		
ROM.16:27				27to the only wise God, through Jesus Christ be glory forever and ever. Amen.]n	* [16:25–27] This doxology is assigned variously to the end of Rom 14; 15; 16 in the manuscript tradition. Some manuscripts omit it entirely. Whether written by Paul or not, it forms an admirable conclusion to the letter at this point.	
REV. 5:1-5				The Scroll and the Lamb.* 1I saw a scroll* in the right hand of the one who sat on the throne. It had writing on both sides and was sealed with seven seals.a 2Then I saw a mighty angel who proclaimed in a loud voice, "Who is worthy to open the scroll and break its seals?" 3But no one in heaven or on earth or under the earth was able to open the scroll or to examine it. 4I shed many tears because no one was found worthy to open the scroll or to examine it. 5One of the elders said to me, "Do not weep. The lion of the tribe of Judah, the root of David,* has	* [5:1–14] The seer now describes a papyrus roll in God's right hand (Rev 5:1) with seven seals indicating the importance of the message. A mighty angel asks who is worthy to open the scroll, i.e., who can accomplish God's salvific plan (Rev 5:2). There is despair at first when no one in creation can do it (Rev 5:3–4). But the seer is comforted by an elder who tells him that Christ, called the lion of the tribe of Judah, has won the right to open it (Rev 5:5).	This section of the book is the scroll. "Break the seals" in this context means "break the code" or "decode".

SCRIPTURE NUMBER	BEGIN DATE	DAYS (END - BEGIN DATES)	END DATE	SCRIPTURE	BIBLICAL NOTES	COMMENTARY	
REV. 5:1-5				triumphed, enabling him to open the scroll with its seven seals."b			
IS.29:11				11For you the vision of all this has become like the words of a sealed scroll. When it is handed to one who can read, with the request, "Read this," the reply is, "I cannot, because it is sealed."	* [29:9–16] Despite their show of piety, Judah's leaders refused to accept the prophet's words of assurance. They rejected prophetic advice (cf. 30:10–11), did not consult the prophetic oracle in forming their political plans (30:1–2; 31:1), and tried to hide their plans even from God's prophet (v. 15), who, they thought, simply did not understand military and political reality.		
IS.11:1				1But a shoot shall sprout from the stump* of Jesse, and from his roots a bud shall blossom.a	* [11:1] Shoot...stump: the imagery suggests the bankruptcy of the monarchy as embodied in the historical kings, along with the need for a new beginning, to spring from the very origin from which David and his dynasty arose. Jesse: David's father (cf. 1 Sm 16:1–13).		
IS.11:10				10On that day, The root of Jesse, set up as a signal for the peoples— Him the nations will seek out; his dwelling shall be glorious.h	* [11:10–16] This passage, with its reference to God's people in widely scattered lands, is probably from a much later period. God will restore them to their own land. The reconciliation of Ephraim (i.e., the Northern Kingdom) and Judah reverses what Isaiah saw as a disastrous event of the past (cf. 7:17). God's action is likened to a new exodus, analogous to the time God first acquired Israel in bringing them out of the land of Egypt. Pathros: upper Egypt. Elam: east of Babylonia. Shinar: Babylonia. Hamath: on the Orontes River in Syria. Isles: or coastlands, in the Mediterranean.		
ROM.15:12				12And again Isaiah says: "The root of Jesse shall come, raised up to rule the Gentiles; in him shall the Gentiles hope."k			

SCRIPTURE NUMBER	BEGIN DATE	DAYS (END - BEGIN DATES)	END DATE	SCRIPTURE	BIBLICAL NOTES	COMMENTARY
REV. 5:6-10				6Then I saw standing in the midst of the throne and the four living creatures and the elders, a Lamb* that seemed to have been slain. He had seven horns and seven eyes; these are the [seven] spirits of God sent out into the whole world.c 7He came and received the scroll from the right hand of the one who sat on the throne. 8When he took it, the four living creatures and the twenty-four elders fell down before the Lamb. Each of the elders held a harp and gold bowls filled with incense, which are the prayers of the holy ones. 9They sang a new hymn: "Worthy are you to receive the scroll and to break open its seals, for you were slain and with your blood you purchased for God those from every tribe and tongue, people and nation. 10You made them a kingdom and priests for our God, and they will reign on earth."d	Christ then appears as a Lamb, coming to receive the scroll from God (Rev 5:6–7), for which he is acclaimed as at a coronation (Rev 5:8–10). * [5:6] Christ is the Paschal Lamb without blemish, whose blood saved the new Israel from sin and death; cf. Ex 12; Is 53:7; Jn 1:29, 36; Acts 8:32; 1 Pt 1:18–19. This is the main title for Christ in Revelation, used twenty-eight times. Seven horns and seven eyes: Christ has the fullness (see note on Rev 1:4) of power (horns) and knowledge (eyes); cf. Zec 4:7. [Seven] spirits: as in Rev 1:4; 3:1; 4:5.	Receiving the Scroll from the right hand of God to "Break the Seals".
JN.1:29				29The next day he saw Jesus coming toward him and said, "Behold, the Lamb of God,* who takes away the sin of the world.t	* [1:29] The Lamb of God: the background for this title may be the victorious apocalyptic lamb who would destroy evil in the world (Rev 5–7; 17:14); the paschal lamb, whose blood saved Israel (Ex 12); and/or the suffering servant led like a lamb to the slaughter as a sin-offering (Is 53:7, 10).	
EX.19:6				6You will be to me a kingdom of priests,* a holy nation.d That is what you must tell the Israelites.	* [19:6] Kingdom of priests: inasmuch as this phrase is parallel to "holy nation," it most likely means that the whole Israelite nation is set apart from other nations and so consecrated to God, or holy, in the way priests are among the people (cf. Is 61:6; 1 Pt 2:5, 9).	
IS.61:6				6* You yourselves shall be called "Priests of the LORD," "Ministers of our God" you shall be called. You shall eat the wealth of the nations and in their riches you will boast.d	* [61:6] The bestowal of a new name suggests a new identity and mission. The whole people will be priests (cf. Ex 19:6), even ministering to nations who will serve God's people.	

SCRIPTURE NUMBER	BEGIN DATE	DAYS (END - BEGIN DATES)	END DATE	SCRIPTURE	BIBLICAL NOTES	COMMENTARY	
REV. 5:11-14				11I looked again and heard the voices of many angels who surrounded the throne and the living creatures and the elders. They were countless* in number,e 12and they cried out in a loud voice: "Worthy is the Lamb that was slain to receive power and riches, wisdom and strength, honor and glory and blessing." 13Then I heard every creature in heaven and on earth and under the earth and in the sea, everything in the universe, cry out: "To the one who sits on the throne and to the Lamb be blessing and honor, glory and might,forever and ever." 14The four living creatures answered, "Amen," and the elders fell down and worshiped.	This is followed by a doxology of the angels (Rev 5:11–12) and then finally by the heavenly church united with all of creation (Rev 5:13–14). * [5:1] A scroll: a papyrus roll possibly containing a list of afflictions for sinners (cf. Ez 2:9–10) or God's plan for the world. Sealed with seven seals: it is totally hidden from all but God. Only the Lamb (Rev 5:7–9) has the right to carry out the divine plan. * [5:5] The lion of the tribe of Judah, the root of David: these are the messianic titles applied to Christ to symbolize his victory; cf. Rev 22:16; Gn 49:9; Is 11:1, 10; Mt 1:1.		
DN.7:10				10A river of fire surged forth, flowing from where he sat; Thousands upon thousands were ministering to him, and myriads upon myriads stood before him.b The court was convened, and the books were opened.	* [7:9–10] A vision of the heavenly throne of God (the Ancient of Days), who sits in judgment over the nations. Some of the details of the vision, depicting the divine majesty and omnipotence, are to be found in Ezekiel 1. Others are paralleled in 1 Enoch, a contemporary Jewish apocalypse.		
JUDE14-15				14* Enoch, of the seventh generation from Adam, prophesied also about them when he said,l "Behold, the Lord has come with his countless holy ones 15to execute judgment on all and to convict everyone for all the godless deeds that they committed and for all the harsh words godless sinners have uttered against him."	* [14–15] Cited from the apocryphal Book of Enoch 1:9.		
REV. 6:1-2	20-Jan-89	1461	20-Jan-93	The First Six Seals. 1* Then I watched while the Lamb broke open the first of the seven seals, and I heard one of the four living creatures cry out in a voice like thunder, "Come forward." 2I looked, and there was a white horse, and its rider had a bow.* He was given a crown, and he rode forth victorious to further his victories.	* [6:2] White horse...bow: this may perhaps allude specifically to the Parthians on the eastern border of the Roman empire. Expert in the use of the bow, they constantly harassed the Romans and won a major victory in A.D. 62; see note on Rev 9:13–21. But the Old Testament imagery typifies the history of oppression of God's people at all times. This chapter provides a symbolic description of the contents of the sealed scroll. The breaking of the first four seals reveals four riders. The first rider (of a white horse) is a conquering power (Rev 6:1–2),	A war in the Biblical land of Babylon (Iraq) ... Desert Storm. President George Herbert Walker Bush, who had a career in the oil business. Desert Storm was a war with a well-defined mission.	THE 1ST SIX SEALS

SCRIPTURE NUMBER	BEGIN DATE	DAYS (END - BEGIN DATES)	END DATE	SCRIPTURE	BIBLICAL NOTES	COMMENTARY	
ZEC.1:8-10				8* I looked out in the night,* and there was a man mounted on a red horse standing in the shadows among myrtle trees; and behind him were red, sorrel, and white horses. 9I asked, "What are these, my lord?"* Then the angel who spoke with me answered, "I will show you what these are." 10Then the man who was standing among the myrtle trees spoke up and said, "These are the ones whom the LORD has sent to patrol the earth."f	* [1:8] In the night: nighttime, or this night. This setting of darkness is meant only for the first vision. * [1:9] My lord: this expression in Hebrew ('adoni) is used as a polite form of address. Angel who spoke with me: angelic being (not identical to the angel of the Lord who is one of the four horsemen) who serves as an interpreter, bringing a message from God to the prophet, who himself is a messenger of God.		
REV.6:3-4	20-Jan-01	2922	20-Jan-09	3When he broke open the second seal, I heard the second living creature cry out, "Come forward." 4* b Another horse came out, a red one. Its rider was given power to take peace away from the earth, so that people would slaughter one another. And he was given a huge sword.	the second (red horse) a symbol of bloody war (Rev 6:3–4),	A war in the Biblical land of Babylon (Iraq) ... Operation Iraqi Freedom. Pres. George Walker Bush, who had a career in the oil business. Red represents: 1) The Republican Party 2)The Passion (in this case, a compelling emotion or feeling of hate) 3) There are multiple designations for red in the Catholic Liturgical Colors. The Iraq War had an ill-defined mission. The Afghan War is a war with a very difficult mission in a land of many conquerors.	THE 1ST SIX SEALS
EZ.12:14-16				14Son of man, prophesy! say: Thus says the LORD: A sword, a sword has been sharpened, a sword, a sword has been burnished:e 15Sharpened to make a slaughter, burnished to flash lightning! Why should I stop now? You have rejected the rod and every judgment! 16I have given it over to the burnisher that he might hold it in his hand, A sword sharpened and burnished to be put in the hands of an executioner.		Sword also represents the Word of God.	

SCRIPTURE NUMBER	BEGIN DATE	DAYS (END - BEGIN DATES)	END DATE	SCRIPTURE	BIBLICAL NOTES	COMMENTARY
REV. 6:5-6	20-Jan-09			5When he broke open the third seal, I heard the third living creature cry out, "Come forward." I looked, and there was a black horse,* and its rider held a scale in his hand. 6I heard what seemed to be a voice in the midst of the four living creatures. It said, "A ration of wheat costs a day's pay,* and three rations of barley cost a day's pay. But do not damage the olive oil or the wine."c	* [6:5] Black horse: this is a symbol of famine, the usual accompaniment of war in antiquity; cf. Lv 26:26; Ez 4:12–13. The scale is a symbol of shortage of food with a corresponding rise in price. * [6:6] A day's pay: literally, "a denarius," a Roman silver coin that constitutes a day's wage in Mt 20:2. Because of the famine, food was rationed and sold at an exorbitant price. A liter of flour was considered a day's ration in the Greek historians Herodotus and Diogenes Laertius. Barley: food of the poor (Jn 6:9, 13; cf. 2 Kgs 7:1, 16, 18); it was also used to feed animals; cf. 1 Kgs 5:8. Do not damage: the olive and the vine are to be used more sparingly in time of famine. the third (black horse) a symbol of famine (Rev 6:5–6),	A war in the Biblical land of Babylon (Iraq) ... Operation Iraqi Freedom. A leader who ended this war: President Barack Obama. He inherited the worst recession this country has endured since the Great Depression. Both the Iraq War and the Afghan war were ongoing when Pres. Obama took office. Operations in the Iraqi Theatre have ceased. The scale is a symbol of shortage of food with a corresponding rise in price. It also represents the scales of justice (constitutional lawyer), truth and fairness.

THE 1ST SIX SEALS

SCRIPTURE NUMBER	BEGIN DATE	DAYS (END - BEGIN DATES)	END DATE	SCRIPTURE	BIBLICAL NOTES	COMMENTARY
LV.26:26				26When I break your staff of bread, ten women will need but one oven for baking your bread, and they shall dole it out to you by weight;o and though you eat, you shall not be satisfied.	* [26:14–46] To encourage obedience, the list of punishments is longer than the blessings (cf. a similar proportion in Dt 28). The punishments are presented in waves (vv. 14–17, 18–20, 21–22, 23–26, 27–39), one group following another if the people do not return to obedience. Punishments involve sickness, pestilence, agricultural failure and famine, attack of wild animals, death of the people's children, destruction of illicit and even licit cults, military defeat, panic, and exile.* [26:14–46] To encourage obedience, the list of punishments is longer than the blessings (cf. a similar proportion in Dt 28). The punishments are presented in waves (vv. 14–17, 18–20, 21–22, 23–26, 27–39), one group following another if the people do not return to obedience. Punishments involve sickness, pestilence, agricultural failure and famine, attack of wild animals, death of the people's children, destruction of illicit and even licit cults, military defeat, panic, and exile.	
EZ.4:16-17				16Then he said to me: Son of man, I am about to break the staff of bread* in Jerusalem so they shall eat bread which they have weighed out anxiously and drink water which they have measured out fearfully.f 17Because they lack bread and water they shall be devastated; each and every one will waste away because of their guilt.g	* [4:16] Break the staff of bread: reducing the supply of bread that supports life as the walking staff supports a traveler; cf. 5:16; 14:13; Lv 26:26; Ps 105:16; Is 3:1.	

THE 1ST SIX SEALS

SCRIPTURE NUMBER	BEGIN DATE	DAYS (END - BEGIN DATES)	END DATE	SCRIPTURE	BIBLICAL NOTES	COMMENTARY	
REV. 6:7-8				7When he broke open the fourth seal, I heard the voice of the fourth living creature cry out, "Come forward." 8I looked, and there was a pale green* horse. Its rider was named Death, and Hades accompanied him. They were given authority over a quarter of the earth, to kill with sword, famine, and plague, and by means of the beasts of the earth.d	* [6:8] Pale green: symbol of death and decay; cf. Ez 14:21. the fourth (pale green horse) a symbol of Death himself, accompanied by Hades (the netherworld) as his page (Rev 6:7–8).	The Tea Party. Their unwillingness to negotiate with the moderate Republicans and Democrats has stalled legislation relating to job growth, healthcare, and the environment. In the CNN / Tea Party Express Debate on Sept. 12, 2011 in Tampa, Fla., Wolf Blitzer asked Rep. Ron Paul, "Congressman, are you saying that society should just let him (someone who did not have health insurance) die?" to which a small number of audience members shouted "Yeah!". I get a vision of Christ standing next to Pilate, with a crowd yelling "crucify him". How have we lost our way from Christ's Greatest Commandments? Mt.22:37-40. The "Wild Beasts of the Earth" are the oil / coal companies and their destruction of the Earth. If the Tea Party ever gains power in the Executive and Legislative Branches, they will push for war between Israel and Iran, destabilizing the Middle East, and creating an environment of domestic "drill, baby, drill" sentiment due to the instability of foreign oil imports. We must phase out oil (foreign and domestic) with the use of Natural Gas as a bridge to renewable energy.	**THE 1ST SIX SEALS**
EZ.14:21				21Thus says the Lord GOD: Even though I send against Jerusalem my four evil punishments—sword, famine, wild beasts, and plague—to cut off from it human being and beast alike,i	* [14:12–23] According to Ezekiel, the people in Jerusalem deserve destruction because they are corrupt. Yet he admits an exception to the principle of individual responsibility when he affirms that some of those deserving death will survive and be reunited with family in exile. The depravity of Jerusalem testifies that the punishment of Jerusalem was just and necessary.		

SCRIPTURE NUMBER	BEGIN DATE	DAYS (END - BEGIN DATES)	END DATE	SCRIPTURE	BIBLICAL NOTES	COMMENTARY
REV. 6:9-11				9When he broke open the fifth seal, I saw underneath the altar* the souls of those who had been slaughtered because of the witness they bore to the word of God. 10They cried out in a loud voice, "How long will it be, holy and true master,* before you sit in judgment and avenge our blood on the inhabitants of the earth?" 11Each of them was given a white robe, and they were told to be patient a little while longer until the number was filled of their fellow servants and brothers who were going to be killed as they had been.	The breaking of the fifth seal reveals Christian martyrs in an attitude of sacrifice as blood poured out at the foot of an altar begging God for vindication, which will come only when their quota is filled; but they are given a white robe symbolic of victory (Rev 6:9–11).	Christian martyrs who were slain by pagan civilizations and morally corrupt entities.
REV. 6:12-17				12* Then I watched while he broke open the sixth seal, and there was a great earthquake; the sun turned as black as dark sackcloth* and the whole moon became like blood.e 13The stars in the sky fell to the earth like unripe figs* shaken loose from the tree in a strong wind. 14Then the sky was divided* like a torn scroll curling up, and every mountain and island was moved from its place.f 15The kings of the earth, the nobles,* the military officers, the rich, the powerful, and every slave and free person hid themselves in caves and among mountain crags. 16They cried out to the mountains and the rocks, "Fall on us and hide us from the face of the one who sits on the throne and from the wrath of the Lamb,g 17because the great day of their* wrath has come and who can withstand it?"	The breaking of the sixth seal reveals typical apocalyptic signs in the sky and the sheer terror of all people at the imminent divine judgment (Rev 6:12–17).	Rev. 6:12 6.5 Earthquake in Iran on 12/20/10 @ 12:41p.m. CST. Lunar eclipse "the whole moon became like blood" on 12/21/10 @ 1:41 a.m. CST, exactly 13 hrs. (Rev.1:3) after the 6.5 Earthquake. Rev. 6:13 Geminid Meteor Shower 12-13-10 Ursids Meteor Shower 12-21-10.

THE 1ST SIX SEALS

TRIBULATION - CHAPTER 6 - THE SCROLL

SCRIPTURE NUMBER	BEGIN DATE	DAYS (END - BEGIN DATES)	END DATE	SCRIPTURE	BIBLICAL NOTES	COMMENTARY	
Jl.3:4				4The sun will darken, the moon turn blood-red, Before the day of the LORD arrives, that great and terrible day.b	* [3:1–5] In many places in the Old Testament, Hebrew ruah is God's power, or spirit, bestowed on chosen individuals. The word can also mean "breath" or "wind." In this summary introduction to his second speech, Joel anticipates that the Lord will someday renew faithful Judahites with the divine spirit. In Acts 2:17–21 the author has Peter cite Joel's words to suggest that the newly constituted Christian community, filled with divine life and power, inaugurates the Lord's Day, understood as salvation for all who believe that Jesus of Nazareth is the Christ.		
MT24:29				29* l "Immediately after the tribulation of those days, the sun will be darkened, and the moon will not give its light, and the stars will fall from the sky, and the powers of the heavens will be shaken.	* [24:1–25:46] The discourse of the fifth book, the last of the five around which the gospel is structured. It is called the "eschatological" discourse since it deals with the coming of the new age (the eschaton) in its fullness, with events that will precede it, and with how the disciples are to conduct themselves while awaiting an event that is as certain as its exact time is unknown to all but the Father (Mt 24:36).		THE 1ST SIX SEALS
IS.34:4				4All the host of heaven shall rot; the heavens shall be rolled up like a scroll. All their host shall wither away, as the leaf wilts on the vine, or as the fig withers on the tree.d	* [34:1–35:10] These two chapters form a small collection which looks forward to the vindication of Zion, first by defeat of its enemies (chap. 34), then by its restoration (chap. 35). They are generally judged to be later than the time of Isaiah (eighth century), perhaps during the Babylonian exile or thereafter; they are strongly influenced by Deutero-Isaiah (sixth century). In places they reflect themes from other parts of the Isaian collection.		
IS.16:20				20* Every island fled, and mountains disappeared.	* [16:20–21] See note on Rev 6:12–14. Hailstones: as in the seventh Egyptian plague (Ex 9:23–24); cf. Rev 8:7. Like huge weights: literally, "weighing a talent," about one hundred pounds.		
IS.2:19				19People will go into caves in the rocks and into holes in the earth, At the terror of the LORD and the splendor of his majesty, as he rises to overawe the earth.			

SCRIPTURE NUMBER	BEGIN DATE	DAYS (END - BEGIN DATES)	END DATE	SCRIPTURE	BIBLICAL NOTES	COMMENTARY	
HOS.10:8				8The high places of Aven* will be destroyed, the sin of Israel; thorns and thistles will overgrow their altars. Then they will cry out to the mountains, "Cover us!" and to the hills, "Fall upon us!"d	* [10:8] Aven: wickedness, first of all at Bethel (v. 5), but also at all the high places.		
LK.23:30				30At that time people will say to the mountains, 'Fall upon us!' and to the hills, 'Cover us!'o	* [23:26–32] An important Lucan theme throughout the gospel has been the need for the Christian disciple to follow in the footsteps of Jesus. Here this theme comes to the fore with the story of Simon of Cyrene who takes up the cross and follows Jesus (see Lk 9:23; 14:27) and with the large crowd who likewise follow Jesus on the way of the cross. See also note on Mk 15:21.		THE 1ST SIX SEALS
REV. 7:1-3				The 144,000 Sealed. 1After this I saw four angels standing at the four corners of the earth,* holding back the four winds of the earth so that no wind could blow on land or sea or against any tree.a 2Then I saw another angel come up from the East,* holding the seal of the living God. He cried out in a loud voice to the four angels who were given power to damage the land and the sea, 3"Do not damage the land or the sea or the trees until we put the seal on the foreheads of the servants of our God."b	* [7:1] The four corners of the earth: the earth is seen as a table or rectangular. In the first vision. * [7:2] East: literally, "rising of the sun." The east was considered the source of light and the place of paradise (Gn 2:8). Seal: whatever was marked by the impression of one's signet ring belonged to that person and was under his protection. (Rev 7:1–8), the elect receive the seal of the living God as protection against the coming cataclysm; cf. Rev 14:1; Ez 9:4–6; 2 Cor 1:22; Eph 1:13; 4:30.	This Pentecost or Holy Spirit Cross (9th Cross in the Key of David) shaped plaque depicts the Holy Spirit surrounded by images of the Annunciation, Pentecost, and the Baptism of Jesus in the Jordan. The Cross also shows the 7 Gifts of the Holy Spirit: Wisdom, Knowledge, Counsel, Fortitude, Understanding, Piety, and Fear of the Lord. The seal is either the impression of a signet ring and/or the symbol of the Holy Spirit, a dove.	
JER.49:36				36I will bring upon Elam the four winds from the four ends of the heavens: I will scatter them to all these winds, until there is no nation to which the outcasts of Elam have not gone.			
ZEC.6:5				5The angel answered me, "These are the four winds of the heavens,* which are coming forth after presenting themselves before the LORD of all the earth.b	* [6:5] Four winds of the heavens: four compass directions and therefore the whole world.		

SCRIPTURE NUMBER	BEGIN DATE	DAYS (END - BEGIN DATES)	END DATE	SCRIPTURE	BIBLICAL NOTES	COMMENTARY
EX.12:7-14				7They will take some of its blood and apply it to the two doorposts and the lintel of the houses in which they eat it. 8They will consume its meat that same night, eating it roasted with unleavened bread and bitter herbs. 9Do not eat any of it raw or even boiled in water, but roasted, with its head and shanks and inner organs. 10You must not keep any of it beyond the morning; whatever is left over in the morning must be burned up. 11This is how you are to eat it: with your loins girt, sandals on your feet and your staff in hand, you will eat it in a hurry. It is the LORD's Passover. 12For on this same night I will go through Egypt, striking down every firstborn in the land, human being and beast alike, and executing judgment on all the gods of Egypt—I, the LORD!b 13But for you the blood will mark the houses where you are. Seeing the blood, I will pass over you; thereby, when I strike the land of Egypt, no destructive blow will come upon you.c 14This day will be a day of remembrance for you, which your future generations will celebrate with pilgrimage to the LORD; you will celebrate it as a statute forever.		
EZ.9:4				4c and the LORD said to him:* Pass through the city, through the midst of Jerusalem, and mark an X on the foreheads of those who grieve and lament over all the abominations practiced within it.	* [9:4] Ezekiel emphasizes personal accountability; the innocent inhabitants of Jerusalem are spared while the idolatrous are punished. An X: lit., the Hebrew letter taw.	
2COR.1:22				22he has also put his seal upon us and given the Spirit in our hearts as a first installment.n	* [1:21–22] The commercial terms gives us security, seal, first installment are here used analogously to refer to the process of initiation into the Christian life, perhaps specifically to baptism. The passage is clearly trinitarian. The Spirit is the first installment or "down payment" of the full messianic benefits that God guarantees to Christians. Cf. Eph 1:13–14.	

SCRIPTURE NUMBER	BEGIN DATE	DAYS (END - BEGIN DATES)	END DATE	SCRIPTURE	BIBLICAL NOTES	COMMENTARY
EPH 1:13				13In him you also, who have heard the word of truth, the gospel of your salvation, and have believed in him, were sealed* with the promised holy Spirit,l	* [1:13] Sealed: by God, in baptism; cf. Eph 4:30; 2 Cor 1:22.	
EPH. 4:30				30And grieve not the holy Spirit of God, whereby ye are sealed unto the day of redemption.		
REV. 7:4-6				4I heard the number of those who had been marked with the seal, one hundred and forty-four thousand marked* from every tribe of the Israelites:c 5twelve thousand were marked from the tribe of Judah,* twelve thousand from the tribe of Reuben, twelve thousand from the tribe of Gad, 6twelve thousand from the tribe of Asher, twelve thousand from the tribe of Naphtali, twelve thousand from the tribe of Manasseh,	* [7:4–9] One hundred and forty-four thousand: the square of twelve (the number of Israel's tribes) multiplied by a thousand, symbolic of the new Israel (cf. Rev 14:1–5; Gal 6:16; Jas 1:1) that embraces people from every nation, race, people, and tongue (Rev 7:9).	This could be an inference that the New Jerusalem (Rev.21:9-14) is New York City: 1) 1,000 or multiples of 1,000 represent immensity 2) People from every nation, race, people, and tongue 3) 2nd largest urban population of Jews in the world, next to Tel Aviv. 4) Rev.10:1-11 Statue of Liberty, New Collossus by Emma Lazarus, Ellis Island: 11Then someone said to me, "You must prophesy again about many peoples, nations, tongues, and kings."*
REV.7:7-8				7twelve thousand from the tribe of Simeon, twelve thousand from the tribe of Levi, twelve thousand from the tribe of Issachar, 8twelve thousand from the tribe of Zebulun, twelve thousand from the tribe of Joseph, and twelve thousand were marked from the tribe of Benjamin.	[7:5–8] Judah is placed first because of Christ; cf. "the Lion of the tribe of Judah" (Rev 5:5). Dan is omitted because of a later tradition that the antichrist would arise from it.	The Key of David has a dimension of 78" spanning across 3 of the upper crosses. The upper crosses are arranged with Cross 14, the "Love Cross" (1Cor.13:13) in the north, Cross 13, Isaiah 43:1 "Redemption Cross" in the center, and Cross 12, the Crucifix, in the south. I started looking at the Tribes of Zebulun, Joseph, and Benjamin and the people within the tribes. Per a map The Twelve Tribes of Israel (see below), the 3 tribes are geographically contiguous with Zebulun to the north, Joseph (consisting of W. Manasseh and Ephraim) in the center, and Benjamin in the south. Its widely accepted that Nazareth was located within the boundary of Zebulun. Jerusalem is located within the boundary of what was Benjamin. These 2 cities along with Bethlehem are referred to as the Holy Lands. Christ spent his youth and adulthood in

SCRIPTURE NUMBER	BEGIN DATE	DAYS (END - BEGIN DATES)	END DATE	SCRIPTURE	BIBLICAL NOTES	COMMENTARY
REV.7:7-8						Nazareth. (Mt.2:23) (Mt.4:12-16). Christ traversed a path from Galilee (Zebulun), through Samaria (Joseph) and through Jericho, to Jerusalem (Benjamin). The 12th and 14th Crosses match positions of Benjamin and Zebulun, respectively, on each side of Joseph, which is the 13th cross. In addition, the religious representation of the different crosses: The 14th Cross, Love and representing Jn.3:16. The 12th Cross being The Crucifix and the Death and Resurrection of Christ in Jerusalem. Cross 13, Isaiah 43:1 "Redemption Cross" in the center represents God's redemption of the Jews for their persecution and His crucifixion in Jerusalem. The Devine message from Scripture, given to me on June 16, 2012 by the Holy Spirit, is Jn 3:16, Is. 43.1, Jn:17-30...Walk the Path of Christ, Forgiveness of Our Sins, and Redemption of the Hebrews.

SCRIPTURE NUMBER	BEGIN DATE	DAYS (END - BEGIN DATES)	END DATE	SCRIPTURE	BIBLICAL NOTES	COMMENTARY
MT.4:13-17				**The Beginning of the Galilean Ministry.** * 12g When he heard that John had been arrested, he withdrew to Galilee. 13He left Nazareth and went to live in Capernaum by the sea, in the region of Zebulun and Naphtali,h 17* From that time on, Jesus began to preach and say,k "Repent, for the kingdom of heaven is at hand."	* [4:12–17] Isaiah's prophecy of the light rising upon Zebulun and Naphtali (Is 8:22–9:1) is fulfilled in Jesus' residence at Capernaum. The territory of these two tribes was the first to be devastated (733–32 B.C.) at the time of the Assyrian invasion. In order to accommodate Jesus' move to Capernaum to the prophecy, Matthew speaks of that town as being "in the region of Zebulun and Naphtali" (Mt 4:13), whereas it was only in the territory of the latter, and he understands the sea of the prophecy, the Mediterranean, as the sea of Galilee.	Its widely accepted that Nazareth was located within the Tribe of Zebulun.

SCRIPTURE NUMBER	BEGIN DATE	DAYS (END - BEGIN DATES)	END DATE	SCRIPTURE	BIBLICAL NOTES	COMMENTARY

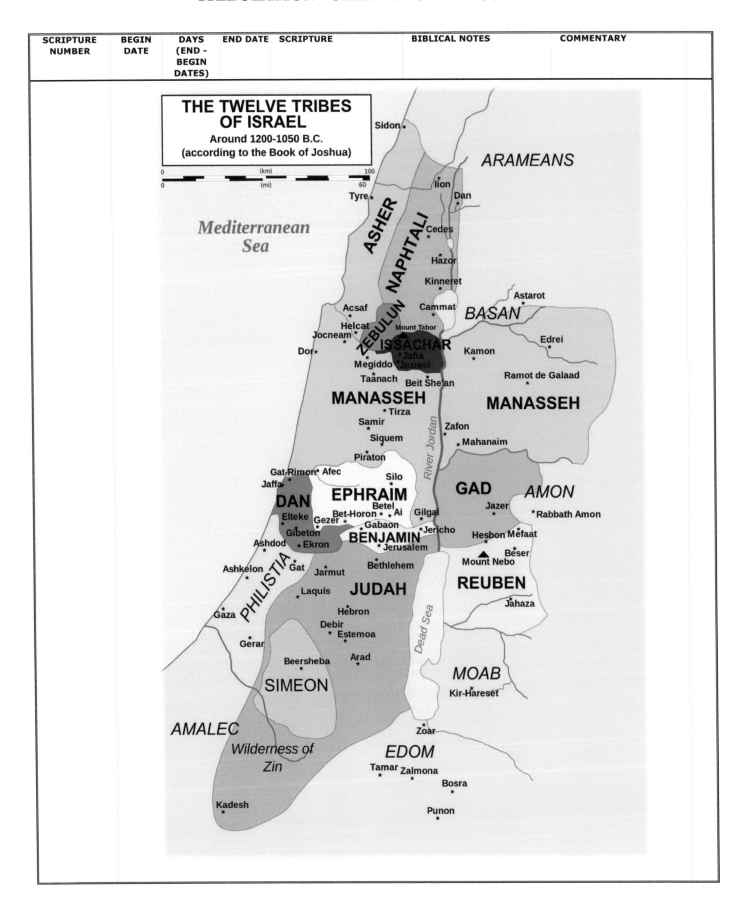

SCRIPTURE NUMBER	BEGIN DATE	DAYS (END - BEGIN DATES)	END DATE	SCRIPTURE	BIBLICAL NOTES	COMMENTARY
MT.4:13-17	Created on June 16, 2012:					

REV. 7:8 12,000 FROM THE TRIBE OF ZEBULUN

12,000 FROM THE TRIBE OF JOSEPH

12,000 FROM THE TRIBE OF BENJAMIN

JOSEPH 39"

BENJAMIN

CRUCIFIX

IS. 43:1 CROSS 39"

ZEBULUN 39"

LOVE CROSS JOHN 3:16

ISAIAH 43:1 REDEMPTION

THROUGH JOSEPH FORGIVENESS FOR THE SINS

LAND OF JOSEPH

NAZARETH

JERUSALEM

TO HIS DEATH & RESURRECTION

HOME

WALK THE PATH OF CHRIST 78"

SCRIPTURE NUMBER	BEGIN DATE	DAYS (END - BEGIN DATES)	END DATE	SCRIPTURE	BIBLICAL NOTES	COMMENTARY
MT.4:13-17						

SCRIPTURE NUMBER	BEGIN DATE	DAYS (END - BEGIN DATES)	END DATE	SCRIPTURE	BIBLICAL NOTES	COMMENTARY
REV.7:9-11				Triumph of the Elect. 9After this I had a vision of a great multitude, which no one could count, from every nation, race, people, and tongue. They stood before the throne and before the Lamb, wearing white robes and holding palm branches* in their hands. 10They cried out in a loud voice: "Salvation comes from* our God, who is seated on the throne, and from the Lamb." 11All the angels stood around the throne and around the elders and the four living creatures. They prostrated themselves before the throne, worshiped God,	* [7:9] White robes…palm branches: symbols of joy and victory; see note on Rev 3:5. * [7:10] Salvation comes from: literally, "(let) salvation (be ascribed) to." A similar hymn of praise is found at the fall of the dragon (Rev 12:10) and of Babylon (Rev 19:1).	Symbolic of the new Israel (cf. Rev 14:1–5; Gal 6:16; Jas 1:1) that embraces people from every nation, race, people, and tongue (Rev 7:9). "Palm Branches": Jn12:12-13 This is symbolic of Palm Sunday and the arrival of Jesus to Jerusalem. He who comes in the name of the Lord: referred in Ps 118:26 to a pilgrim entering the temple gates, but here a title for Jesus (see notes on Mt 11:3 and Jn 6:14; 11:27). The New Israel may very well be New York City (people from every nation, race, people, and tongue). Also symbolic of the United Nations. I now live in New Canaan, CT.
JN.12:12-13				The Entry into Jerusalem.* 12i On the next day, when the great crowd that had come to the feast heard that Jesus was coming to Jerusalem, 13they took palm branches* and went out to meet him, and cried out: "Hosanna! Blessed is he who comes in the name of the Lord, [even] the king of Israel."j	* [12:12–19] In John, the entry into Jerusalem follows the anointing whereas in the synoptics it precedes. In John, the crowd, not the disciples, are responsible for the triumphal procession.	
REV.7:12-15				12and exclaimed: "Amen. Blessing and glory, wisdom and thanksgiving, honor, power, and might be to our God forever and ever. Amen." 13Then one of the elders spoke up and said to me, "Who are these wearing white robes, and where did they come from?" 14I said to him, "My lord, you are the one who knows." He said to me, "These are the ones who have survived the time of great distress;* they have washed their robes and made them white in the blood of the Lamb.d 15"For this reason they stand before God's throne and worship him day and night in his temple.The one who sits on the throne will shelter them.	* [7:14] Time of great distress: fierce persecution by the Romans; cf. Introduction.	
MT.24:21				21* i for at that time there will be great tribulation, such as has not been since the beginning of the world until now, nor ever will be.	* [24:21] For the unparalleled distress of that time, see Dn 12:1.	

SCRIPTURE NUMBER	BEGIN DATE	DAYS (END - BEGIN DATES)	END DATE	SCRIPTURE	BIBLICAL NOTES	COMMENTARY
DAN.7:13				13As the visions during the night continued, I saw coming with the clouds of heavenc One like a son of man.* When he reached the Ancient of Days and was presented before him,	* [7:13–14] One like a son of man: In contrast to the worldly kingdoms opposed to God, which are represented as grotesque beasts, the coming Kingdom of God is represented by a human figure. Scholars disagree as to whether this figure should be taken as a collective symbol for the people of God (cf. 7:27) or identified as a particular individual, e.g., the archangel Michael (cf. 12:1) or the messiah. The phrase "Son of Man" becomes a title for Jesus in the gospels, especially in passages dealing with the Second Coming (Mk 13 and parallels).	
REV.7:16-17				16They will not hunger or thirst anymore, nor will the sun or any heat strike them.e 17For the Lamb who is in the center of the throne will shepherd them and lead them to springs of life-giving water,* and God will wipe away every tear from their eyes."f	* [7:17] Life-giving water: literally, "the water of life," God's grace, which flows from Christ; cf. Rev 21:6; 22:1, 17; Jn 4:10, 14.	Keep in mind, the Big Dipper and Little Dipper each have 7 stars in the their astronomical formations, which could also represent "The one who holds the seven stars in his right hand" leading them to the "life-giving water" described in Rev.7:17: "will shepherd them and lead them to springs of life-giving water", means leading them to repentance and salvation as described in 2 Ptr 3:8-10.
IS.49:10				10They shall not hunger or thirst; nor shall scorching wind or sun strike them; For he who pities them leads them and guides them beside springs of water.g		
IS.25:8				8He will destroy death forever. The Lord GOD will wipe away the tears from all faces; The reproach of his people he will remove from the whole earth; for the LORD has spoken.d	* [25:1–9] These verses praise God for carrying out his plan to destroy the enemy and to save the poor of his people in Zion (14:32), and they announce the victory banquet to be celebrated in the Lord's city.	

SCRIPTURE NUMBER	BEGIN DATE	DAYS (END - BEGIN DATES)	END DATE	SCRIPTURE	BIBLICAL NOTES	COMMENTARY	
REV. 8:1-4				The Seven Trumpets. 1When he broke open the seventh seal, there was silence in heaven*for about half an hour.a 2And I saw that the seven angels who stood before God were given seven trumpets.b The Gold Censer. 3Another angel came and stood at the altar,* holding a gold censer. He was given a great quantity of incense to offer, along with the prayers of all the holy ones, on the gold altar that was before the throne.c 4The smoke of the incense along with the prayers of the holy ones went up before God from the hand of the angel.	* [8:1] Silence in heaven: as in Zep 1:7, a prelude to the eschatological woes that are to follow; cf. Introduction.* [8:3] Altar: there seems to be only one altar in the heavenly temple, corresponding to the altar of holocausts in Rev 6:9, and here to the altar of incense in Jerusalem; cf. also Rev 9:13; 11:1; 14:18; 16:7.	When I raised the 7th Cross from 79" to 92", the number of 13" dimensions went from 12 to 13 and the number of 18" dimensions went from 6 to 7. This should symbolize the Ascension of Christ and the Exaltation of the Virgin Mary which represents the 7th Seal and the 7 Thunders.	7 TRUMPETS / 7TH SEAL
HEB.2:2				2For if the word announced through angels proved firm, and every transgression and disobedience received its just recompense,a	The word announced through angels (Heb 2:2), the Mosaic law, is contrasted with the more powerful word that Christians have received (Heb 2:3–4). Christ's supremacy strengthens Christians against being carried away from their faith.		
ZEP.1:7				7Silence in the presence of the Lord GOD! for near is the day of the LORD, Yes, the LORD has prepared a sacrifice, he has consecrated his guests.* c	* [1:7] He has consecrated his guests: God has consecrated the troops, presumably foreign, who have been invited to share in the spoil on the day of slaughter.		
ZEC.2:17				17Silence, all people, in the presence of the LORD, who stirs forth from his holy dwelling.k			1ST 6 TRUMPETS
TB.12:15				15I am Raphael, one of the seven angels who stand and serve before the Glory of the Lord."e			
PS.141:2				2Let my prayer be incense* before you; my uplifted hands* an evening offering.a	* [141:2] Incense: lit., "smoke," i.e., the fragrant fumes arising from the altar at the burning of sacrificial animals or of aromatic spices; also used in Rev 5:8 as a symbol of prayer. My uplifted hands: the gesture of supplication, cf. Ps 28:2; 63:5; 88:10; 119:48; 134:2; 143:6.		

SCRIPTURE NUMBER	BEGIN DATE	DAYS (END - BEGIN DATES)	END DATE	SCRIPTURE	BIBLICAL NOTES	COMMENTARY	
TB.12:12				12d Now when you, Tobit, and Sarah prayed, it was I who presented the record of your prayer before the Glory of the Lord; and likewise whenever you used to bury the dead.*	* [12:12] Raphael is one of the seven Angels of the Presence, specially designated intercessors who present prayers to God. Angelology was developing in this period. The names of two other of these seven angels are given in the Bible: Gabriel (Dn 8:16; 9:21; Lk 1:19, 26) and Michael (Dn 10:13, 21; 12:1; Jude 9; Rev 12:7). See 1 Enoch for the names of the rest.	The 4 remaining Archangels are Uriel (or Anael), Simiel, Oriphiel and Zachariel.	
SIR.22:27				27Who will set a guard over my mouth, an effective seal on my lips, That I may not fail through them, and my tongue may not destroy me?e			
REV.8:5-7				5Then the angel took the censer, filled it with burning coals from the altar, and hurled it down to the earth. There were peals of thunder, rumblings, flashes of lightning, and an earthquake.d The First Four Trumpets. 6The seven angels who were holding the seven trumpets prepared to blow them.e 7When the first one blew his trumpet, there came hail and fire mixed with blood, which was hurled down to the earth. A third of the land was burned up, along with a third of the trees and all green grass.*	A minor liturgy (Rev 8:3-5) is enclosed by a vision of seven angels (Rev 8:2, 6). [8:7] This woe resembles the seventh plague of Egypt (Ex 9:23-24); cf. Jl 3:3. Then follow the first four trumpet blasts, each heralding catastrophes modeled on the plagues of Egypt affecting the traditional prophetic third (cf. Ez 5:12) of the earth, sea, fresh water, and stars (Rev 8:7-12). * [8:13] Woe! Woe! Woe: each of the three woes pronounced by the angel represents a separate disaster; cf. Rev 9:12; 11:14. The final woe, released by the seventh trumpet blast, includes the plagues of Rev 16.	In Cypress, 85" (REV.8:5 is the dimension across the arched opening (the door) leading out of the foyer. The censer is used in several Christian rituals (benedictions, processions, important Masses), particularly in the Roman Catholic and Christian Orthodox churches. So where the Manhattan Key of David, at the doorway, symbolizes Catholic and Protestant religions, the Cypress Key of David, at the doorway, symbolizes the calamity described in Rev. 8:5. This may very well may coincide with events described in Rev.16:8-9, 16:17-21.	**1ST 6 TRUMPETS**
EZ.10:2				2* And he said to the man dressed in linen: Go within the wheelwork under the cherubim; fill both your hands with burning coals from the place among the cherubim, then scatter them over the city. As I watched, he entered.b	* [10:2-13] The burning coals, a sign of the divine presence (cf. 28:14; Ps 18:9), represent the judgment of destruction that God is visiting upon the city; they may also represent the judgment of purification that prepares the land to become the Lord's sanctuary (cf. Is 6:6-7).	Similar calamitous events are described in this supporting scripture to Rev.8:5-7:	
PS.11:6				6And rains upon the wicked fiery coals and brimstone, a scorching wind their allotted cup.*d	* [11:6] Their allotted cup: the cup that God gives people to drink is a common figure for their destiny, cf.		

SCRIPTURE NUMBER	BEGIN DATE	DAYS (END - BEGIN DATES)	END DATE	SCRIPTURE	BIBLICAL NOTES	COMMENTARY
REV. 8:8-11	21-Apr-10			8* When the second angel blew his trumpet, something like a large burning mountain was hurled into the sea. A third of the sea turned to blood,f 9a third of the creatures living in the sea* died, and a third of the ships were wrecked. 10When the third angel blew his trumpet, a large star burning like a torch fell from the sky. It fell on a third of the rivers and on the springs of water.g 11The star was called "Wormwood,"* and a third of all the water turned to wormwood. Many people died from this water, because it was made bitter.h	* [8:8–11] The background of these two woes is the first plague of Egypt (Ex 7:20–21). * [8:9] Creatures living in the sea: literally, "creatures in the sea that had souls."	Deepwater Horizon, the horrendous oil spill disaster, starting in mid-April 2010 and lasting for 3 months. The "large burning mountain" is the oil production platform flaming as it eventually sank into the sea. A 3rd of the Sea turned to blood (wine of God's wrath) which in actuality was oil which looked like blood in the Gulf of Mexico. 3rd of the Creatures died. The damage to wildlife is still being discovered and evaluated. [8:9] Creatures living in the sea: literally, "creatures in the sea that had souls." This probably best represents bottlenose dolphins and marine mammals affected by the spill.
EX.7:20				20This, then, is what Moses and Aaron did, exactly as the LORD had commanded. Aaron raised his staff and struck the waters in the Nile in full view of Pharaoh and his servants, and all the water in the Nile was changed into blood.		
IS.14:12				12How you have fallen from the heavens, O Morning Star,* son of the dawn! How you have been cut down to the earth, you who conquered nations!i		
JER.9:14				14therefore, thus says the LORD of hosts, the God of Israel: See now, I will give this people wormwood to eat and poisoned water to drink.h		
REV. 8:12-13				12When the fourth angel blew his trumpet, a third of the sun, a third of the moon, and a third of the stars were struck, so that a third of them became dark. The day lost its light for a third of the time, as did the night.i 13Then I looked again and heard an eagle flying high overhead cry out in a loud voice, "Woe! Woe! Woe* to the inhabitants of the earth from the rest of the trumpet blasts that the three angels are about to blow!"	Then follow the first four trumpet blasts, each heralding catastrophes modeled on the plagues of Egypt affecting the traditional prophetic third (cf. Ez 5:12) of the earth, sea, fresh water, and stars (Rev 8:7-12). Finally, there is a vision of an eagle warning of the last three trumpet blasts (Rev 8:13). * [8:13] Woe! Woe! Woe: each of the three woes pronounced by the angel represents a separate disaster; cf. Rev 9:12; 11:14. The final woe, released by the seventh trumpet blast, includes the plagues of Rev 16.	

1ST 6 TRUMPETS

SCRIPTURE NUMBER	BEGIN DATE	DAYS (END - BEGIN DATES)	END DATE	SCRIPTURE	BIBLICAL NOTES	COMMENTARY
EX.10:23-24				23People could not see one another, nor could they get up from where they were, for three days. But all the Israelites had light where they lived. 24Pharaoh then summoned Moses and Aaron and said, "Go, serve the LORD. Only your flocks and herds will be detained. Even your little ones may go with you."		
REV. 9:1-4				The Fifth Trumpet.* 1Then the fifth angel blew his trumpet, and I saw a star* that had fallen from the sky to the earth. It was given the key for the passage to the abyss. 2It opened the passage to the abyss,a and smoke came up out of the passage like smoke from a huge furnace. The sun and the air were darkened by the smoke from the passage.b 3Locusts came out of the smoke onto the land, and they were given the same power as scorpions* of the earth.c 4They were told not to harm the grass of the earth or any plant or any tree, but only those people who did not have the seal of God on their foreheads.	* [9:1] A star: late Judaism represented fallen powers as stars (Is 14:12–15; Lk 10:18; Jude 13), but a comparison with Rev 1:20 and Rev 20:1 suggests that here it means an angel. The passage to the abyss: referring to Sheol, the netherworld, where Satan and the fallen angels are kept for a thousand years, to be cast afterwards into the pool of fire; cf. Rev 20:7–10. The abyss was conceived of as a vast subterranean cavern full of fire. Its only link with the earth was a kind of passage or mine shaft, which was kept locked. * [9:3] Scorpions: their poisonous sting was proverbial; Ez 2:6; Lk 11:12.	My interpretation of the star is a Seraph, a type of celestial or heavenly being in the Abrahamic religions. This "burning angel" is traditionally placed in the FIFTH rank of ten in the Jewish angelic hierarchy and the highest rank in the Christian angelic hierarchy. God has sent the Seraph to earth, with the keys to the abyss (See Rev. 20:1), to open the abyss, releasing the locusts who will protect the flora and protect God's people and who will torment those who do not have the seal of God on their foreheads: Rev.9:3 Locusts are helicopters and scorpions are tanks. Locusts given the same power as scorpions: Locust is something like an AC 130 gunship or an Apache AH-64 helicopter having the same power as a M-1a-1/2 Abrams tank. In April 2005, Boeing delivered the first AH-64D Apache Helicopters to the Israeli Air Force (IAF). The IAF has named the AH-64D Saraph (שרף, also as "Seraph", Hebrew for flaming angel). Commentary on Rev.9:5-8. See Scripture and Biblical Notes for Is.6:2-3. Scripture and Biblical Notes above represent an armed conflict of God's people against evil. Wisdom is needed here before a preemptive act.

1ST 6 TRUMPETS

SCRIPTURE NUMBER	BEGIN DATE	DAYS (END - BEGIN DATES)	END DATE	SCRIPTURE	BIBLICAL NOTES	COMMENTARY

<u>REV.1:18</u> the one who lives. Once I was dead, but now I am alive forever and ever. I hold the keys to death and the netherworld.* Netherworld: Greek Hades, Hebrew Sheol, the abode of the dead; cf. Rev 20:13–14; Nm 16:33. <u>REV.11:18</u> The nations raged, but your wrath has come, and the time for the dead to be judged, and to recompense your servants, the prophets, and the holy ones and those who fear your name, the small and the great alike, and to <u>DESTROY</u> those who <u>DESTROY</u> the earth."g

THE REVELATION 9   *The key to the pit*

hail and fire mixed with blood were thrown down upon the earth. One-third of the earth was set on fire so that one-third of the trees were burned, and all the green grass.

8,9 Then the second angel blew his trumpet, and what appeared to be a huge burning mountain was thrown into the sea, destroying a third of all the ships; and a third of the sea turned red as[a] blood; and a third of the fish were killed.

10 The third angel blew, and a great flaming star fell from heaven upon a third of the rivers and springs. 11 The star was called "Bitterness"[b] because it poisoned a third of all the water on the earth and many people died.

12 The fourth angel blew his trumpet and immediately a third of the sun was blighted and darkened, and a third of the moon and the stars, so that the daylight was dimmed by a third, and the nighttime darkness deepened. 13 As I watched, I saw a solitary eagle flying through the heavens crying loudly, "Woe, woe, woe to the people of the earth because of the terrible things that will soon happen when the three remaining angels blow their trumpets."

9 THEN THE FIFTH angel blew his trumpet and I saw one[a] who was fallen to earth from heaven, and to him was given the key to the bottomless pit. 2 When he opened it, smoke poured out as though from some huge furnace, and the sun and air were darkened by the smoke.

3 Then locusts came from the smoke and descended onto the earth and were given power to sting like scorpions. 4 They were told not to hurt the grass or plants or trees, but to attack those people who did not have the mark of God on their foreheads. 5 They were not to kill them, but to torture them for five months with agony like the pain of scorpion stings. 6 In those days men will try to kill themselves but won't be able to—death will not come. They will long to die—but death will flee away!

7 The locusts looked like horses armored for battle. They had what looked like golden crowns on their heads, and their faces looked like men's. 8 Their hair was long like women's, and their teeth were those of lions. 9 They wore breastplates that seemed to be of iron, and their wings roared like an army of chariots rushing into battle. 10 They had stinging tails like scorpions, and their power to hurt, given to them for five months, was in their tails. 11 Their king is the Prince of the bottomless pit whose name in Hebrew is Abaddon, and in Greek, Apollyon [and in English, the Destroyer[b]].

12 One terror now ends, but there are two more coming!

13 The sixth angel blew his trumpet and I heard a voice speaking from the four horns of the golden altar that stands before the throne of God, 14 saying to the sixth angel, "Release the four mighty demons[c] held bound at the great River Euphrates." 15 They had been kept in readiness for that year and month and day and hour, and now they were turned loose to kill a third of all mankind. 16 They led an army of 200,000,-000[d] warriors[e]—I heard an announcement of how many there were.

17,18 I saw their horses spread out before me in my vision; their riders wore fiery-red breastplates, though some were sky-blue and others yellow. The horses' heads looked much like lions', and smoke and fire and flaming sulphur billowed from their mouths, killing one-third of all mankind. 19 Their power of death was not only in their mouths, but in their tails as well, for their tails were similar to serpents' heads that struck and bit with fatal wounds.

20 But the men left alive after these plagues *still refused to worship God!* They would not renounce their demon-worship, nor their idols made of gold and silver, brass, stone, and wood—which neither see nor hear nor walk! 21 Neither did they change their mind and attitude about all their murders and witchcraft, their immo-

1ST 6 TRUMPETS

8a Literally, "became blood."   8b Literally, "Wormwood."   9a Literally, "a star fallen from heaven"; it is unclear whether this person is of satanic origin, as most commentators believe, or whether the reference is to Christ.   9b Implied.   9c Literally, "(fallen) angels."   9d If this is a literal figure, it is no longer incredible, in view of a world population of 6,000,000,000 in the near future. In China alone, in 1961, there were an "estimated 200,000,000 armed and organized militiamen" (Associated Press Release, April 24, 1964). 9e Literally, "horsemen."

1010

The above Scripture and Biblical Notes are from the Living Bible (Paraphrased), 42nd Printing 1974. Note 9a: Literally, "a star fallen from Heaven"; it is unclear whether this person is of satanic origin, as most commentators believe, or whether the reference is to Christ. My commentary: The angel of the abyss (<u>"THE DESTROYER" as translated from Greek and Hebrew</u>), is a Seraph. Satan is doomed to perdition; therefore why would he be given the keys to the Abyss (his own jail cell).

SCRIPTURE NUMBER	BEGIN DATE	DAYS (END - BEGIN DATES)	END DATE	SCRIPTURE	BIBLICAL NOTES	COMMENTARY
GN.19:28				28As he looked down toward Sodom and Gomorrah and the whole region of the Plain,* he saw smoke over the land rising like the smoke from a kiln.k	* [19:28–29] In a deft narrative detail, Abraham looks down from the height east of Hebron, from which he could easily see the region at the southern end of the Dead Sea, where the cities of the Plain were probably located.	
EX.10:12-15				12b The LORD then said to Moses: Stretch out your hand over the land of Egypt for the locusts, that they may come upon it and eat up all the land's vegetation, whatever the hail has left. 13So Moses stretched out his staff over the land of Egypt, and the LORD drove an east wind* over the land all that day and all night. When it was morning, the east wind brought the locusts. 14The locusts came up over the whole land of Egypt and settled down over all its territory. Never before had there been such a fierce swarm of locusts, nor will there ever be again. 15They covered the surface of the whole land, so that it became black. They ate up all the vegetation in the land and all the fruit of the trees the hail had spared. Nothing green was left on any tree or plant in the fields throughout the land of Egypt.	* [10:13] East wind: coming across the desert from Arabia, the strong east wind brings Egypt the burning sirocco and, at times, locusts. Cf. 14:21.	
WIS.16:9				9For the bites of locusts and of flies slew them, and no remedy was found to save their lives because they deserved to be punished by such means;g	9For the bites of locusts and of flies slew them, and no remedy was found to save their lives because they deserved to be punished by such means;g	
REV. 9:5-8		150		5They were not allowed to kill them but only to torment them for five months;* the torment they inflicted was like that of a scorpion when it stings a person. 6During that time these people will seek death but will not find it, and they will long to die but death will escape them.d 7* The appearance of the locusts was like that of horses ready for battle. On their heads they wore what looked like crowns of gold; their faces were like human faces,e 8and they had hair like women's hair. Their teeth were like lions' teeth,f.	* [9:5] For five months: more or less corresponding to the life-span of locusts.* [9:7–10] Eight characteristics are listed to show the eschatological and diabolical nature of these locusts.	Symbolic of an armed conflict. AH-64 Apache Attack Helicopter with Hellfire Missiles. "Rev.9:7 The appearance of the locusts was like that of horses ready for battle." Historical (from the movie, We Were Soldiers): 1st Battalion, 7th Cavalry. Location: Ia Drang Valley (Valley of Death) in 1965, the first major battle between the United States and North Vietnam The 7th Cavalry used helicopters, not horses, for conveyance to the battlefield. Perhaps a 5 month battle in modern day time. AH64 are currently deployed by Egypt, Greece, Israel, Japan, Kuwait,

1ST 6 TRUMPETS

SCRIPTURE NUMBER	BEGIN DATE	DAYS (END - BEGIN DATES)	END DATE	SCRIPTURE	BIBLICAL NOTES	COMMENTARY
REV. 9:5-8						Netherlands, Taiwan, Singapore, UAE, UK, USA. Data provide by Wikipedia.

AH-64 APACHE ATTACK HELICOPTER...FACE & CROWN

AH-64 APACHE ATTACK HELICOPTER...TEETH

AH-64 APACHE ATTACK HELICOPTER...HAIR

AC-130 SPECTRE / SPOOKY / STINGER II ... HAIR

SCRIPTURE NUMBER	BEGIN DATE	DAYS (END - BEGIN DATES)	END DATE	SCRIPTURE	BIBLICAL NOTES	COMMENTARY
JB.3:21				21They wait for death and it does not come; they search for it more than for hidden treasures.		
JL. 2:4				4Their appearance is that of horses; like war horses they run.	* [2:1–11] Joel warns the people about the destruction he sees galloping toward Jerusalem. He combines the imagery of the locust invasion (chap. 1) with language from the holy war tradition in order to describe the Lord leading a heavenly army against the enemy, in this case, Jerusalem.	There are no plans to lead a heavennly army against Jerusalem.

1ST 6 TRUMPETS

SCRIPTURE NUMBER	BEGIN DATE	DAYS (END - BEGIN DATES)	END DATE	SCRIPTURE	BIBLICAL NOTES	COMMENTARY	
JL.1:6				6For a nation* invaded my land, powerful and past counting, With teeth like a lion's, fangs like those of a lioness.	* [1:6] A nation: the locusts are compared to an invading army, whose numbers are overwhelming. The ravaged landscape resembles the wasteland left behind by marauding troops; the order and peace associated with agricultural productivity (1 Kgs 5:5; Mi 4:4) has been destroyed.	Iraq War	
REV. 9:9-12				9and they had chests like iron breastplates. The sound of their wings was like the sound of many horse-drawn chariots racing into battle. 10They had tails like scorpions, with stingers; with their tails they had power to harm people for five months. 11They had as their king the angel of the abyss, whose name in Hebrew is Abaddon* and in Greek Apollyon. 12The first woe has passed, but there are two more to come.	* [9:7–10] Eight characteristics are listed to show the eschatological and diabolical nature of these locusts. * [9:11] Abaddon: Hebrew (more precisely, Aramaic) for destruction or ruin.	Crew protection in the AH-64 is provided by boron armour shielding within the cockpit sides, flooring, and in the bulkhead between the cockpit positions. This shielding is resistant against armour-piercing rounds up to 12.7mm. Sound of many horse-drawn chariots are the main and tail rotors. The tail section and tail rotor, when not operating, looks like a scorpion's tail. (Source: AH64 - Apache http://www.nme.de/cgi-shl/nme/ah64.ph)	
REV.9:13-16				The Sixth Trumpet.* 13Then the sixth angel blew his trumpet, and I heard a voice coming from the [four]* horns of the gold altar before God,g 14telling the sixth angel who held the trumpet, "Release the four angels* who are bound at the banks of the great river Euphrates." 15So the four angels were released, who were prepared for this hour, day, month, and year to kill a third of the human race. 16The number of cavalry troops was two hundred million; I heard their number.	* [9:13–21] The sixth trumpet heralds a woe representing another diabolical attack symbolized by an invasion by the Parthians living east of the Euphrates; see note on Rev 6:2. At the appointed time (Rev 9:15), the frightful horses act as God's agents of judgment. The imaginative details are not to be taken literally; see Introduction and the note on Rev 6:12–14.	"The four angels* who are bound at the banks of the great river Euphrates.": Iran, Iraq, Syria, Turkey. In 2008, the following numbers were the respective populations: Iran 71,956,322, Iraq 30,711,152, Syria 22,581,290, Turkey 73,914,260 totaling 197,163,024 people. In 2011, the following numbers were the respective populations: Iran 75,330,000, Iraq 30,399,752, Syria 22,717,417 Turkey 73,722,988 totaling 202,169,977 people, with Iran having the largest growth of 3,373,678 or 4.7%. Data provided by Wikipedia.	1ST 6 TRUMPETS
EX.30:1-3				1For burning incense you shall make an altar of acacia wood,a 2with a square surface, a cubit long, a cubit wide, and two cubits high, with horns that are of one piece with it. 3Its grate on top, its walls on all four sides, and its horns you shall plate with pure gold. Put a gold molding around it.			

SCRIPTURE NUMBER	BEGIN DATE	DAYS (END - BEGIN DATES)	END DATE	SCRIPTURE	BIBLICAL NOTES	COMMENTARY	
REV.9:17-21				17Now in my vision this is how I saw the horses and their riders. They wore red, blue, and yellow breastplates,* and the horses' heads were like heads of lions, and out of their mouths came fire, smoke, and sulfur.h 18By these three plagues of fire, smoke, and sulfur that came out of their mouths a third of the human race was killed. 19For the power of the horses is in their mouths and in their tails; for their tails are like snakes, with heads that inflict harm. 20The rest of the human race, who were not killed by these plagues, did not repent of the works of their hands,* to give up the worship of demons and idols made from gold, silver, bronze, stone, and wood, which cannot see or hear or walk.i 21Nor did they repent of their murders, their magic potions, their unchastity, or their robberies.	* [9:17] Blue: literally, "hyacinth-colored." Yellow: literally, "sulfurous."	Red, blue and yellow are the 3 primary colors. "Magic potions" are oil and its derivatives.	
JB.41:10-13				10When he sneezes, light flashes forth; his eyes are like the eyelids of the dawn. 11Out of his mouth go forth torches; sparks of fire leap forth. 12From his nostrils comes smoke as from a seething pot or bowl. 13His breath sets coals afire; a flame comes from his mouth.			
PS 135:15-17				15The idols of the nations are silver and gold,k the work of human hands. 16They have mouths but do not speak; they have eyes but do not see; 17They have ears but do not hear; nor is there breath in their mouths.		Idolatry	
IS.17:8				8They shall not turn to the altars, the work of their hands, nor shall they look to what their fingers have made: the asherahs* or the incense stands.	* [17:8] Asherahs: see note on Ex 34:13. Incense stands: small altars on which incense was burned; cf. Is 27:9; Lv 26:30.	Warning against Idolatry	
DN 5-4				4wine from them, they praised their gods of gold and silver, bronze and iron, wood and stone.		Idolatry	

1ST 6 TRUMPETS

SCRIPTURE NUMBER	BEGIN DATE	DAYS (END - BEGIN DATES)	END DATE	SCRIPTURE	BIBLICAL NOTES	COMMENTARY	
REV. 10:1-3				**The Angel with the Small Scroll**. 1* Then I saw another mighty angel come down from heaven wrapped in a cloud, with a halo around his head; his face was like the sun and his feet were like pillars of fire. 2In his hand he held a small scroll that had been opened. He placed his right foot on the sea and his left foot on the land,* 3and then he cried out in a loud voice as a lion roars. When he cried out, the seven thunders* raised their voices, too.a	* [10:1-11:14] An interlude in two scenes (Rev 10:1-11 and Rev 11:1-14) precedes the sounding of the seventh trumpet; cf. Rev 7:1-17. The first vision describes an angel astride sea and land like a COLOSSUS, with a small scroll open, the contents of which indicate that the end is imminent (Rev 10).* [10:2] He placed...on the land: this symbolizes the UNIVERVERSALITY of the angel's message, as does the figure of the small scroll open to be read.* [10:3] The seven thunders: God's voice announcing judgment and doom; cf. Ps 29:3-9, where thunder, as the voice of Yahweh is praised seven times.(Rev.1:8 8"I am the Alpha and the Omega,"* says the Lord God, "the one who is and who was and who is to come, the almighty."g)	The 8th Cross in the Key is a Celtic Cross and what is the Son of Man, is clothed with a white wraparound and the halo around his head symbolizing eternity. The cross is green, blue, and copper colored. "mighty angel come down from heaven wrapped in a cloud, with a halo around his head" The Statue of Liberty. 7 rays (7 thunders) coming from the crown on her head. 2In his hand he held a small scroll. St. John saw the book in Lady Liberty's left hand and proclaimed it the "small scroll"; however the words of "The New Colossus" by Emma Lazarus", in a plaque at the base of the monument, is the content of the scroll. He (she) placed his (her) right foot on the sea and his (her) left foot on the land (she's stepping toward the sea), and then he (she) cried out in a loud voice as a lion roars,* 3and then he cried out in a loud voice as a lion roars. When he (she) cried out, the seven thunders* raised their voices saying: ""Give me your tired, your poor,/Your huddled masses yearning to breathe free".	**7 THUNDERS**

SCRIPTURE NUMBER	BEGIN DATE	DAYS (END - BEGIN DATES)	END DATE	SCRIPTURE	BIBLICAL NOTES	COMMENTARY
REV. 10:1-3				The New Colossus, "Anthem Of Freedom" by Jewish American poet, Emma Lazarus: Not like the brazen giant of Greek fame, With conquering limbs astride from land to land; Here at our sea-washed, sunset gates shall stand A mighty woman with a torch, whose flame Is the imprisoned lightning, and her name Mother of Exiles. From her beacon-hand Glows world-wide welcome; her mild eyes command The air-bridged harbor that twin cities frame. "Keep, ancient lands, your storied pomp!" cries she With silent lips. "Give me your tired, your poor, Your huddled masses yearning to breathe free, The wretched refuse of your teeming shore. Send these, the homeless, tempest-tost to me, I lift my lamp beside the golden door!" 	Regarding Mexican immigrants, I'm proud that my parents taught me that if someone is hungry you feed them, if their clothing is tattered, you give them clothing, if they need shelter, you shelter them. If they need direction, you guide them, because they only want a better life.

7 THUNDERS

SCRIPTURE NUMBER	BEGIN DATE	DAYS (END - BEGIN DATES)	END DATE	SCRIPTURE	BIBLICAL NOTES	COMMENTARY
PS.29:3-9				3The voice of the LORD* is over the waters; the God of glory thunders, the LORD, over the mighty waters. 4The voice of the LORD is power; the voice of the LORD is splendor.b 5The voice of the LORD cracks the cedars; the LORD splinters the cedars of Lebanon, 6Makes Lebanon leap like a calf, and Sirion* like a young bull. 7The voice of the LORD strikes with fiery flame; 8the voice of the LORD shakes the desert; the LORD shakes the desert of Kadesh. 9*The voice of the LORD makes the deer dance and strips the forests bare. All in his Temple say, "Glory!"	* [29:3] The voice of the LORD: the sevenfold repetition of the phrase imitates the sound of crashing thunder and may allude to God's primordial slaying of Leviathan, the seven-headed sea monster of Canaanite mythology. * [29:6] Sirion: the Phoenician name for Mount Hermon, cf. Dt 3:9. * [29:9b–10] Having witnessed God's supreme power (Ps 29:3–9a), the gods acknowledge the glory that befits the king of the divine and human world.	
JER.25:30				30As for you, prophesy against them all these words and say to them: The LORD roars from on high, from his holy dwelling he raises his voice; Mightily he roars over his sheepfold, a shout like that of vintagers echoesn over all the inhabitants of the earth.		
AM.3:8				8The lion has roared, who would not fear?c The Lord GOD has spoken, who would not prophesy?	* [3:3–8] The metaphors in these sayings illustrate the principle of cause and effect, and lead up to the conclusion in v. 8.	
REV. 10:4-7	24-Mar-12			4When the seven thunders had spoken, I was about to write it down; but I heard a voice from heaven say, "Seal up what the seven thunders have spoken, but do not write it down." 5Then the angel I saw standing on the sea and on the land raised his right hand to heaven 6and swore by the one who lives forever and ever, who created heaven and earth and sea* and all that is in them, "There shall be no more delay.b 7At the time when you hear the seventh angel blow his trumpet, the mysterious plan of God* shall be fulfilled, as he promised to his servants the prophets."c	* [10:6] Heaven and earth and sea: the three parts of the universe. No more delay: cf. Dn 12:7; Heb 2:3. * [10:7] The mysterious plan of God: literally, "the mystery of God," the end of the present age when the forces of evil will be put down (Rev 17:1–19:4, 11–21; 20:7–10; cf. 2 Thes 2:6–12; Rom 16:25–26), and the establishment of the reign of God when all creation will be made new (Rev 21:1–22:5).	6and swore by the one who lives forever and ever, who created heaven and earth and sea* and all that is in them, "There shall be no more delay.b 7At the time when you hear the seventh angel blow his trumpet, the mysterious plan of God* shall be fulfilled, as he promised to his servants the prophets."c [10:3] The seven thunders: Ps 29:3-9, where thunder, as the voice of Yahweh, is praised seven times. (Rev.1:8 8"I am the Alpha and the Omega,"* says the Lord God, "the one who is and who was and who is to come, the almighty.")g) 7 measurements of 18" on the Key of David.s See dimensioned drawing (Key of David - Manhattan).

7 THUNDERS

TRIBULATION - CHAPTER 6 - THE SCROLL

SCRIPTURE NUMBER	BEGIN DATE	DAYS (END - BEGIN DATES)	END DATE	SCRIPTURE	BIBLICAL NOTES	COMMENTARY
DT.32:40				40For I raise my hand to the heavens and will say: As surely as I live forever,		
DN.12:7		1260		7The man clothed in linen,d who was upstream, lifted his hands to heaven; and I heard him swear by him who lives forever that it should be for a time, two times, and half a time;* and that, when the power of the destroyer of the holy people was brought to an end, all these things should end.	* [12:7] A time, two times, and half a time: see note on 7:25.	
EZ.12:28				28Say to them therefore: Thus says the Lord GOD: None of my words shall be delayed any longer. Whatever I say is final; it shall be done—oracle of the Lord GOD.	* [12:22–28] This proverb conveys the skepticism the people of Jerusalem have; cf. Jer 20:7–9.	
AM.3:7				7(Indeed, the Lord GOD does nothing without revealing his plan to his servants the prophets.)	* [3:3–8] The metaphors in these sayings illustrate the principle of cause and effect, and lead up to the conclusion in v. 8.	
REV. 10:8-11				8Then the voice that I had heard from heaven spoke to me again and said, "Go, take the scroll that lies open in the hand of the angel who is standing on the sea and on the land." 9So I went up to the angel and told him to give me the small scroll. He said to me, "Take and swallow it. It will turn your stomach sour, but in your mouth it will taste as sweet* as honey." 10I took the small scroll from the angel's hand and swallowed it. In my mouth it was like sweet honey, but when I had eaten it, my stomach turned sour.d 11Then someone said to me, "You must prophesy again about many peoples, nations, tongues, and kings."*	* [10:9–10] The small scroll was sweet because it predicted the final victory of God's people; it was sour because it also announced their sufferings. Cf. Ez 3:1–3.* [10:11] This further prophecy is contained in chaps. 12–22.	"Take and swallow it" means open, read, and accept the scroll. Then someone said to me, "You must prophesy again about many peoples, nations, tongues, and kings."*: The immigrants who went through Ellis Island. The "melting pot" of New York City with a population of approx. 8MM people. The United Nations. This Angel, the Statue of Liberty, gives people Hope. The book she's holding gives the date of the signing of the Declaration of Independence. With words that were once sweet, they are now sour because of the hypocrisy towards the Mexican immigrants to the south.

7 THUNDERS

SCRIPTURE NUMBER	BEGIN DATE	DAYS (END - BEGIN DATES)	END DATE	SCRIPTURE	BIBLICAL NOTES	COMMENTARY
EZ.3:1-3				1He said to me: Son of man, eat what you find here: eat this scroll, then go, speak to the house of Israel. 2So I opened my mouth, and he gave me the scroll to eat. 3a Son of man, he said to me, feed your stomach and fill your belly with this scroll I am giving you. I ate it, and it was as sweet as honey* in my mouth.	* [3:3] As sweet as honey: though the prophet must foretell terrible things, the word of God is sweet to the one who receives it.	
REV. 11-1-4		1260		The Two Witnesses. 1* a Then I was given a measuring rod like a staff and I was told, "Come and measure the temple of God and the altar, and count those who are worshiping in it. 2But exclude the outer court* of the temple; do not measure it, for it has been handed over to the Gentiles, who will trample (See Dn.8:14) the holy city for forty-two months. 3I will commission my two witnesses* to prophesy for those twelve hundred and sixty days, wearing sackcloth." 4b These are the two olive trees and the two lampstands* that stand before the Lord of the earth.	* [11:1] The temple and altar symbolize the new Israel; see note on Rev 7:4–9. The worshipers represent Christians. The measuring of the temple (cf. Ez 40:3–42:20; 47:1–12; Zec 2:5–6) suggests that God will preserve the faithful remnant (cf. Is 4:2–3) who remain true to Christ (Rev 14:1–5). * [11:2] The outer court: the Court of the Gentiles. Trample…forty-two months: the duration of the vicious persecution of the Jews by Antiochus IV Epiphanes (Dn 7:25; 12:7); this persecution of three and a half years (half of seven, counted as 1260 days in Rev 11:3; 12:6) became the prototype of periods of trial for God's people; cf. Lk 4:25; Jas 5:17. The reference here is to the persecution by the Romans; cf. Introduction.	Sackcloth, a rough cloth made of animal hair, symbolizes mourning, lamenting, or repenting. In this case lamenting over the declining physical condition of the earth.
EZ. 40:3-5				3He brought me there, and there standing in the gateway was a man whose appearance was like bronze! He held in his hand a linen cord and a measuring rod.c 4The man said to me, "Son of man, look carefully and listen intently. Pay strict attention to everything I show you, for you have been brought here so that I might show it to you. Then you must tell the house of Israel everything you see." 5There an outer wall completely surrounded the temple. The measuring rod in the man's hand was six cubits long, each cubit being a cubit plus a handbreadth;* he measured the width of the structure, one rod, and its height, one rod.	3He brought me there, and there standing in the gateway was a man whose appearance was like bronze! He held in his hand a linen cord and a measuring rod.c 4The man said to me, "Son of man, look carefully and listen intently. Pay strict attention to everything I show you, for you have been brought here so that I might show it to you. Then you must tell the house of Israel everything you see." 5There an outer wall completely surrounded the temple. The measuring rod in the man's hand was six cubits long, each cubit being a cubit plus a handbreadth;* he measured the width of the structure, one rod, and its height, one rod.	

7 THUNDERS

TRIBULATION - CHAPTER 6 - THE SCROLL

SCRIPTURE NUMBER	BEGIN DATE	DAYS (END - BEGIN DATES)	END DATE	SCRIPTURE	BIBLICAL NOTES	COMMENTARY
ZEC.2:5-9				Third Vision: The Man with the Measuring Cord. 5I raised my eyes and looked, and there was a man with a measuring cord* in his hand.c 6I asked, "Where are you going?" And he said, "To measure Jerusalem—to see how great its width is and how great its length." 7Then the angel who spoke with me advanced as another angel came out to meet him 8and he said to the latter, "Run, speak to that official:* Jerusalem will be unwalled, because of the abundance of people and beasts in its midst.d 9I will be an encircling wall of fire*for it—oracle of the LORD—and I will be the glory in its midst."e	* [2:5] Measuring cord: a string for measuring, as opposed to a builder's string, 1:16. * [2:8] That official: probably the man with the measuring cord of v. 5. * [2:9] Encircling wall of fire: divine protection for an unwalled Jerusalem. Urban centers were generally walled, and Jerusalem's walls were eventually rebuilt in the late fifth century B.C. (Neh 2:17–20).	
ZEC.4:3,14				3And beside it are two olive trees,* one on the right of the bowl and one to its left." lord." 14Then he said, "These are the two anointed ones* who stand by the Lord of the whole earth."d	* [4:3] Olive trees: visionary image that picks up the botanical language describing the Israelite cultic lampstands, with the olive trees specifically connoting fertility, permanence, and righteousness.* [4:14] Two anointed ones: two leadership positions in the ideal restored nation. The concept of a state headed by both priestly and political leaders harks back to premonarchic traditions (Aaron and Moses) and finds an echo in the two messianic figures—a Davidic and a levitical messiah—in the Dead Sea Scrolls and in apocryphal literature. See also the two crowns of 6:11–14.	
REV. 11:5-7				5* If anyone wants to harm them, fire comes out of their mouths and devours their enemies. In this way, anyone wanting to harm them is sure to be slain. 6They also have the power to close up the sky so that no rain can fall during the time of their prophesying. They also have power to turn water into blood and to afflict the earth with any plague as often as they wish.c 7When they have finished their testimony, the beast that comes up from the abyss* will wage war against them and conquer them and kill them.d	* [11:5–6] These details are derived from stories of Moses, who turned water into blood (Ex 7:17–20), and of Elijah, who called down fire from heaven (1 Kgs 18:36–40; 2 Kgs 1:10) and closed up the sky for three years (1 Kgs 17:1; cf. 18:1). * [11:7] The beast...from the abyss: the Roman emperor Nero, who symbolizes the forces of evil, or the antichrist (Rev 13:1, 8; 17:8); cf. Dn 7:2-8, 11–12, 19–22 and Introduction.	The documentation and prophecy of Climate Change and Environmental Pollution: "They have the power to close up the sky so that no rain can fall during the time of their prophesying." At least 2 years of severe record-setting drought and serious fires. "Turning water into blood" are offshore oil spills. Their powers are the documentation they provide. Because of their testimony against the oil and coal companies, these companies (and their bought-and-paid-for politicians like Gov. Rick Perry, Former Gov. Mitt Romney and Rep. Paul Ryan) will wage war against them and try to kill (eliminate) them.

SCRIPTURE NUMBER	BEGIN DATE	DAYS (END - BEGIN DATES)	END DATE	SCRIPTURE	BIBLICAL NOTES	COMMENTARY
REV. 11:5-7						The 2 Witnesses are the Environmental Protection Agency (EPA) and the Department of Energy (DOE).
EX.7:17				17Thus says the LORD: This is how you will know that I am the LORD. With the staff here in my hand, I will strike the water in the Nile and it will be changed into blood.d		
DN.7:21				21For, as I watched, that horn made war against the holy ones and was victorious		
REV.11:8-11		3.5		8Their corpses will lie in the main street of the great city,* which has the symbolic names "Sodom" and "Egypt," where indeed their Lord was crucified. 9* Those from every people, tribe, tongue, and nation will gaze on their corpses for three and a half days, and they will not allow their corpses to be buried. 10The inhabitants of the earth will gloat over them and be glad and exchange gifts because these two prophets tormented the inhabitants of the earth. 11But after the three and a half days, a breath of life from God entered them. When they stood on their feet, great fear fell on those who saw them.e	* [11:8] The great city: this expression is used constantly in Revelation for Babylon, i.e., Rome; cf. Rev 14:8; 16:19; 17:18; 18:2, 10, 21. "Sodom" and "Egypt": symbols of immorality (cf. Is 1:10) and oppression of God's people (cf. Ex 1:11–14). Where indeed their Lord was crucified: not the geographical but the symbolic Jerusalem that rejects God and his witnesses, i.e., Rome, called Babylon in Rev 16–18; see note on Rev 17:9 and Introduction. * [11:9–12] Over the martyrdom (Rev 11:7) of the two witnesses, now called prophets, the ungodly rejoice for three and a half days, a symbolic period of time; see note on Rev 11:2. Afterwards they go in triumph to heaven, as did Elijah (2 Kgs 2:11).	"Sodom" and "Egypt" in this case is Harris County, TX. Gov. Rick Perry has continually fought the EPA regarding environmental matters in Texas. Because of the lawful environmental restrictions to the oil and coal companies, there is a continuing desire by the Tea Party and their candidates to eliminate these 2 cabinet positions. The Tea Party will rejoice if they are eliminated.
EZ.37:5				5Thus says the Lord GOD to these bones: Listen! I will make breath enter you so you may come to life.	* [37:1–14] This account is a figurative description of God's creation of a new Israel. Even though that creation begins with the remains of the old Israel, the exiles under the image of dry bones, depicting a totally hopeless situation, the new Israel is radically different: it is an ideal people, shaped by God's spirit to live the covenant faithfully, something the old Israel, exiles included, were unable to do. While this passage in its present context is not about the doctrine of individual or communal resurrection, many Jewish and Christian commentators suggest that the doctrine is foreshadowed here.	

SCRIPTURE NUMBER	BEGIN DATE	DAYS (END - BEGIN DATES)	END DATE	SCRIPTURE	BIBLICAL NOTES	COMMENTARY
EZ.37:10				10I prophesied as he commanded me, and the breath entered them; they came to life and stood on their feet, a vast army.c		
REV. 11:12-14				12Then they heard a loud voice from heaven say to them, "Come up here." So they went up to heaven in a cloud as their enemies looked on.f 13At that moment there was a great earthquake, and a tenth of the city fell in ruins. Seven thousand people* were killed during the earthquake; the rest were terrified and gave glory to the God of heaven. 14The second woe has passed, but the third is coming soon.	* [11:13] Seven thousand people: a symbolic sum to represent all social classes (seven) and large numbers (thousands); cf. Introduction.	
2KGS.2:11				11As they walked on still conversing, a fiery chariot and fiery horses came between the two of them, and Elijah went up to heaven in a whirlwind,c		
REV. 11-15				The Seventh Trumpet.* 15Then the seventh angel blew his trumpet. There were loud voices in heaven, saying, "The kingdom of the world now belongs to our Lord and to his Anointed, and he will reign forever and ever." 16The twenty-four elders who sat on their thrones before God prostrated themselves and worshiped God 17and said: "We give thanks to you, Lord God almighty, 18The nations raged, but your wrath has come, and the time for the dead to be judged, and to recompense your servants, the prophets, and the holy ones and those who fear your name, the small and the great alike, and to destroy those who destroy the earth."g	* [11:15–19] The seventh trumpet proclaims the coming of God's reign after the victory over diabolical powers; see note on Rev 10:7.	Diabolical powers = Tea Party and the oil/coal companies which fund and follow them.

7TH TRUMPET

SCRIPTURE NUMBER	BEGIN DATE	DAYS (END - BEGIN DATES)	END DATE	SCRIPTURE	BIBLICAL NOTES	COMMENTARY	
REV. 11:16-18				Revelation 11:16 And the four and twenty elders, which sat before God on their seats, fell upon their faces, and worshipped God, Revelation 11:17 Saying, We give thee thanks, O Lord God Almighty, which art, and wast, and art to come; because thou hast taken to thee thy great power, and hast reigned. Revelation 11:18 And the nations were angry, and thy wrath is come, and the time of the dead, that they should be judged, and that thou shouldest give reward unto thy servants the prophets, and to the saints, and <u>them that fear thy name, small and great; and shouldest destroy them which destroy the earth.</u>		And the nations were angry, and thy wrath is come, and the time of the dead, that they should be judged, and that thou shouldest give reward unto thy servants the prophets, and to the saints, and them that fear thy name, small and great; and shouldest destroy them which destroy the earth. UNREST IN THE MIDDLE EAST BY THE FOLLOWING COUNTRIES: TUNISIA, YEMEN, BAHRAIN, IRAN, EGYPT, LIBYA, ALGERIA AND SYRIA. As of this writing, the bloodiest fighting is in Syria. See Is.10:5-27 Judgment of Assyria. Is.14:24-27 God's Plan for Assyria.	**7TH TRUMPET**
PS.2:1,5				1Why do the nations protest and the peoples conspire in vain?a 5Then he speaks to them in his anger,			
AM.3:7				7(Indeed, the Lord GOD does nothing without revealing his plan to his servants the prophets.)	* [3:3–8] The metaphors in these sayings illustrate the principle of cause and effect, and lead up to the conclusion in v. 8.		
REV. 11:19				19Then God's temple in heaven was opened, and the ark of his covenant could be seen in the temple. There were flashes of lightning, rumblings, and peals of thunder, an earthquake, and a violent hailstorm.			
REV. 12:1-4	18-Jun-03	1258	27-Nov-06	**The Woman and the Dragon.** 1* A great sign appeared in the sky, a woman* clothed with the sun, with the moon under her feet, and on her head a crown of twelve stars.a 2She was with child and wailed aloud in pain as she labored to give birth.* 3Then another sign appeared in the sky; it was a huge red dragon,* with seven heads and ten horns, and on its heads were seven diadems.b 4Its tail swept away a third of the stars in the sky and hurled them down to the earth. Then the dragon stood before the woman about to give birth, to	* [12:1] The woman adorned with the sun, the moon, and the stars (images taken from Gn 37:9–10) symbolizes God's people in the Old and the New Testament. The Israel of old gave birth to the Messiah (Rev 12:5) and then became the new Israel, the church, which suffers persecution by the dragon (Rev 12:6, 13–17); cf. Is 50:1; 66:7; Jer 50:12. This corresponds to a widespread myth throughout the ancient world that a goddess pregnant with a savior was pursued by a horrible monster; by miraculous intervention, she bore a son who then killed the monster. * [12:2] Because of Eve's sin, the woman gives birth in	**The First Tribulation.** Symbolism: On entry into my home in Cypress, TX (See attached floor plan and pictures), the Virgin Mary and the 7th Cross are hidden from people entering the front door. Earlier Symbol: My Rebirth. I moved with my wife and kids from Shiloh, TX to Katy, TX in June 2003. My mom and dad moved from Shiloh, TX to Trinity (Wilderness) and lived there for 3.5 years. They then bought a home in Temple, TX in late Nov. 2006. They lived there until October 4, 2007, when they died in a murder-suicide.	

SCRIPTURE NUMBER	BEGIN DATE	DAYS (END - BEGIN DATES)	END DATE	SCRIPTURE	BIBLICAL NOTES	COMMENTARY
REV. 12:1-4				devour her child when she gave birth.c	distress and pain (Gn 3:16; cf. Is 66:7–14). * [12:3] Huge red dragon: the Devil or Satan (cf. Rev 12:9; 20:2), symbol of the forces of evil, a mythical monster known also as Leviathan (Ps 74:13–14) or Rahab (Jb 26:12–13; Ps 89:11). Seven diadems: these are symbolic of the fullness of the dragon's sovereignty over the kingdoms of this world; cf. Christ with many diadems (Rev 19:12).	
GN.37:9				9Then he had another dream, and told it to his brothers. "Look, I had another dream," he said; "this time, the sun and the moon and eleven stars were bowing down to me."	* [37:5–10] Joseph's dreams of ruling his brothers appear at first glance to be merely adolescent grandiosity, and they bring him only trouble. His later successes make it clear, however, that they were from God. Another confirmation of their divine source is the doubling of dreams (cf. 41:32).	
DN.7:7				7* After this, in the visions of the night I saw a fourth beast, terrifying, horrible, and of extraordinary strength; it had great iron teeth with which it devoured and crushed, and it trampled with its feet what was left. It differed from the beasts that preceded it. It had ten horns.	* [7:7–8] Alexander's empire was different from all the others in that it was Western rather than Eastern in inspiration, and far exceeded the others in power. The ten horns represent the kings of the Seleucid dynasty, the only part of the Hellenistic empire that concerned the author. The little horn is Antiochus IV Epiphanes (175–164 B.C.), who usurped the throne and persecuted the Jews.	Antiochus IV Epiphanes can be compared to a modern day Mahmoud Ahmadinejad, sixth and current President of the Islamic Republic of Iran. See later commentary Dan. 7:21.
REV. 12:5-8		1260		5She gave birth to a son, a male child, destined to rule all the nations with an iron rod.* Her child was caught up to God and his throne.d 6The woman herself fled into the desert where she had a place prepared by God, that there she might be taken care of for twelve hundred and sixty days.* 7* Then war broke out in heaven; Michael* and his angels battled against the dragon. The dragon and its angels fought back, 8but they did not prevail and there was no longer any place for them in heaven.	* [12:5] Rule...iron rod: fulfilled in Rev 19:15; cf. Ps 2:9. Was caught up to God: reference to Christ's ascension. * [12:6] God protects the persecuted church in the desert, the traditional Old Testament place of refuge for the afflicted, according to the typology of the Exodus; see note on Rev 11:2. * [12:7–12] Michael, mentioned only here in Revelation, wins a victory over the dragon. A hymn of praise follows. * [12:7] Michael: the archangel, guardian and champion of Israel; cf. Dn 10:13, 21; 12:1; Jude 9. In Hebrew, the name Michael means "Who can compare with God?"; cf. Rev 13:4.	
IS.66:7				7* Before she is in labor, she gives birth;f Before her pangs come upon her, she delivers a male child.	* [66:7–9] The renewal of Zion is pictured in terms of a miraculous, instantaneous birth, facilitated by God's intervention.	

SCRIPTURE NUMBER	BEGIN DATE	DAYS (END - BEGIN DATES)	END DATE	SCRIPTURE	BIBLICAL NOTES	COMMENTARY
PS.2:9				9With an iron rod you will shepherd them, like a potter's vessel you will shatter them."f	* [Psalm 2] A royal Psalm. To rebellious kings (Ps 2:1–3) God responds vigorously (Ps 2:4–6). A speaker proclaims the divine decree (in the legal adoption language of the day), making the Israelite king the earthly representative of God (Ps 2:7–9) and warning kings to obey (Ps 2:10–11). The Psalm has a messianic meaning for the Church; the New Testament understands it of Christ (Acts 4:25–27; 13:33; Heb 1:5).	
REV. 12:8-10				8but they did not prevail and there was no longer any place for them in heaven. 9The huge dragon, the ancient serpent,* who is called the Devil and Satan, who deceived the whole world, was thrown down to earth, and its angels were thrown down with it.e 10Then I heard a loud voice in heaven say: "Now have salvation and power come, and the kingdom of our God and the authority of his Anointed. For the accuser* of our brothers is cast out, who accuses them before our God day and night.	* [12:9] The ancient serpent: who seduced Eve (Gn 3:1–6), mother of the human race; cf. Rev 20:2; Eph 6:11–12. Was thrown down: allusion to the expulsion of Satan from heaven; cf. Lk 10:18. * [12:10] The accuser: the meaning of the Hebrew word "Satan," found in Rev 12:9; Jb 1–2; Zec 3:1; 1 Chr 21:1; he continues to accuse Christ's disciples.	
GN.3:1-4				1Now the snake was the most cunning* of all the wild animals that the LORD God had made. He asked the woman, "Did God really say, 'You shall not eat from any of the trees in the garden'?" 2The woman answered the snake: "We may eat of the fruit of the trees in the garden; 3a it is only about the fruit of the tree in the middle of the garden that God said, 'You shall not eat it or even touch it, or else you will die.'" 4But the snake said to the woman: "You certainly will not die!b	* [3:1] Cunning: there is a play on the words for "naked" (2:25) and "cunning/wise" (Heb. 'arum). The couple seek to be "wise" but end up knowing that they are "naked."	
LK.10:18				18Jesus said, "I have observed Satan fall like lightning* from the sky.p		

SCRIPTURE NUMBER	BEGIN DATE	DAYS (END - BEGIN DATES)	END DATE	SCRIPTURE	BIBLICAL NOTES	COMMENTARY
REV.12:11-14				11They conquered him by the blood of the Lamb and by the word of their testimony; love for life did not deter them from death. 12Therefore, rejoice, you heavens, and you who dwell in them. But woe to you, earth and sea, for the Devil has come down to you in great fury, for he knows he has but a short time." 13When the dragon saw that it had been thrown down to the earth, it pursued the woman who had given birth to the male child.f 14But the woman was given the two wings of the great eagle,* so that she could fly to her place in the desert, where, far from the serpent, she was taken care of for a year, two years, and a half-year.g	* [12:14] Great eagle: symbol of the power and swiftness of divine help; cf. Ex 19:4; Dt 32:11; Is 40:31.	
GN.3:15				15I will put enmity between you and the woman, and between your offspring and hers; They will strike at your head, while you strike at their heel.* g	* [3:15] They will strike...at their heel: the antecedent for "they" and "their" is the collective noun "offspring," i.e., all the descendants of the woman. Christian tradition has seen in this passage, however, more than unending hostility between snakes and human beings. The snake was identified with the devil (Wis 2:24; Jn 8:44; Rev 12:9; 20:2), for fallen humankind, the protoevangelium. Irenaeus of Lyons (ca. A.D. 130–200), in his Against Heresies 5.21.1, followed by several other Fathers of the Church, interpreted the verse as referring to Christ, and cited Gal 3:19 and 4:4 to support the reference. Another interpretive translation is ipsa, "she," and is reflected in Jerome's Vulgate. "She" was thought to refer to Mary, the mother of the messiah. In Christian art Mary is sometimes depicted with her foot on the head of the serpent.whose eventual defeat seemed implied in the verse. Because "the Son of God was revealed to destroy the works of the devil" (1 Jn 3:8), the passage was understood as the first promise of a redeemer	
EX.19:4				4You have seen how I treated the Egyptians and how I bore you up on eagles' wings and brought you to myself.b		

SCRIPTURE NUMBER	BEGIN DATE	DAYS (END - BEGIN DATES)	END DATE	SCRIPTURE	BIBLICAL NOTES	COMMENTARY
DN.7:25		1260		25He shall speak against the Most High and wear down the holy ones of the Most High, intending to change the feast days and the law.* They shall be handed over to him for a time, two times, and half a time.	* [7:25] The reference is to the persecution of Antiochus IV and specifically to the disruption of the Temple cult (1 Mc 1:41–64). A time, two times, and half a time: an indefinite, evil period of time. Probably here, three and a half years, which becomes the standard period of tribulation in apocalyptic literature (Rev 11:2; 13:5 [in months]; 11:3 [in days]; and cf. 12:14). As seven is the Jewish "perfect" number, half of it signifies great imperfection. Actually, the Temple was desecrated for three years (1 Mc 4:52–54). The duration of the persecution was a little longer, since it was already under way before the Temple was desecrated.	
DN.12:7		1260		7The man clothed in linen,d who was upstream, lifted his hands to heaven; and I heard him swear by him who lives forever that it should be for a time, two times, and half a time;* and that, when the power of the destroyer of the holy people was brought to an end, all these things should end.	* [12:7] A time, two times, and half a time: see note on 7:25.	
REV. 12:15-18				15The serpent,* however, spewed a torrent of water out of his mouth after the woman to sweep her away with the current. 16But the earth helped the woman and opened its mouth and swallowed the flood that the dragon spewed out of its mouth. 17Then the dragon became angry with the woman and went off to wage war against the rest of her offspring, those who keep God's commandments and bear witness to Jesus.* 18It took its position* on the sand of the sea.h	* [12:15] The serpent is depicted as the sea monster; cf. Rev 13:1; Is 27:1; Ez 32:2; Ps 74:13–14. * [12:17] Although the church is protected by God's special providence (Rev 12:16), the individual Christian is to expect persecution and suffering. * [12:17] It took its position: many later manuscripts and versions read "I took my position," thus connecting the sentence to the following paragraph.	Symbolism: Rev.12:6 The torrent of water was from Hurricane Rita on Sep.23, 2005. Water was swallowed up by Lake Livingston, sparing my parents home, and the dam was damaged which caused the lake level to be lowered for a significant period of time. Lake Belton also "swallowed" a significant amount of water in the flood of the summer of 2007 while my parents were living in **Temple,** TX. "Position on the sand of the sea" The Cameron Highway Oil Pipeline System (CHOPS) traverses Cameron Parish LA. on its way to feed refineries and terminals in

SCRIPTURE NUMBER	BEGIN DATE	DAYS (END - BEGIN DATES)	END DATE	SCRIPTURE	BIBLICAL NOTES	COMMENTARY
REV. 12:15-18						the Beaumont / Port Arthur, TX area. The Pipeline Company is a 50/50 partnership between Enterprise Product Partners (NYSE: EPD) (my former employer) and Genesis Energy (NYSE:GEL). Enterprise serves as the operator of the system. Genesis Energy acquired its interest in November 2010. Cameron Parish was hit the hardest from Hurricane Rita, with the towns of Creole, Cameron, Grand Chenier, Johnson's Bayou, and Holly Beach being totally demolished. The Beaumont / Port Arthur, TX areas were significantly impacted by the storm. Rev. 12:18 "It (the dragon) took its position* on the sand of the sea.h", is symbolically represented on the book cover as the oil tapped from the bottom of the sea, by the beast (See book cover). The story of this particular scripture is continued in Rev.13:1-5.
REV.13:1-3				The First Beast.* 1Then I saw a beast come out of the sea with ten horns and seven heads; on its horns were ten diadems, and on its heads blasphemous name[s].a 2The beast I saw was like a leopard, but it had feet like a bear's, and its mouth was like the mouth of a lion.* b To it the dragon gave its own power and throne, along with great authority. 3I saw that one of its heads seemed to have been mortally wounded, but this mortal wound was healed.* Fascinated, the whole world followed after the beast.	* [13:1-10] This wild beast, combining features of the four beasts in Dn 7:2–28, symbolizes the Roman empire; the seven heads represent the emperors; see notes on Rev 17:10 and Rev 17:12–14. The blasphemous names are the divine titles assumed by the emperors. * [13:2] Satan (Rev 12:9), the prince of this world (Jn 12:31), commissioned the beast to persecute the church (Rev 13:5–7). * [13:3] This may be a reference to the popular legend that Nero would come back to life and rule again after his death (which occurred in A.D. 68 from a self-inflicted stab wound in the throat); cf. Rev 13:14; Rev 17:8. Domitian (A.D. 81–96) embodied all the	Coming "out of the sea" represents oil / gas drilling rigs and production platforms. The large letter "A" on the book cover is representative of that. The "beast" represents an oil / coal company or companies and 10 horns are ten of the 12 members of OPEC: Iran, Iraq, Kuwait, Saudi Arabia, Venezuela, Qatar, Libya, UAE, Algeria, Nigeria, Angola, and Ecuador. Biblically, a horn is a symbol of power with a (diadem) or crown symbolizing royal dignity or authority: Oil Minister or Sheik. When discussing Babylon, the 7 heads are the 7 U.S. Congressional Districts in

SCRIPTURE NUMBER	BEGIN DATE	DAYS (END - BEGIN DATES)	END DATE	SCRIPTURE	BIBLICAL NOTES	COMMENTARY
						Harris County, Texas: Dist. 2 - Ted Poe (R), Dist. 7 - John Culberson (R), Dist. 9 - Al Green (D), Dist. 10 - Michael McCaul (R), Dist. 18 - Sheila Jackson Lee (D), Dist. 22 - Pete Olson (R), Dist. 29 - Gene Green (D). Leopard: Lattice work or oil spills throughout the structure would be black spots. "Bear's feet" are the feet of a "jack up" rig. Lion's mouth would be the actual drill bit at the end of the drill stem. See Dn.7:19 where Daniel best describes the rig as "devouring and crushing with its iron teeth and bronze claws, and trampling with its feet what was left". The blasphemous names are Greek and Roman gods: Poseidon, Hermes, Hera, Dionysis, Athena, Atlas, Neptune, Brutus, Mars, Pluto, Thunder Horse (Pegasus), Triton, Ursa. Jupiter, Trident, Hercules, Polaris, Helios (BP Company Logo), Vulcan, Zeus. "Whole world followed after the beast": World reliance on fossil fuels and their derivatives (primarily gasoline and diesel). The world is constantly monitoring the prices of oil, gasoline, and diesel because they can have such financially adverse affects on our lives. Those adverse affects can be mitigated with competion from natural gas and renewable energy.
DN. 12:11-13	23-Jul-07	1335	19-Mar-11	11* From the time that the daily sacrifice is abolished and the desolating abomination is set up, there shall be one thousand two hundred and ninety days. 12Blessed are they who have patience and persevere for the one thousand three hundred and thirty-five days. 13Go, take your rest, you shall rise for your reward at the end of days."	* [12:11] The specific numbers of days given in vv. 11–12 represent attempts to calculate the precise duration of the three and a half years. Most probably, when the first date (1,290 days) passed, the author attempted another calculation. Another, earlier calculation is preserved in 8:14. It is noteworthy, however, that the contradictory numbers were allowed to stand in the text; this is a reminder that it is not possible to calculate a precise date for God's judgment; cf. Mk 13:32.	**The Second Tribulation.** The "desolating abomination" in this case is the Independence Hub (the symbol of a beast and my former employer) which went into service on July 23. 2007. 1335 days later, I left New York after signing an apartment lease and making a commitment to move here and write this book..."my reward".

SCRIPTURE NUMBER	BEGIN DATE	DAYS (END - BEGIN DATES)	END DATE	SCRIPTURE	BIBLICAL NOTES	COMMENTARY
MT. 24:15				The Great Tribulation.* 15g "When you see the desolating abomination* spoken of through Daniel the prophet standing in the holy place (let the reader understand),	* [24:15] The desolating abomination: in 167 B.C. the Syrian king Antiochus IV Epiphanes desecrated the temple by setting up in it a statue of Zeus Olympios (see 1 Mc 1:54). That event is referred to in Dn 12:11 LXX as the "desolating abomination" (NAB "horrible abomination") and the same Greek term is used here; cf. also Dn 9:27; 11:31. Although the desecration had taken place before Daniel was written, it is presented there as a future event, and Matthew sees that "prophecy" fulfilled in the desecration of the temple by the Romans. In the holy place: the temple; more precise than Mark's where he should not (Mk 13:14). Let the reader understand: this parenthetical remark, taken from Mk 13:14 invites the reader to realize the meaning of Daniel's "prophecy."	This confirms the Comment section of REV.13:1-3 regarding "blasphemous names".
2THES.2:3-12				3Let no one deceive you in any way. For unless the apostasy comes first and the lawless one is revealed,* the one doomed to perdition, 4c who opposes and exalts himself above every so-called god and object of worship, so as to seat himself in the temple of God,* claiming that he is a god— 5do you not recall that while I was still with you I told you these things? 6And now you know what is restraining,* that he may be revealed in his time. 7* For the mystery of lawlessness is already at work. But the one who restrains is to do so only for the present, until he is removed from the scene.d 8And then the lawless one will be revealed, whom the Lord [Jesus] will kill with the breath of his mouth and render powerless by the manifestation of his coming,e 9the one whose coming springs from the power of Satan in every mighty deed and in signs and wonders that lie,f 10and in every wicked deceit for those who are perishing because they have not accepted the love of truth so that they may be saved.	* [2:3b–5] This incomplete sentence (anacoluthon, 2 Thes 2:4) recalls what the Thessalonians had already been taught, an apocalyptic scenario depicting, in terms borrowed especially from Dn 11:36–37 and related verses, human self-assertiveness against God in the temple of God itself. The lawless one represents the climax of such activity in this account. * [2:4] Seat himself in the temple of God: a reflection of the language in Dn 7:23–25; 8:9–12; 9:27; 11:36–37; 12:11 about the attempt of Antiochus IV Epiphanes to set up a statue of Zeus in the Jerusalem temple and possibly of the Roman emperor Caligula to do a similar thing (Mk 13:14). Here the imagery suggests an attempt to install someone in the place of God, claiming that he is a god (cf. Ez 28:2). Usually, it is the Jerusalem temple that is assumed to be meant; on the alternative view sketched above (see note on 2 Thes 2:1–17), the temple refers to the Christian community. * [2:6–7] What is restraining...the one who restrains: neuter and masculine, respectively, of a force and person holding back the lawless one. The Thessalonians know what is meant (2 Thes 2:6), but the terms, seemingly found only in	

TRIBULATION - CHAPTER 6 - THE SCROLL

SCRIPTURE NUMBER	BEGIN DATE	DAYS (END - BEGIN DATES)	END DATE	SCRIPTURE	BIBLICAL NOTES	COMMENTARY
2THES.2:3-12				11Therefore, God is sending them a deceiving power so that they may believe the lie, 12that all who have not believed the truth but have approved wrongdoing may be condemned.	this passage and in writings dependent on it, have been variously interpreted. Traditionally, 2 Thes 2:6 has been applied to the Roman empire and 2 Thes 2:7 to the Roman emperor (in Paul's day, Nero) as bulwarks holding back chaos (cf. Rom 13:1–7). A second may underlie the imagery.	
DAN.7:3-7				3from which emerged four immense beasts,a each different from the others. 4The first was like a lion, but with eagle's wings.* While I watched, the wings were plucked; it was raised from the ground to stand on two feet like a human being, and given a human mind. 5The second beast was like a bear;* it was raised up on one side, and among the teeth in its mouth were three tusks. It was given the order, "Arise, devour much flesh." 6After this I looked and saw another beast, like a leopard;* on its back were four wings like those of a bird, and it had four heads. To this beast dominion was given. 7* After this, in the visions of the night I saw a fourth beast, terrifying, horrible, and of extraordinary strength; it had great iron teeth with which it devoured and crushed, and it trampled with its feet what was left. It differed from the beasts that preceded it. It had ten horns.	* [7:4] In ancient times the Babylonian empire was commonly represented as a winged lion, in the rampant position (raised up on one side). The two wings that were plucked may represent Nebuchadnezzar and Belshazzar. On two feet like a human being...a human mind: contrasts with what is said in 4:13, 30. * [7:5] A bear: represents the Median empire, its three tusks symbolizing its destructive nature; hence, the command: "Arise, devour much flesh." * [7:6] A leopard: used to symbolize the swiftness with which Cyrus the Persian established his kingdom. Four heads: corresponding to the four Persian kings of 11:2	See the similarities between Dan.7:4-6 and Rev.13:1-3: 4The first was like a lion, but with eagle's wings.* While I watched, the wings were plucked; it was raised from the ground to stand on two feet like a human being, and given a human mind. 5The second beast was like a bear;* it was raised up on one side, and among the teeth in its mouth were three tusks. It was given the order, "Arise, devour much flesh." 6After this I looked and saw another beast, like a leopard;* on its back were four wings like those of a bird, and it had four heads. To this beast dominion was given. versus Rev.13:2 2The beast I saw was like a leopard, but it had feet like a bear's, and its mouth was like the mouth of a lion.* This exemplifies many of the visions of the Old Testament Prophets and similar visions from St. John.

SCRIPTURE NUMBER	BEGIN DATE	DAYS (END - BEGIN DATES)	END DATE	SCRIPTURE	BIBLICAL NOTES	COMMENTARY
DAN.7:3-7						Left to right: 1) Onshore platform; 2) Fixed platform; 3) Jackup rig; The jackup rig's legs raise as it travels to its drilling destination, then lower to the sea bottom upon arriving at its destination, thereby anchoring the rig. This could very well signify "and it trampled with its feet what was left." in Dan.7:7 and The beast I saw was like a leopard, but it had feet like a bear's, and its mouth was like the mouth of a lion.* in Rev.13:2 The leopard spots are either the view through the lattice work or the oil spots from spills.

SCRIPTURE NUMBER	BEGIN DATE	DAYS (END - BEGIN DATES)	END DATE	SCRIPTURE	BIBLICAL NOTES	COMMENTARY
DAN.7:3-7				**Dan.7:5 The second beast was like a bear;* it was raised up on one side, and among the teeth in its mouth were three tusks. Dan.7:7* After this, in the visions of the night I saw a fourth beast, terrifying, horrible, and of extraordinary strength; it had great iron teeth with which it devoured and crushed, and it trampled with its feet what was left. It differed from the beasts that preceded it. It had ten horns. Rev.13:2 The beast I saw was like a leopard, but it had feet like a bear's, and its mouth was like the mouth of a lion.*** **The 3 "tusks" are a "3 cone, or tricone rock bit (like the one in the attached picture) "with its great iron teeth", with which it devours and crushes (through rock formations), and it tramples with its feet (of a conventional fixed platform or jack up rig).**	**The largest oil drill bit in the world is on display at the Petroleum Museum in Norway. It is three ft in diameter and weighs nearly 4000 lbs. Photo: Jan A. Tjemsland/Norwegian Petroleum Museum** 	
REV. 13:4-7		1260		4They worshiped the dragon because it gave its authority to the beast; they also worshiped the beast* and said, "Who can compare with the beast or who can fight against it?" 5* The beast was given a mouth uttering proud boasts and blasphemies,c and it was given authority to act for forty-two months.*6It opened its mouth to utter blasphemies against God, blaspheming his name and his dwelling and those who dwell in heaven. 7It was also allowed to wage war against the holy ones and conquer them, and it was granted authority over every tribe, people, tongue, and nation.d	* [13:4] Worshiped the beast: allusion to emperor worship, which Domitian insisted upon and ruthlessly enforced. Who can compare with the beast:perhaps a deliberate parody of the name Michael; see note on Rev 12:7. * [13:5–6] Domitian, like Antiochus IV Epiphanes (Dn 7:8, 11, 25), demanded that he be called by divine titles such as "our lord and god" and "Jupiter." See note on Rev 11:2. * [13:5] Forty-two months: this is the same duration as the profanation of the holy city (Rev 11:2), the prophetic mission of the two witnesses (Rev 11:3), and the retreat of the woman into the desert (Rev 12:6, 14)	"The dragon gave its authority to the beast", meaning the exploration and production companies, with their downstream refining and petrochemical businesses The marketing and distribution of oil, coal and derivatives to the public; thereby holding them hostage, through fossil fuel energy reliance, with a low priority on renewable / clean energy.

SCRIPTURE NUMBER	BEGIN DATE	DAYS (END - BEGIN DATES)	END DATE	SCRIPTURE	BIBLICAL NOTES	COMMENTARY
DAN.7:8,11,25		1260		8I was considering the ten horns it had, when suddenly another, a little horn, sprang out of their midst, and three of the previous horns were torn away to make room for it. This horn had eyes like human eyes, and a mouth that spoke arrogantly. 11I watched, then, from the first of the arrogant words which the horn spoke, until the beast was slain and its body destroyed and thrown into the burning fire. 25He shall speak against the Most High and wear down the holy ones of the Most High, intending to change the feast days and the law.* They shall be handed over to him for a time, two times, and half a time.	* [7:7–8] Alexander's empire was different from all the others in that it was Western rather than Eastern in inspiration, and far exceeded the others in power. The ten horns represent the kings of the Seleucid dynasty, the only part of the Hellenistic empire that concerned the author. The little horn is Antiochus IV Epiphanes (175–164 B.C.), who usurped the throne and persecuted the Jews. * [7:25] The reference is to the persecution of Antiochus IV and specifically the disruption of the Temple cult (1 Mc 1:41–64). A time, two times, and half a time: an indefinite, evil period of time. Probably here, three and a half years, which becomes the standard period of tribulation in apocalyptic literature (Rev 11:2; 13:5 [in months]; 11:3 [in days]; and cf. 12:14). As seven is the Jewish "perfect" number, half of it signifies great imperfection. Actually, the Temple was desecrated for three years (1 Mc 4:52–54). The duration of the persecution was a little longer, since it was already under way before the Temple was desecrated.	See commentary Rev.13:4-7, 11-14. Rev. 13-7: 7It was also allowed to wage war against the holy ones and conquer them, and it was granted authority over every tribe, people, tongue, and nation.d Dn. 7:25 25He shall speak against the Most High and wear down the holy ones of the Most High, intending to change the feast days and the law.* They shall be handed over to him for 3.5 years. This scripture eludes to the control over us that the oil and coal companies have possessed since the 19th century. The Holy Ones being those who fought the oil / coal companies regarding air and water pollution and its destruction of the Earth, as described in Is.24:5,6,10, and Rev.11:18
IS.24:5, 6, 10				5The earth is polluted because of its inhabitants, 6Therefore a curse devours the earth, and its inhabitants pay for their guilt; Therefore they who dwell on earth have dwindled, and only a few are left.e 10Broken down is the city of chaos,* every house is shut against entry.i	* [24:5] Ancient covenant: God's commandments to all humankind (cf. Gn 9:4–6). * [24:10] City of chaos: a godless city which appears several times in chaps. 24–27; see note on 24:1–27:13. Of particular interest is an unnamed city (24:10–13; 25:2; 26:5–6; 27:10–11), a wicked city, doomed to destruction; to the extent that it is identifiable, it may be Babylon, but more generally it symbolizes all forces hostile to God. And it stands in contrast to another city, also unnamed but no doubt to be identified with Jerusalem (26:1–2).	"A curse devours the earth" The "curse" is climate change. The unnamed City of Chaos or Babylon reference would be the new Babylon described as "Babylon the Great" in Rev. Chapters 17 and 18. This will be identified as Harris County, Texas in further commentary to Rev. Chapters 14 and 16. The new Jerusalem would be New York City described in further commentary of Rev. Chapters 1, 7, 10, 18, 21. The City of Chaos in this prophesy is shuttered because of its godless acts.
DAN.8:13				13I heard a holy one speaking, and another said to whichever one it was that spoke, "How long shall the events of this vision last concerning the daily sacrifice, the desolating sin,* the giving over of the sanctuary and the host for trampling?"	* [8:13] The desolating sin: the Hebrew contains a wordplay (shomem) on the name Baal Shamem ("lord of the heavens," identified by some as the Greek Zeus Olympios). The reference is to some object with which Antiochus profaned the Temple of Jerusalem (2 Mc 6:2), most probably a pagan altar.	This also confirms the Comment section of REV.13:1-3 regarding "blasphemous names".

SCRIPTURE NUMBER	BEGIN DATE	DAYS (END - BEGIN DATES)	END DATE	SCRIPTURE	BIBLICAL NOTES	COMMENTARY
DAN.8:14		2300		14He answered him, "For two thousand three hundred evenings and mornings; then the sanctuary shall be set right."		
DAN.9:27				27For one week* he shall make a firm covenant with the many; Half the week he shall abolish sacrifice and offering; In their place shall be the desolating abomination until the ruin that is decreed is poured out upon the desolator."d	* [9:27] One week: the final phase of the period in view, the time of Antiochus' persecution. He: Antiochus himself. The many: the faithless Jews who allied themselves with the Seleucids; cf. 1 Mc 1:11–13. Half the week: three and a half years; the Temple was desecrated by Antiochus from 167 to 164 B.C. The desolating abomination: see note on 8:13; probably a pagan altar. Jesus refers to this passage in his prediction of the destruction of Jerusalem in Mt 24:15.	
DAN.11:36				36"The king shall do as he wills, exalting himself and making himself greater than any god; he shall utter dreadful blasphemies against the God of gods. He shall prosper only till the wrath is finished, for what is determined must take place.		
DAN.12:7		1260		7The man clothed in linen,d who was upstream, lifted his hands to heaven; and I heard him swear by him who lives forever that it should be for a time, two times, and half a time;* and that, when the power of the destroyer of the holy people was brought to an end, all these things should end.	* [12:7] A time, two times, and half a time: see note on 7:25.	

SCRIPTURE NUMBER	BEGIN DATE	DAYS (END - BEGIN DATES)	END DATE	SCRIPTURE	BIBLICAL NOTES	COMMENTARY
DAN.7:21				21For, as I watched, that horn made war against the holy ones and was victorious		The small horn is the False Prophet, also described in Rev.13:11-1 as 2 small horns. Mahmoud Ahmadinejad has never been shy about his disdain for Israel, much more so than any of the other Muslim countries. He's denied the Holocaust and has repeatedly threatened Israel and remains a continuous threat. The Holy Ones in this case: Iranians seeking free and fair elections and free society, Christians, and Jews. Ahmadinejad's denial of the holocaust, is his effort to deny the last triumph over the Jews ("the holy ones") by Nazi Germany. He thinks if the holocaust never happened, then he would be the conquering king in Dan.7:21 and he would probably convince the hierarchy of Iran of this to justify an unprovoked attack against Israel. Israel and all of the nations of the world should take this prophesy and the Iranian threat very seriously.
REV. 13:8-10				8All the inhabitants of the earth will worship it, all whose names were not written from the foundation of the world in the book of life, which belongs to the Lamb who was slain.e 9Whoever has ears ought to hear these words.f 10Anyone destined for captivity goes into captivity. Anyone destined to be slain by the sword shall be slain by the sword.g Such is the faithful endurance of the holy ones.		
MT.13:9				9Whoever has ears ought to hear."		
JER.15:2				2If they ask you, "Where should we go?" tell them, Thus says the LORD: Whoever is marked for death, to death; whoever is marked for the sword, to the sword; whoever is marked for famine, to famine; whoever is marked for captivity, to captivity.b		

SCRIPTURE NUMBER	BEGIN DATE	DAYS (END - BEGIN DATES)	END DATE	SCRIPTURE	BIBLICAL NOTES	COMMENTARY
REV. 13:11-14				The Second Beast.* 11Then I saw another beast come up out of the earth; it had two horns like a lamb's but spoke like a dragon. 12It wielded all the authority of the first beast in its sight and made the earth and its inhabitants worship the first beast, whose mortal wound had been healed. 13It performed great signs, even making fire come down from heaven to earth in the sight of everyone.h 14It deceived the inhabitants of the earth with the signs it was allowed to perform in the sight of the first beast, telling them to make an image for the beast who had been wounded by the sword and revived.	* [13:11–18] The second beast is described in terms of the false prophets (cf. Rev 16:13; 19:20; 20:10) who accompany the false messiahs (the first beast); cf. Mt 24:24; Mk 13:22; 2 Thes 2:9; cf. also Dt 13:2–4. Christians had either to worship the emperor and his image or to suffer martyrdom.	2 of the 12 OPEC countries. The 2 horns may very well represent Iran and Iraq. These 2 horns, coming up out of the earth, are considered to be the false prophets. Both Saddam Hussein and Mahmoud Ahmadinejad have never been shy about their disdain for Israel, much more so than any of the other Muslim countries. Saddam's brutality was akin to that of Nero or Domitian, both of whom were suspected of being the antichrist by early Christians. Saddam Hussein attacked Israel in Desert Storm in a desperate attempt to unite Muslim countries against the Jewish State. Saddam is dead...Thank God! Mahmoud Ahmadinejad has now inherited the position of chief tormenter of Israel. He continues to spew his venomous denials about the Holocaust being a lie. He now not only threatens Israel, but other regional countries with his suspected development of WMD (weapons of mass destruction). Therefore, he establishes himself with the moniker: False Prophet who speaks like the Dragon (with deceit...ONE BIG LIE!). Unfortunately, we must take this despot seriously with his threats of destruction. One of the things supporting The Revelation is prophecy from St. John which agrees with the prophets of the Old Testament. This happens throughout the Holy Bible. In the case of the Beasts; Daniel prophesized this in Chapter 7 (Dn.7:7-8,19-28); however, there are 10 horns, in which 3 of the 10 horns were torn away to make way room for an 11th horn; which bears the characteristics of the aforementioned false prophet and makes a bit more sense since Saddam is now dead. Rev.13:13 It performed great signs, even making fire come down from heaven to earth in the sight of everyone.h "Fire come down from heaven to earth" was Scud missiles from Iraq launched against Israel in

SCRIPTURE NUMBER	BEGIN DATE	DAYS (END - BEGIN DATES)	END DATE	SCRIPTURE	BIBLICAL NOTES	COMMENTARY
REV. 13:11-14						Operation Desert Storm. For the future, it could mean missiles launched by Iran at Israel.
MT.24:24				24False messiahs and false prophets will arise, and they will perform signs and wonders so great as to deceive, if that were possible, even the elect.		
2THES.2:9-10				9the one whose coming springs from the power of Satan in every mighty deed and in signs and wonders that lie,f 10and in every wicked deceit for those who are perishing because they have not accepted the love of truth so that they may be saved.	* [2:7–12] The lawless one and the one who restrains are involved in an activity or process, the mystery of lawlessness, behind which Satan stands (2 Thes 2:9). The action of the Lord [Jesus] in overcoming the lawless one is described in Old Testament language (with the breath of his mouth; cf. Is 11:4; Jb 4:9; Rev 19:15). His coming is literally the Lord's "parousia." The biblical concept of the "holy war," eschatologically conceived, may underlie the imagery.	

SCRIPTURE NUMBER	BEGIN DATE	DAYS (END - BEGIN DATES)	END DATE	SCRIPTURE	BIBLICAL NOTES	COMMENTARY
REV. 13:15-18				15It was then permitted to breathe life into the beast's image, so that the beast's image could speak and [could] have anyone who did not worship it put to death.i 16It forced all the people, small and great, rich and poor, free and slave, to be given a stamped image on their right hands or their foreheads,j 17so that no one could buy or sell except one who had the stamped image of the beast's name or the number that stood for its name. 18* k Wisdom is needed here; one who understands can calculate the number of the beast, for it is a number that stands for a person. His number is six hundred and sixty-six.	* [13:11–18] The second beast is described in terms of the false prophets (cf. Rev 16:13; 19:20; 20:10) who accompany the false messiahs (the first beast); cf. Mt 24:24; Mk 13:22; 2 Thes 2:9; cf. also Dt 13:2–4. Christians had either to worship the emperor and his image or to suffer martyrdom. * [13:18] Each of the letters of the alphabet in Hebrew as well as in Greek has a numerical value. Many possible combinations of letters will add up to 666, and many candidates have been nominated for this infamous number. The most likely is the emperor Caesar Nero (see note on Rev 13:3), the Greek form of whose name in Hebrew letters gives the required sum. (The Latin form of this name equals 616, which is the reading of a few manuscripts.) Nero personifies the emperors who viciously persecuted the church. It has also been observed that "6" represents imperfection, falling short of the perfect number "7," and is represented here in a triple or superlative form.	From the Book "The Rite" by Matt Baglio: In Chapter 10, a Franciscan priest named Father Daniel, during an exorcism, told of a woman who vomited seven black two-inch-long nails—six of which had dissolved into a dark liquid but the seventh he kept. The symbolism here being 6 as the imperfect number related to Satan, the dark liquid being the Dragon or Satan (oil) and the seventh nail, not dissolving, being the reality or authenticity of Christ.
DAN.3:5-7, 15				5* when you hear the sound of the horn, pipe, zither, dulcimer, harp, double-flute, and all the other musical instruments, you must fall down and worship the golden statue which King Nebuchadnezzar has set up. 6Whoever does not fall down and worship shall be instantly cast into a white-hot furnace." 7Therefore, as soon as they heard the sound of the horn, pipe, zither, dulcimer, harp, double-flute, and all the other musical instruments, the nations and peoples of every language all fell down and worshiped the golden statue which King Nebuchadnezzar had set up.15Now, if you are ready to fall down and worship the statue I made, whenever you hear the sound of the horn, pipe, zither, dulcimer, harp, double-flute, and all the other musical instruments, then all will be well;* if not, you shall be instantly cast into the white-hot furnace;		

SCRIPTURE NUMBER	BEGIN DATE	DAYS (END - BEGIN DATES)	END DATE	SCRIPTURE	BIBLICAL NOTES	COMMENTARY
DAN.3:5-7, 15				and who is the God who can deliver you out of my hands?"		
REV. 14:1-3				**The Lamb's Companions.*** 1Then I looked and there was the Lamb standing on Mount Zion,* and with him a hundred and forty-four thousand who had his name and his Father's name written on their foreheads.a 2I heard a sound from heaven like the sound of rushing water or a loud peal of thunder. The sound I heard was like that of harpists playing their harps. 3They were singing [what seemed to be] a new hymn before the throne, before the four living creatures and the elders. No one could learn this hymn except the hundred and forty-four thousand who had been ransomed from the earth.b	* [14:1–5] Now follows a tender and consoling vision of the Lamb and his companions. * [14:1] Mount Zion: in Jerusalem, the traditional place where the true remnant, the Israel of faith, is to be gathered in the messianic reign; cf. 2 Kgs 19:30–31; Jl 3:5; Ob 17; Mi 4:6–8; Zep 3:12–20. A hundred and forty-four thousand: see note on Rev 7:4–9. His Father's name…foreheads: in contrast to the pagans who were marked with the name or number of the beast (Rev 13:16–17).	The multiple of 1,000 means immense.
Jl:3:5				5Then everyone who calls upon the name of the LORD will escape harm. For on Mount Zion there will be a remnant, as the LORD has said, And in Jerusalem survivors whom the LORD will summon.c	* [3:1–5] In many places in the Old Testament, Hebrew ruah is God's power, or spirit, bestowed on chosen individuals. The word can also mean "breath" or "wind." In this summary introduction to his second speech, Joel anticipates that the Lord will someday renew faithful Judahites with the divine spirit. In Acts 2:17–21 the author has Peter cite Joel's words to suggest that the newly constituted Christian community, filled with divine life and power, inaugurates the Lord's Day, understood as salvation for all who believe that Jesus of Nazareth is the Christ.	
OB 17				17But on Mount Zion there will be some who escape;* the mountain will be holy, And the house of Jacob will take possession of those who dispossessed them.g	* [17–19] The Israelites will be restored and will occupy the lands of those who oppressed them. The survivors of Judah will be rejoined by the returned exiles from northern Israel.	
ACTS. 2:21				21and it shall be that everyone shall be saved who calls on the name of the Lord.'i	* [2:14–36] The first of six discourses in Acts (along with Acts 3:12–26; 4:8–12; 5:29–32; 10:34–43; 13:16–41) dealing with the resurrection of Jesus and its messianic import. Five of these are attributed to Peter, the final one to Paul. Modern scholars term these discourses in Acts the "kerygma," the Greek word for proclamation (cf. 1 Cor 15:11).	

SCRIPTURE NUMBER	BEGIN DATE	DAYS (END - BEGIN DATES)	END DATE	SCRIPTURE	BIBLICAL NOTES	COMMENTARY
PS.33:3				3Sing to him a new song; skillfully play with joyful chant.	* [Psalm 33] A hymn in which the just are invited (Ps 33:1–3) to praise God,	
PS.96:1				1Sing to the LORD a new song;a sing to the LORD, all the earth.	* [Psalm 96] A hymn inviting all humanity to praise the glories of Israel's God (Ps 96:1–3),	
PS.98:1				1A psalm. I Sing a new song to the LORD, for he has done marvelous deeds.a His right hand and holy arm have won the victory.*b	* [98:1] Marvelous deeds...victory: the conquest of all threats to the peaceful existence of Israel, depicted in the Psalms variously as a cosmic force such as sea, or nations bent on Israel's destruction, or evildoers seemingly triumphant. His right hand and holy arm: God is pictured as a powerful warrior.	God's message is clear: Protect Israel from any threat to their peace, be it Iran or any other country.
IS.42:10				10Sing to the LORD a new song, his praise from the ends of the earth: Let the sea and what fills it resound, the coastlands, and those who dwell in them.		
REV. 14:4-6				4These are they who were not defiled with women; they are virgins* and these are the ones who follow the Lamb wherever he goes. They have been ransomed as the firstfruits of the human race for God and the Lamb.c 5On their lips no deceit* has been found; they are unblemished.d The Three Angels.* 6Then I saw another angel flying high overhead, with everlasting good news* to announce to those who dwell on earth, to every nation, tribe, tongue, and people.	* [14:6–13] Three angels proclaim imminent judgment on the pagan world, calling all peoples to worship God the creator. Babylon (Rome) will fall, and its supporters will be tormented forever. * [14:6] Everlasting good news: that God's eternal reign is about to begin; see note on Rev 10:7.	Babylon (also known as the Harlot) is a city. Most likely a port city whose primary business is marketing, trading, processing and distributing oil and its derivatives. Given the 85" apocalyptic dimension (Rev.8:5) in the Cypress Key of David, Babylon is probably Houston (Harris County) Texas. When you take into account all of the discussion and evidence of oil and idolatry, it makes sense. The 7 heads of the beast being the 7 U.S. Congressional Districts in Harris County. The image of the beast representing Houston, be it the oil derrick "A" on the book cover or an old Houston Oiler oil derrick logo. I saw this threat 3 years ago: In this vision a deepwater oil tanker, sailing under a friendly (possibly Israeli flag as deception by the "lawless one") coming into the port of Houston or port of Valdez. This a "sum of all fears" scenario in which a bomb would be ignited in the bay of either port, before the "pilot" boarded and took control the ship. This would allow positioning the ship at a distance from an industrial hub to maximize destruction

SCRIPTURE NUMBER	BEGIN DATE	DAYS (END - BEGIN DATES)	END DATE	SCRIPTURE	BIBLICAL NOTES	COMMENTARY
REV. 14:4-6						based on atmospheric conditions at the time. This would explain a devastating earthquake, city burning forever, splitting the city into 3 parts, blood (oil) as high as a horses bridle for 200 miles in the local tributaries of the San Jacinto and Buffalo watersheds. Only God knows what will happen. He gave the prophets the information that He wanted them to have. They did not have the real-life-experiencel to distinguish a giant earthquake from a giant explosion. You can compare this scenario to the fertilizer ship exploding at a Texas City, TX dock in 1947, but on a significantly larger scale.
JER.2:2				2Go, cry out this message for Jerusalem to hear! I remember the devotion* of your youth, how you loved me as a bride, Following me in the wilderness, in a land unsown.a	* [2:1–3:5] These chapters may contain some of Jeremiah's early preaching. He portrays Israel as the wife of the Lord, faithful only in the beginning, when she walked behind him (2:2–3, 5; 3:1). Consistent with the marriage metaphor, he describes her present unfaithfulness as adultery (2:20; 3:2–3); now she walks behind the Baals. * [2:2] Devotion: Heb. hesed; Israel's gratitude, fidelity, and love for God.	Don't test God's love with pagans or anyone else.
JAS.1:18				18i He willed to give us birth by the word of truth that we may be a kind of firstfruits of his creatures.*	* [1:18] Acceptance of the gospel message, the word of truth, constitutes new birth (Jn 3:5–6) and makes the recipient the firstfruits (i.e., the cultic offering of the earliest grains, symbolizing the beginning of an abundant harvest) of a new creation; cf. 1 Cor 15:20; Rom 8:23.	
ZEP.3:13				13the remnant of Israel. They shall do no wrong and speak no lies; Nor shall there be found in their mouths a deceitful tongue; They shall pasture and lie down with none to disturb them.g		

SCRIPTURE NUMBER	BEGIN DATE	DAYS (END - BEGIN DATES)	END DATE	SCRIPTURE	BIBLICAL NOTES	COMMENTARY
REV. 14:7-10				7He said in a loud voice, "Fear God and give him glory, for his time has come to sit in judgment. Worship him who made heaven and earth and sea and springs of water."e 8A second angel followed, saying: "Fallen, fallen is Babylon the great,f that made all the nations drink the wine of her licentious passion."* 9A third angel followed them and said in a loud voice, "Anyone who worships the beast or its image, or accepts its mark on forehead or hand, 10will also drink the wine of God's fury,* poured full strength into the cup of his wrath, and will be tormented in burning sulfur before the holy angels and before the Lamb.	* [14:8] This verse anticipates the lengthy dirge over Babylon (Rome) in Rev 18:1–19:4. The oracle of Is 21:9 to Babylon is applied here. * [14:10–11] The wine of God's fury: image taken from Is 51:17; Jer 25:15–16; 49:12; 51:7; Ez 23:31–34. Eternal punishment in the fiery pool of burning sulfur (or "fire and brimstone"; cf. Gn 19:24) is also reserved for the Devil, the beast, and the false prophet (Rev 19:20; 20:10; 21:8).	The wine of God's fury and "made all the nations drink the wine of her licentious passion. "are symbols for oil. God's fury occurred through the Mesozoic Era when he destroyed the dinosaurs (Dragons) and millions of years later, their aftermath is fossil fuels. "Burning sulfur" is "fire and brimstone" and probably represents crude oil with a higher sulfur content. Heavy Sour (Sulfuric) Crude vs. Light Sweet (non-Sulfuric) Crude. "Fallen, fallen is Babylon the great. A phase out of oil and its derivatives (gasoline and diesel) which would not only decimate the economy of Harris County, TX, it would do the same to the state. What brought the nations riches will ultimately poison them because of idolatry and their choice of greed over the welfare of the Earth.

SCRIPTURE NUMBER	BEGIN DATE	DAYS (END - BEGIN DATES)	END DATE	SCRIPTURE	BIBLICAL NOTES	COMMENTARY
DT:32:28-39				28For they are a nation devoid of reason,* having no understanding. 29If they had insight they would realize this, they would understand their end: 30"How could one rout a thousand, or two put ten thousand to flight, Unless it was because their Rock sold them, the LORD delivered them up?" 31Indeed, their "rock" is not like our Rock; our enemies are fools. 32For their vine is from the vine of Sodom, from the vineyards of Gomorrah. Their grapes are grapes of poison, and their clusters are bitter.w 33Their wine is the venom of serpents, the cruel poison of vipers. 34Is not this stored up with me, sealed up in my storehouses? 35Vengeance is mine and recompense, for the time they lose their footing; Because the day of their disaster is at hand and their doom is rushing upon them!x 36Surely, the LORD will do justice for his people; on his servants he will have pity. When he sees their strength is gone, and neither bond nor free* is left,y 37He will say, Where are their gods,z the rock in whom they took refuge, 38Who ate the fat of their sacrifices and drank the wine of their libations? Let them rise up now and help you! Let them be your protection! 39See now that I, I alone, am he, and there is no god besides me. It is I who bring both death and life, I who inflict wounds and heal them, and from my hand no one can deliver.a	* [32:28–35] The reference is to the nations, not to Israel.	See commentary 13:1-3 and 14:7-10." 32For their vine is from the vine of Sodom, from the vineyards of Gomorrah. Their grapes are grapes of poison, and their clusters are bitter.w 33Their wine is the venom of serpents, the cruel poison of vipers." Oil.
MT.10:28				28And do not be afraid of those who kill the body but cannot kill the soul; rather, be afraid of the one who can destroy both soul and body in Gehenna.r		
IS.21:9				9Here he comes— a single chariot, a pair of horses— He calls out and says, 'Fallen, fallen is Babylon! All the images of her gods are smashed to the ground!'"h		
JER.51:8				8Babylon suddenly falls and is broken: wail over her! Bring balm for her wounds, in case she can be healed.f		

SCRIPTURE NUMBER	BEGIN DATE	DAYS (END - BEGIN DATES)	END DATE	SCRIPTURE	BIBLICAL NOTES	COMMENTARY
IS 51:17				17Wake up, wake up! Arise, Jerusalem, You who drank at the LORD's hand the cup of his wrath; Who drained to the dregs the bowl of staggering!g		
JER.25:15-17				The Cup of Judgment on the Nations. 15* For thus said the LORD, the God of Israel, to me: Take this cup of the wine of wrath* from my hand and have all the nations to whom I will send you drink it.j 16They shall drink, and retch, and go mad, because of the sword I will send among them.k 17I took the cup from the hand of the LORD and gave it as drink to all the nations to whom the LORD sent me:	* [25:15–17] Jeremiah is a prophet to the nations (cf. 1:5) as well as to his own people. All the nations mentioned here appear again in the more extensive collection of Jeremiah's oracles against the nations in chaps. 46–51.	
REV. 14:11-14				11The smoke of the fire that torments them will rise forever and ever, and there will be no relief day or night for those who worship the beast or its image or accept the mark of its name."g 12Here is what sustains the holy ones who keep God's commandments.h and their faith in Jesus.* 13i I heard a voice from heaven say, "Write this: Blessed are the dead who die in the Lord from now on." "Yes," said the Spirit, "let them find rest from their labors, for their works accompany them."* The Harvest of the Earth.* 14Then I looked and there was a white cloud, and sitting on the cloud one who looked like a son of man, with a gold crown on his head and a sharp sickle in his hand.j	* [14:12] In addition to faith in Jesus, the seer insists upon the necessity and value of works, as in Rev 2:23; 20:12–13; 22:12; cf. Mt 16:27; Rom 2:6. * [14:13] See note on Rev 1:3. According to Jewish thought, people's actions followed them as witnesses before the court of God. * [14:14–20] The reaping of the harvest symbolizes the gathering of the elect in the final judgment, while the reaping and treading of the grapes symbolizes the doom of the ungodly (cf. Jl 4:12–13; Is 63:1–6) that will come in Rev 19:11–21.	"The smoke of the fire (either fires as a result of the city being shuttered or fires from a large explosion) that torments them will rise forever and ever, and there will be no relief day or night for those who worship the beast or its image or accept the mark of its name."
MT.11:28-29				**The Gentle Mastery of Christ**. 28* "Come to me, all you who labor and are burdened,* and I will give you rest. 29* p Take my yoke upon you and learn from me, for I am meek and humble of heart; and you will find rest for your selves.	* [11:28] Who labor and are burdened: burdened by the law as expounded by the scribes and Pharisees (Mt 23:4). * [11:29] In place of the yoke of the law, complicated by scribal interpretation, Jesus invites the burdened to take the yoke of obedience to his word, under which they will find rest; cf. Jer 6:16.	

SCRIPTURE NUMBER	BEGIN DATE	DAYS (END - BEGIN DATES)	END DATE	SCRIPTURE	BIBLICAL NOTES	COMMENTARY
2THES.1:7				7and to grant rest along with us to you who are undergoing afflictions, at the revelation of the Lord Jesus from heaven with his mighty angels,	* [1:3–12] On the thanksgiving, see note on Rom 1:8 and cf. 1 Thes 1:2–10. Paul's gratitude to God for the faith and love of the Thessalonians (2 Thes 1:3) and his Christian pride in their faithful endurance (2 Thes 1:4–5) contrast with the condemnation announced for those who afflict them, a judgment to be carried out at the parousia (2 Thes 1:6–10), which is described in vivid language drawn from Old Testament apocalyptic. A prayer for the fulfillment of God's purpose in the Thessalonians (2 Thes 1:11–12) completes the section, as is customary in a Pauline letter (cf. 1 Thes 1:2–3). * [1:10] Among his holy ones: in the Old Testament, this term can refer to an angelic throng.	
HEB.4:10				10And whoever enters into God's rest, rests from his own works as God did from his.		
DAN.7:13				13As the visions during the night continued, I saw coming with the clouds of heaven One like a son of man.* When he reached the Ancient of Days and was presented before him,	* [7:13–14] One like a son of man: In contrast to the worldly kingdoms opposed to God, which are represented as grotesque beasts, the coming Kingdom of God is represented by a human figure. Scholars disagree as to whether this figure should be taken as a collective symbol for the people of God (cf. 7:27) or identified as a particular individual, e.g., the archangel Michael (cf. 12:1) or the messiah. The phrase "Son of Man" becomes a title for Jesus in the gospels, especially in passages dealing with the Second Coming (Mk 13 and parallels).	"In contrast to the worldly kingdoms opposed to God, which are represented as grotesque beasts,":Pagan and idolatrous nations.

SCRIPTURE NUMBER	BEGIN DATE	DAYS (END - BEGIN DATES)	END DATE	SCRIPTURE	BIBLICAL NOTES	COMMENTARY
REV. 14:15-18				15Another angel came out of the temple, crying out in a loud voice to the one sitting on the cloud, "Use your sickle and reap the harvest, for the time to reap has come, because the earth's harvest is fully ripe."k 16So the one who was sitting on the cloud swung his sickle over the earth, and the earth was harvested. 17Then another angel came out of the temple in heaven who also had a sharp sickle.18Then another angel [came] from the altar,* [who] was in charge of the fire, and cried out in a loud voice to the one who had the sharp sickle, "Use your sharp sickle and cut the clusters from the earth's vines, for its grapes are ripe."	* [14:18] Altar: there was only one altar in the heavenly temple; see notes above on Rev 6:9; 8:3; 11:1.	
JL.4:13				13Wield the sickle,g for the harvest is ripe; Come and tread, for the wine press is full; The vats overflow, for their crimes are numerous.*	* [4:13] Their crimes are numerous: the nations are ripe for punishment. Joel uses the vocabulary of the autumn grape harvest to describe the assault of the Lord's army against these nations. In Is 63:1–6, grape harvest imagery also controls the description of the Lord's return from Edom with blood-spattered clothing after having trod his enemies into the ground as if they were grapes (cf. Jer 25:30).	

SCRIPTURE NUMBER	BEGIN DATE	DAYS (END - BEGIN DATES)	END DATE	SCRIPTURE	BIBLICAL NOTES	COMMENTARY
MT.13:36-43				The Explanation of the Parable of the Weeds. 36Then, dismissing the crowds,* he went into the house. His disciples approached him and said, "Explain to us the parable of the weeds in the field." 37*He said in reply, "He who sows good seed is the Son of Man, 38the field is the world,* the good seed the children of the kingdom. The weeds are the children of the evil one, 39and the enemy who sows them is the devil. The harvest is the end of the age,* and the harvesters are angels. 40Just as weeds are collected and burned [up] with fire, so will it be at the end of the age. 41The Son of Man will send his angels, and they will collect out of his kingdom* all who cause others to sin and all evildoers. 42m They will throw them into the fiery furnace, where there will be wailing and grinding of teeth. 43* n Then the righteous will shine like the sun in the kingdom of their Father. Whoever has ears ought to hear.	* [13:36] Dismissing the crowds: the return of Jesus to the house marks a break with the crowds, who represent unbelieving Israel. From now on his attention is directed more and more to his disciples and to their instruction. The rest of the discourse is addressed to them alone. * [13:37–43] In the explanation of the parable of the weeds emphasis lies on the fearful end of the wicked, whereas the parable itself concentrates on patience with them until judgment time. * [13:38] The field is the world: this presupposes the resurrection of Jesus and the granting to him of "all power in heaven and on earth" (Mt 28:18). * [13:39] The end of the age: this phrase is found only in Matthew (13:40, 49; 24:3; 28:20). * [13:41] His kingdom: the kingdom of the Son of Man is distinguished from that of the Father (Mt 13:43); see 1 Cor 15:24–25. The church is the place where Jesus' kingdom is manifested, but his royal authority embraces the entire world; see note on Mt 13:38. * [13:43] See Dn 12:3.	
REV.14:19-20				19So the angel swung his sickle over the earth and cut the earth's vintage. He threw it into the great wine press of God's fury.l 20The wine press was trodden outside the city and blood poured out of the wine press to the height of a horse's bridle for two hundred miles.*	* [14:20] Two hundred miles: literally sixteen hundred stades. The stadion, a Greek unit of measurement, was about 607 feet in length, approximately the length of a furlong.	(See below map) 200 miles of Buffalo / San Jacinto watershed tributaries leading into Buffalo Bayou, the San Jacinto River, and ultimately the Houston Ship Channel and the Gulf of Mexico ("many waters" as described in Rev.. 17:1) with an explosion or a storm which would push water upstream into these tributaries and water sheds, carrying a "stew" of toxic and flammable materials, oil based, which would give the appearance of blood. Outside the city (Harris County) would be in some place like Galveston Bay or the Gulf of Mexico.

SCRIPTURE NUMBER	BEGIN DATE	DAYS (END - BEGIN DATES)	END DATE	SCRIPTURE	BIBLICAL NOTES	COMMENTARY
REV.14:19-20				Below is a map of Harris County, TX, and approximately 200 miles of highlighted tributaries in the Buffalo / San Jacinto watershed (in red) within the county, leading into Buffalo Bayou, the San Jacinto River, and ultimately the Houston Ship Channel and the Gulf of Mexico. ("many waters" as described in Rev. 17:1)		

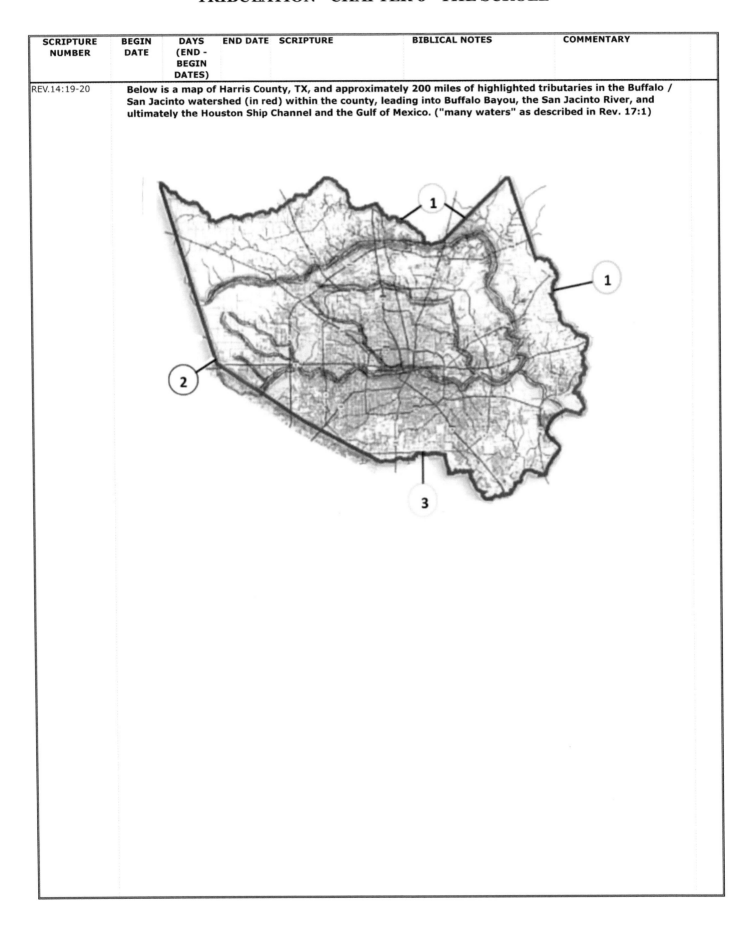

SCRIPTURE NUMBER	BEGIN DATE	DAYS (END - BEGIN DATES)	END DATE	SCRIPTURE	BIBLICAL NOTES	COMMENTARY
REV.14:19-20				Below is a map of the Buffalo Watershed leading into Buffalo Bayou, the San Jacinto River, and ultimately the Houston Ship Channel and the Gulf of Mexico. ("many waters" as described in Rev. 17:1).		

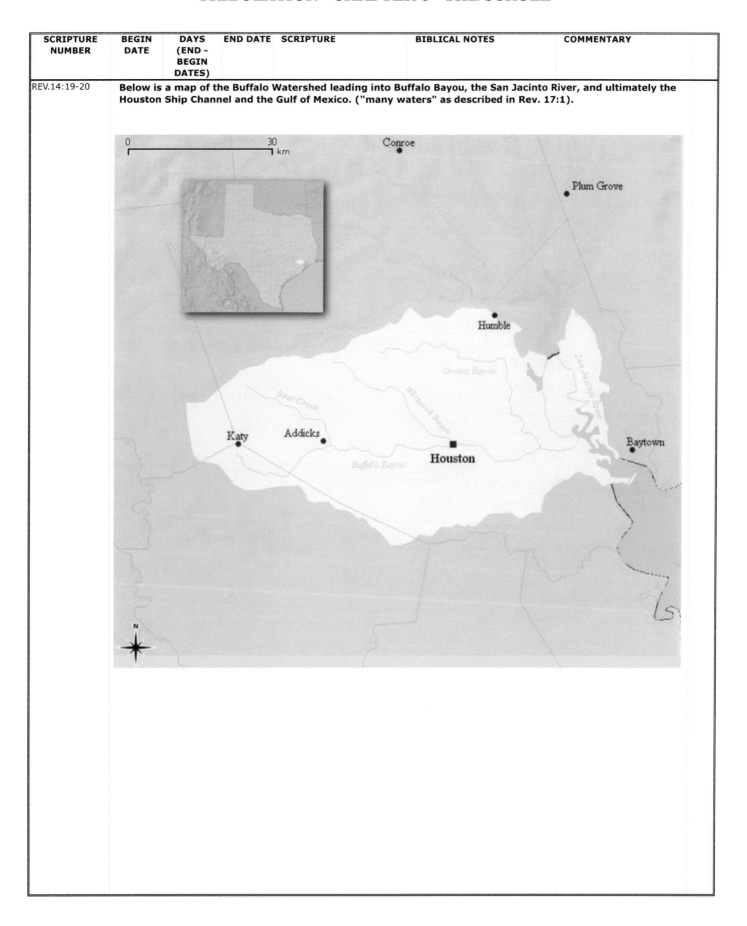

SCRIPTURE NUMBER	BEGIN DATE	DAYS (END - BEGIN DATES)	END DATE	SCRIPTURE	BIBLICAL NOTES	COMMENTARY
REV.14:19-20				Below is a map of the San Jacinto Watershed (including Cypress Creek) leading into Buffalo Bayou, the San Jacinto River, and ultimately the Houston Ship Channel and the Gulf of Mexico. ("many waters" as described in Rev. 17:1).		

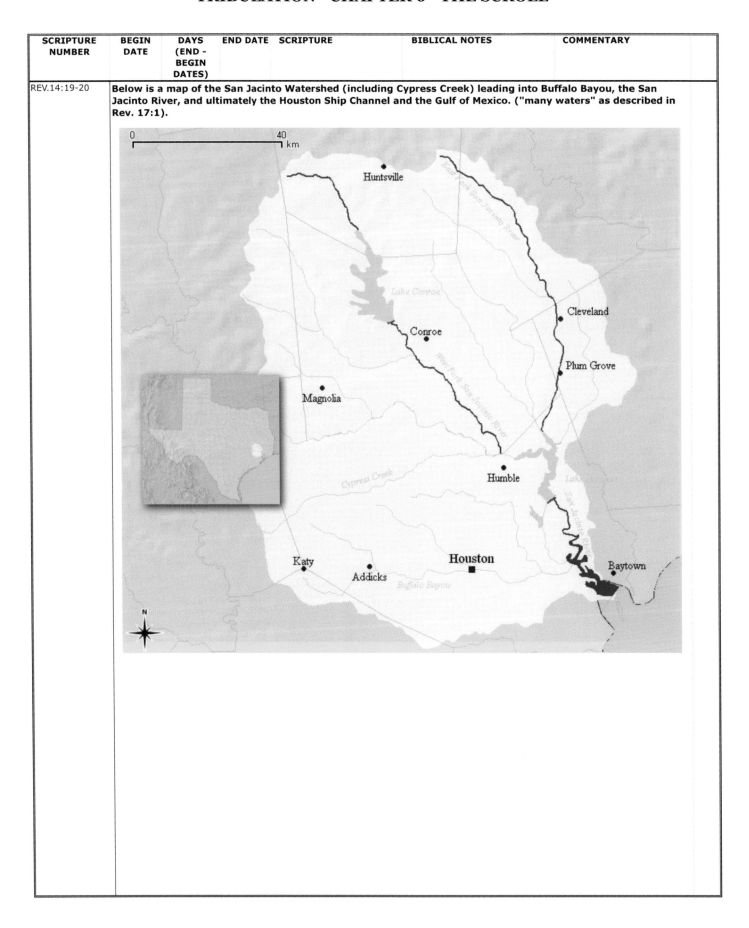

SCRIPTURE NUMBER	BEGIN DATE	DAYS (END - BEGIN DATES)	END DATE	SCRIPTURE	BIBLICAL NOTES	COMMENTARY
IS.63:1-6				1Who is this that comes from Edom, in crimsoned garments, from Bozrah? Who is this, glorious in his apparel, striding in the greatness of his strength? "It is I, I who announce vindication, mighty to save."a 2Why is your apparel red, and your garments like one who treads the wine press?b 3"The wine press I have trodden alone, and from the peoples no one was with me. I trod them in my anger, and trampled them down in my wrath; Their blood spurted on my garments, all my apparel I stained. 4For a day of vindication was in my heart, my year for redeeming had come.c 5I looked about, but there was no one to help, I was appalled that there was no one to lend support; So my own arm brought me victory and my own wrath lent me support.d 6I trampled down the peoples in my anger, I made them drunk in my wrath, and I poured out their blood upon the ground."	* [63:1-6] Two questions are raised at the approach of a majestic figure coming from Edom. It is the Lord, his garments red with the blood from the judgment battle. Edom (its capital Bozrah) plundered Judah after the fall of Jerusalem; cf. 34:5-17. Wine press: here a symbol of a bloody judgment; cf. Lam 1:15; Jl 4:13.	
REV.15:1-3				The Seven Last Plagues. 1* Then I saw in heaven another sign,* great and awe-inspiring: seven angels with the seven last plagues, for through them God's fury is accomplished. 2Then I saw something like a sea of glass mingled with fire.* On the sea of glass were standing those who had won the victory over the beast and its image and the number that signified its name. They were holding God's harps,a 3and they sang the song of Moses,* the servant of God, and the song of the Lamb: "Great and wonderful are your works, Lord God almighty. Just and true are your ways, O king of the nations.b	* [15:1-16:21] The seven bowls, the third and last group of seven after the seven seals and the seven trumpets, foreshadow the final cataclysm. Again, the series is introduced by a heavenly prelude, in which the victors over the beast sing the canticle of Moses (Rev 15:2-4). * [15:1-4] A vision of the victorious martyrs precedes the vision of woe in Rev 15:5-16:21; cf. Rev 7:9-12. * [15:2] Mingled with fire: fire symbolizes the sanctity involved in facing God, reflected in the trials that have prepared the victorious Christians or in God's wrath. * [15:3] The song of Moses: the song that Moses and the Israelites sang after their escape from the oppression of Egypt (Ex 15:1-18). The martyrs have escaped from the oppression of the Devil. Nations: many other Greek manuscripts and versions read "ages."	

THE 7 PLAGUES AND BOWLS

SCRIPTURE NUMBER	BEGIN DATE	DAYS (END - BEGIN DATES)	END DATE	SCRIPTURE	BIBLICAL NOTES	COMMENTARY
PS.92:6				6How great are your works, LORD!c How profound your designs!	* [Psalm 92] A hymn of praise and thanks for God's faithful deeds (Ps 92:2–5). The wicked, deluded by their prosperity (Ps 92:6–9), are punished (Ps 92:10), whereas the psalmist has already experienced God's protection (Ps 92:11–15).	
PS.98:1				1A psalm. I Sing a new song to the LORD, for he has done marvelous deeds.a His right hand and holy arm have won the victory.*b	* [98:1] Marvelous deeds...victory: the conquest of all threats to the peaceful existence of Israel, depicted in the Psalms variously as a cosmic force such as sea, or nations bent on Israel's destruction, or evildoers seemingly triumphant. His right hand and holy arm: God is pictured as a powerful warrior.	
DT.32:4				4The Rock—how faultless are his deeds, how right all his ways! A faithful God, without deceit, just and upright is he!b	* [32:1–43] The whole song is a poetic sermon, having for its theme the Lord's benefits to Israel (vv. 1–14) and Israel's ingratitude and idolatry in turning to the gods of the nations; these sins will be punished by the nations themselves (vv. 15–29); in turn, the foolish pride of the nations will be punished, and the Lord's honor will be vindicated (vv. 30–43).	
PS.145:17				17The LORD is just in all his ways, merciful in all his works.l		
REV. 15:4-8				4Who will not fear you, Lord, or glorify your name? For you alone are holy. All the nations will come and worship before you, for your righteous acts have been revealed."c 5* After this I had another vision. The temple that is the heavenly tent of testimony* opened, 6and the seven angels with the seven plagues came out of the temple. They were dressed in clean white linen, with a gold sash around their chests.d 7One of the four living creatures gave the seven angels seven gold bowls filled with the fury of God, who lives forever and ever. 8Then the temple became so filled with the smoke from God's glory and might that no one could enter it until the seven plagues of the seven angels had been accomplished.e	* [15:5–8] Seven angels receive the bowls of God's wrath. * [15:5] Tent of testimony: the name of the meeting tent in the Greek text of Ex 40. Cf. 2 Mc 2:4–7.	The "tent of testimony" also describes the tent in Canaan, at Shiloh, where the Hebrews kept the Ark of the Covenant. Jos.18:1 The fury of God, also referred to in Rev. 14:9 and 16:19, is a reference to the mass extinction of animal life during the Mesozoic Era and during the flood of Noah. Therefore, oil is the product or "wine" off God's fury. Refer to the Seven Bowls in Rev. 16:1-21. If you remember the horrendous oil spill from the Deepwater Horizon disaster, starting in mid-April 2010 and lasting for 3 months, the oil on the surface of the water looked like blood. Reference my commentary to Rev. 14:9 and 16:19 in the Scroll and a vision of a related calamitous event in Harris County, TX.

THE 7 PLAGUES AND BOWLS

SCRIPTURE NUMBER	BEGIN DATE	DAYS (END - BEGIN DATES)	END DATE	SCRIPTURE	BIBLICAL NOTES	COMMENTARY
JOS.18:1				1The whole community of the Israelites assembled at Shiloh, where they set up the tent of meeting; and the land was subdued before them.a		The Israelites found a resting place for the Ark of the Covenant in Shiloh: After the children of Israel entered Canaan and the war was over, the whole congregation assembled at Shiloh to set up the tent of meeting there (see Joshua 18.1). http://biblocality.com/forums/showthread.php?2087-The-Ark-in-the-Tent-at-Shiloh.
1SAM.4:4,5,10,11				Loss of the Ark. 4So the people sent to Shiloh and brought from there the ark of the LORD of hosts, who is enthroned upon the cherubim.* The two sons of Eli, Hophni and Phinehas, accompanied the ark of God.b 5When the ark of the LORD arrived in the camp, all Israel shouted so loudly that the earth shook. 10The Philistines fought and Israel was defeated; everyone fled to their own tents.* It was a disastrous defeat; Israel lost thirty thousand foot soldiers. 11The ark of God was captured, and Eli's two sons, Hophni and Phinehas, were dead.c	* [4:4] Enthroned upon the cherubim: this divine title first occurs in the Old Testament at the sanctuary at Shiloh (cf. 2 Sm 6:2); God is represented seated upon a throne borne through the heavens by cherubim, creatures partly human being, partly beast (cf. Ez 1 and 10). * [4:10] To their own tents: the defeat is so catastrophic that the soldiers abandon the army for home; cf. 2 Sm 18:17.	
PS.78:60-61				61He gave up his might into captivity, his glorious ark into the hands of the foe.g 62God delivered his people to the sword; he was enraged against his heritage.	* [Psalm 78] A recital of history to show that past generations did not respond to God's gracious deeds and were punished by God making the gift into a punishment. Will Israel fail to appreciate God's act—the choosing of Zion and of David? The tripartite introduction invites Israel to learn the lessons hidden in its traditions	Let us understand that the Lord did not forsake the tent of Shiloh because the ark had been taken captive; rather, the ark was captured because the Lord had first abandoned the tent at Shiloh. Once God's ark left the tent of Shiloh, it never again returned to it. Oh how very serious is this matter. If anyone should imagine that he will be victorious by vainly repeating such words as "I have God"—"In the name of the Lord"—"God surely is with us"—he commits the same error as the Israelites of old. The nation of Israel was beaten before the Philistines because they forgot to deal with their sins. They did not keep in mind that as long as their sins were left, not dealt with, they would never be victorious. http://biblocality.com/forums/showthread.php?2087-The-Ark-in-the-Tent-at-Shiloh The Ark returns in Rev. 11:19. Itgs final resting place in Heaven. ALL SHOULD HEED THIS HISTORY.

THE 7 PLAGUES AND BOWLS

SCRIPTURE NUMBER	BEGIN DATE	DAYS (END - BEGIN DATES)	END DATE	SCRIPTURE	BIBLICAL NOTES	COMMENTARY
PS.86:9-10				9All the nations you have made shall come to bow before you, Lord, and give honor to your name.e 10For you are great and do wondrous deeds ;and you alone are God.		
JER.10:7				7Who would not fear you, King of the nations, for it is your due! Among all the wisest of the nations, and in all their domains, there is none like you.f		
1KGS.8:10				10c When the priests left the holy place, the cloud filled the house of the LORD		
IS.6:4				4At the sound of that cry, the frame of the door shook and the house was filled with smoke.* c	* [6:4] Smoke: reminiscent of the clouds which indicated God's presence at Mount Sinai (Ex 19:16–19; Dt 4:11) and which filled the tabernacle (Ex 40:34–38) and the Temple (1 Kgs 8:10–11) at their dedication.	
REV 16:1-3				The Seven Bowls.* 1I heard a loud voice speaking from the temple to the seven angels, "Go and pour out the seven bowls of God's fury upon the earth." 2The first angel went and poured out his bowl on the earth. Festering and ugly sores broke out on those who had the mark of the beast or worshiped its image.* 3* The second angel poured out his bowl on the sea. The sea turned to blood like that from a corpse; every creature living in the sea died.	* [16:1–21] These seven bowls, like the seven seals (Rev 6:1–17; 8:1) and the seven trumpets (Rev 8:2–9:21; 11:15–19), bring on a succession of disasters modeled in part on the plagues of Egypt (Ex 7–12). See note on Rev 6:12–14. * [16:2] Like the sixth Egyptian plague (Ex 9:8–11). * [16:3–4] Like the first Egyptian plague (Ex 7:20–21). The same woe followed the blowing of the second trumpet (Rev 8:8–9).	One vision could be Red Tide. A significant source of water toxicity from increased nutrient loading from human activities.[14] The growth of marine phytoplankton (one causal factor of red tide) is generally limited by the availability of nitrates and phosphates (fertilizers), which can be abundant in agricultural run-off as well as coastal upwelling zones. Coastal water pollution produced by humans and systematic increase in sea water temperature (climate change) have also been implicated as contributing factors in red tides. Coupled with a water stagnation could cause significant red tide impacts to fish and other marine species due to oxygen depletion in seawater.

THE 7 PLAGUES AND BOWLS

SCRIPTURE NUMBER	BEGIN DATE	DAYS (END - BEGIN DATES)	END DATE	SCRIPTURE	BIBLICAL NOTES	COMMENTARY
REV 16:4-7				4The third angel poured out his bowl on the rivers and springs of water. These also turned to blood.a 5Then I heard the angel in charge of the waters say: "You are just, O Holy One, who are and who were, in passing this sentence.b 6For they have shed the blood of the holy ones and the prophets, and you [have] given them blood to drink; it is what they deserve."c 7Then I heard the altar cry out, "Yes, Lord God almighty, your judgments are true and just."d	EX. 7:14-24 First Plague: Water Turned into Blood.* 14Then the LORD said to Moses: Pharaoh is obstinate* in refusing to let the people go. 15In the morning, just when he sets out for the water, go to Pharaoh and present yourself by the bank of the Nile, holding in your hand the staff that turned into a snake.* 16Say to him: The LORD, the God of the Hebrews, sent me to you with the message: Let my people go to serve me in the wilderness. But as yet you have not listened. 17Thus says the LORD: This is how you will know that I am the LORD. With the staff here in my hand, I will strike the water in the Nile and it will be changed into blood.d 18The fish in the Nile will die, and the Nile itself will stink so that the Egyptians will be unable to drink water from the Nile. 19The LORD then spoke to Moses: Speak to Aaron: Take your staff and stretch out your hand over the waters of Egypt—its streams, its canals, its ponds, and all its supplies of water—that they may become blood. There will be blood throughout the land of Egypt, even in the wooden pails and stone jars. 20This, then, is what Moses and Aaron did, exactly as the LORD had commanded. Aaron raised his staff and struck the waters in the Nile in full view of Pharaoh and his servants, and all the water in the Nile was changed into blood. 21The fish in the Nile died, and the Nile itself stank so that the Egyptians could not drink water from it. There was blood throughout the land of Egypt. 22But the Egyptian magicians did the same* by their magic arts. So Pharaoh hardened his heart and would not listen to them, just as the LORD had said. 23Pharaoh turned away and went into his house, with no concern even for this. 24All the Egyptians had to dig round about the Nile for drinking water, since they could not drink any water from the Nile.	See commentary Rev.16:1-3.

THE 7 PLAGUES AND BOWLS

SCRIPTURE NUMBER	BEGIN DATE	DAYS (END - BEGIN DATES)	END DATE	SCRIPTURE	BIBLICAL NOTES	COMMENTARY	
EZ.35:6				6therefore, as I live—oracle of the Lord GOD—you are guilty of blood, and blood, I swear, shall pursue you.	* [35:1–15] After the fall of Jerusalem, Edom assisted the Babylonians in devastating the land and subduing the population in order to occupy part of Judah's former territory. For this reason these oracles against Edom are found in the context of the city's fall.		
MT.23:34-35				34* q Therefore, behold, I send to you prophets and wise men and scribes; some of them you will kill and crucify, some of them you will scourge in your synagogues and pursue from town to town, 35so that there may come upon you all the righteous blood shed upon earth, from the righteous blood of Abel to the blood of Zechariah, the son of Barachiah, whom you murdered between the sanctuary and the altar.	* [23:34–36] There are important differences between the Matthean and the Lucan form of this Q material; cf. Lk 11:49–51. In Luke the one who sends the emissaries is the "wisdom of God." If, as many scholars think, that is the original wording of Q, Matthew, by making Jesus the sender, has presented him as the personified divine wisdom. In Luke, wisdom's emissaries are the Old Testament "prophets" and the Christian "apostles." Matthew's prophets and wise men and scribes are probably Christian disciples alone; cf. Mt 10:41 and see note on Mt 13:52. You will kill: see Mt 24:9. Scourge in your synagogues…town to town: see Mt 10:17, 23 and the note on Mt 10:17. All the righteous blood shed upon the earth: the slaying of the disciples is in continuity with all the shedding of righteous blood beginning with that of Abel. The persecution of Jesus' disciples by this generation involves the persecutors in the guilt of their murderous ancestors. The blood of Zechariah: see note on Lk 11:51. By identifying him as the son of Barachiah Matthew understands him to be Zechariah the Old Testament minor prophet; see Zec 1:1.		**THE 7 PLAGUES AND BOWLS**
DAN.3:27				27For you are just in all you have done; all your deeds are faultless, all your ways right, and all your judgments proper.	* [3:24–90] These verses are additions to the Aramaic text of Daniel, translated from the Greek form of the book. They were probably first composed in Hebrew or Aramaic, but are no longer extant in the original language. The Roman Catholic Church has always regarded them as part of the canonical Scriptures.		
TB.3:2				2"You are righteous, Lord, and all your deeds are just; All your ways are mercy and fidelity; you are judge of the world.a			

SCRIPTURE NUMBER	BEGIN DATE	DAYS (END - BEGIN DATES)	END DATE	SCRIPTURE	BIBLICAL NOTES	COMMENTARY
REV. 16:8-11				8The fourth angel poured out his bowl on the sun. It was given the power to burn people with fire. 9People were burned by the scorching heat and blasphemed the name of God who had power over these plagues, but they did not repent or give him glory.e 10f The fifth angel poured out his bowl on the throne of the beast.* Its kingdom was plunged into darkness, and people bit their tongues in pain 11and blasphemed the God of heaven because of their pains and sores. But they did not repent of their works.g	* [16:10] The throne of the beast: symbol of the forces of evil. Darkness: like the ninth Egyptian plague (Ex 10:21–23); cf. Rev 9:2.	Climate change. Texas drought surpassed the worst drought in 1956 and July 2011 was the warmest month on record since data collection started in 1895. Record wildfires in Arizona and Texas in 2011. 2012 was the warmest year on record. Possibly elevated peak solar activity in May 2013. It is NOT predicted to be record setting solar activity. (http://en.wikipedia.org/wiki /Solar_cycle_24) Record wildfires happen in New Mexico and Colorado because of the tinderbox of vegetation created by climate change.
AM 4:6				6Though I made your teeth clean of food in all your cities, and made bread scarce in all your dwellings, Yet you did not return to me— oracle of the LORD.a		
EX.10:21-23				Ninth Plague: the Darkness. 21c Then the LORD said to Moses: Stretch out your hand toward the sky, that over the land of Egypt there may be such darkness* that one can feel it. 22So Moses stretched out his hand toward the sky, and there was dense darkness throughout the land of Egypt for three days. 23People could not see one another, nor could they get up from where they were, for three days. But all the Israelites had light where they lived.	* [10:21] Darkness: commentators note that at times a storm from the south, called the khamsin, blackens the sky of Egypt with sand from the Sahara; the dust in the air is then so thick that the darkness can, in a sense, "be felt." But such observations should not obscure the fact that for the biblical author what transpires in each of the plagues is clearly something extraordinary, an event which witnesses to the unrivaled power of Israel's God.	The sandstorms in July 2011 and July 2012 in Phoenix, AZ would be symbolic of this scripture.
EX.9:8-11				9It will turn into fine dust over the whole land of Egypt and cause festering boils* on human being and beast alike throughout the land of Egypt. 10So they took the soot from a kiln and appeared before Pharaoh. When Moses scattered it toward the sky, it caused festering boils on human being and beast alike. 11Because of the boils the magicians could not stand in Moses' presence, for there were boils on the magicians as well as on the rest of the Egyptians.	* [9:9] Boils: the exact nature of the disease is not clear. Semitic cognates, for example, suggest the Hebrew root means "to be hot" and thus point to some sort of inflammation. The fact that soot taken from the kiln is the agent of the disease would point in the same direction. See further Lv 13:18–23; Dt 28:35; 2 Kgs 20:7.	

THE 7 PLAGUES AND BOWLS

SCRIPTURE NUMBER	BEGIN DATE	DAYS (END - BEGIN DATES)	END DATE	SCRIPTURE	BIBLICAL NOTES	COMMENTARY
JER.5:3				3LORD, do your eyes not search for honesty? You struck them, but they did not flinch; you laid them low, but they refused correction; They set their faces harder than stone, and refused to return.a		
REV. 16:12-14				12The sixth angel emptied his bowl on the great river Euphrates. Its water was dried up to prepare the way for the kings of the East.* 13I saw three unclean spirits like frogs* come from the mouth of the dragon, from the mouth of the beast, and from the mouth of the false prophet.h 14These were demonic spirits who performed signs. They went out to the kings of the whole world to assemble them for the battle on the great day of God the almighty.i	* [16:12] The kings of the East: Parthians; see notes on Rev 6:2 and Rev 17:12–13. East: literally, "rising of the sun," as in Rev 7:2. * [16:13] Frogs: possibly an allusion to the second Egyptian plague (Ex 7:25–8:11). The false prophet: identified with the two-horned second beast (Rev 13:11–18 and the note there).	Per a NY Times article in 2009 (http://www.nytimes.com/2009/07/14/world/middleeast/14euphrates.html), the Euphrates River has been drying up due to drought in Iraq, Syria and Turkey, misuse for years by Iraq and its farmers and 2 Wars in Iraq. During various periods of time from 2005 though current day, the "kings of the East" would have been Saddam Hussein (in hiding in Iraq since from 2003 to 2006), Mahmoud Ahmadinejad (Iran since 2005), Bashar Hafez al-Assad (Syria since 2000) for the respective Biblical lands of Babylon, Persia, and Assyria. An Old Testament respective comparison, in ancient times (Between the 5th and 7th century B.C.E.) could be Nebuchadnezzar II (Babylon), Haman (Persia), and Ashurbanipal (Assyria). History has a habit of repeating itself. From the Book "The Rite" by Matt Baglio, in Chapter 12, during an exorcism, Father Carmine De Filippis saw "a woman vomit a small black toad that was alive. When he went to catch it, it fizzled away into BLACK SALIVA". Symbolism in this case would be that the black saliva represented the Dragon (Satan) or, oil and the frog, an unclean spirit.
EX.8:2-3				2So Aaron stretched out his hand over the waters of Egypt, and the frogs came up and covered the land of Egypt. 3But the magicians did the same by their magic arts and made frogs overrun the land of Egypt.		
1COR.1:8				8He will keep you firm to the end, irreproachable on the day of our Lord Jesus [Christ].d		

THE 7 PLAGUES AND BOWLS

SCRIPTURE NUMBER	BEGIN DATE	DAYS (END - BEGIN DATES)	END DATE	SCRIPTURE	BIBLICAL NOTES	COMMENTARY
REV. 16-15-18				15("Behold, I am coming like a thief."* Blessed is the one who watches and keeps his clothes ready, so that he may not go naked and people see him exposed.)j 16They then assembled the kings in the place that is named Armageddon* in Hebrew. 17The seventh angel poured out his bowl into the air. A loud voice came out of the temple from the throne, saying, "It is done."k 18Then there were lightning flashes, rumblings, and peals of thunder, and a great earthquake. It was such a violent earthquake that there has never been one like it since the human race began on earth.l	* [16:15] Like a thief: as in Rev 3:3 (cf. Mt 24:42–44; 1 Thes 5:2). Blessed: see note on Rev 1:3. * [16:16] Armageddon: in Hebrew, this means "Mountain of Megiddo." Since Megiddo was the scene of many decisive battles in antiquity (Jgs 5:19–20; 2 Kgs 9:27; 2 Chr 35:20–24), the town became the symbol of the final disastrous rout of the forces of evil.	Megiddo, near the Holy city of Nazareth where Christ spent most of has life, and near the city of Haifa (prone to many Hezbollah rocket attacks) is the Hebrew name for Armageddon. "a great earthquake. It was such a violent earthquake that there has never been one like it since the human race began on earth.l" The prophet St. John was seeing a vision from God through Christ and an angel. He may not have had the ability to disseminate an earthquake from a tremendous explosion.
MT.24:42-44				42* s Therefore, stay awake! For you do not know on which day your Lord will come. 43t Be sure of this: if the master of the house had known the hour of night when the thief was coming, he would have stayed awake and not let his house be broken into. 44So too, you also must be prepared, for at an hour you do not expect, the Son of Man will come.		
IS.66:6				6A voice roaring from the city, a voice from the temple; The voice of the LORD rendering recompense to his enemies!e Blessings of Prosperity and Consolation	* [66:3–6] The sacrificial abuses listed will only merit punishment. The true worshipers, the downtrodden, are those who "tremble" (vv.2, 5) at God's word. Although they are ridiculed by those who reject them (v. 5), the latter will be afflicted with divine punishment; their "choice" will be met by the Lord's choice (v. 4).	
MK.13:19				19For those times will have tribulation such as has not been since the beginning of God's creation until now, nor ever will be.i		

THE 7 PLAGUES AND BOWLS

SCRIPTURE NUMBER	BEGIN DATE	DAYS (END - BEGIN DATES)	END DATE	SCRIPTURE	BIBLICAL NOTES	COMMENTARY
REV. 16:19-21				19The great city* was split into three parts, and the gentile cities fell. But God remembered great Babylon, giving it the cup filled with the wine of his fury and wrath. 20* Every island fled, and mountains disappeared. 21Large hailstones like huge weights came down from the sky on people, and they blasphemed God for the plague of hail because this plague was so severe.m	* [16:19] The great city: Rome and the empire. * [16:20–21] See note on Rev 6:12–14. Hailstones: as in the seventh Egyptian plague (Ex 9:23–24); cf. Rev 8:7. Like huge weights: literally, "weighing a talent," about one hundred pounds.	200 miles of San Jacinto / Buffalo watershed leading into Buffalo Bayou, the San Jacinto River, and ultimately the Houston Ship Channel and the Gulf of Mexico ("many waters" as described in Rev.. 17:1) with an explosion or a storm which would push water upstream into the water shed carrying a "stew" of toxic, and flammable, materials, oil based, which would give the appearance of blood. See the below map which shows splitting the city into 3 parts, based on the described event and the location of the main tributaries of the watershed. "cup filled with the wine of his fury and wrath"=Oil and its derivatives.
REV. 16:19-21						

"19The great city* was split into three parts, and the gentile cities fell." The parts are separated by the San Jacinto Watershed tributaries to: Part 1 - East and North Harris County. Part 2 - Central Harris County. Part 3 - Southern Harris County.

SCRIPTURE NUMBER	BEGIN DATE	DAYS (END - BEGIN DATES)	END DATE	SCRIPTURE	BIBLICAL NOTES	COMMENTARY	
EX.9:22-26				22The LORD then said to Moses: Stretch out your hand toward the sky, that hail may fall upon the entire land of Egypt, on human being and beast alike and all the vegetation of the fields in the land of Egypt. 23So Moses stretched out his staff toward the sky, and the LORD sent forth peals of thunder and hail.c Lightning flashed toward the earth, and the LORD rained down hail upon the land of Egypt. 24There was hail and lightning flashing here and there through the hail, and the hail was so fierce that nothing like it had been seen in Egypt since it became a nation. 25Throughout the land of Egypt the hail struck down everything in the fields, human being and beast alike; it struck down all the vegetation of the fields and splintered every tree in the fields. 26Only in the land of Goshen, where the Israelites were, was there no hail.			
REV. 17:1-3				Babylon the Great. 1* Then one of the seven angels who were holding the seven bowls came and said to me, "Come here. I will show you the judgment on the great harlot* who lives near the many waters.a 2* The kings of the earth have had intercourse with her,b and the inhabitants of the earth became drunk on the wine of her harlotry." 3Then he carried me away in spirit to a deserted place where I saw a woman seated on a scarlet beast* that was covered with blasphemous names, with seven heads and ten horns.c	* [17:1–19:10] The punishment of Babylon is now described as a past event and, metaphorically, under the image of the great harlot who leads people astray into idolatry. * [17:1–6] Babylon, the symbolic name (Rev 17:5) of Rome, is graphically described as "the great harlot." * [17:2] Intercourse...harlotry: see note on Rev 14:4. The pagan kings subject to Rome adopted the cult of the emperor. * [17:3] Scarlet beast: see note on Rev 13:1–10. Blasphemous names: divine titles assumed by the Roman emperors; see note on Rev 13:5–6.	"Kings" could be U.S. Congressional Representatives, oil companies, oil ministers, or OPEC heads of state. Intercourse with her is idolatry. Wine of her harlotry is oil and its derivatives. Regarding "the great harlot* who lives near the many waters", the Harlot is Harris County, TX, Many waters are Buffalo Bayou, Cypress Creek, San Jacinto River, Lake Houston, Cedar Bayou, Houston Ship Channel, Gulf of Mexico." A woman seated on a scarlet beast"* (Harris County, TX) that was covered with blasphemous names, with seven heads and ten horns.c (See Commentary REV.13:1-3)	
JER.50:38				38A drought upon the waters, and they dry up! For it is a land of idols, soon made frantic by phantoms.z			
JER.51:13				13You who dwell by mighty waters, rich in treasure, Your end has come, the time at which you shall be cut off!j			

THE 7 PLAGUES AND BOWLS

SCRIPTURE NUMBER	BEGIN DATE	DAYS (END - BEGIN DATES)	END DATE	SCRIPTURE	BIBLICAL NOTES	COMMENTARY	
JER.51.7				7who pays out her due.d Babylon was a golden cup in the hand of the LORD making the whole earth drunk; The nations drank its wine, thus they have gone mad.e	* [17:6b–18] An interpretation of the vision is here given.		
REV. 17:4-7				4The woman was wearing purple and scarlet and adorned with gold, precious stones, and pearls.d She held in her hand a gold cup that was filled with the abominable and sordid deeds of her harlotry. 5On her forehead was written a name, which is a mystery, "Babylon the great, the mother of harlots and of the abominations of the earth." 6* I saw that the woman was drunk on the blood of the holy ones and on the blood of the witnesses to Jesus. 7The angel said to me, "Why are you amazed? I will explain to you the mystery of the woman and of the beast that carries her, the beast with the seven heads and the ten horns.	* [17:6] Reference to the great wealth and idolatrous cults of Rome. * [17:6b–18] An interpretation of the vision is here given.		
REV. 17:8-9				8* e The beast that you saw existed once but now exists no longer. It will come up from the abyss and is headed for destruction. The inhabitants of the earth whose names have not been written in the book of life from the foundation of the world shall be amazed when they see the beast, because it existed once but exists no longer, and yet it will come again. 9Here is a clue* for one who has wisdom. The seven heads represent seven hills upon which the woman sits. They also represent seven kings:f	* [17:8] Allusion to the belief that the dead Nero would return to power (Rev 17:11); see note on Rev 13:3. * [17:9] Here is a clue: literally, "Here a mind that has wisdom." Seven hills: of Rome.		

SCRIPTURE NUMBER	BEGIN DATE	DAYS (END - BEGIN DATES)	END DATE	SCRIPTURE	BIBLICAL NOTES	COMMENTARY
REV. 17:8-9				Rome and its Seven Hills. Throughout the Revelation (especially in the Notes sections), Rome is referred to as the harlot Babylon symbolizing pagan Rome, the city on seven hills (Rev17:9). 9Here is a clue* for one who has wisdom. The seven heads represent seven hills upon which the woman sits. They also represent seven kings:f		

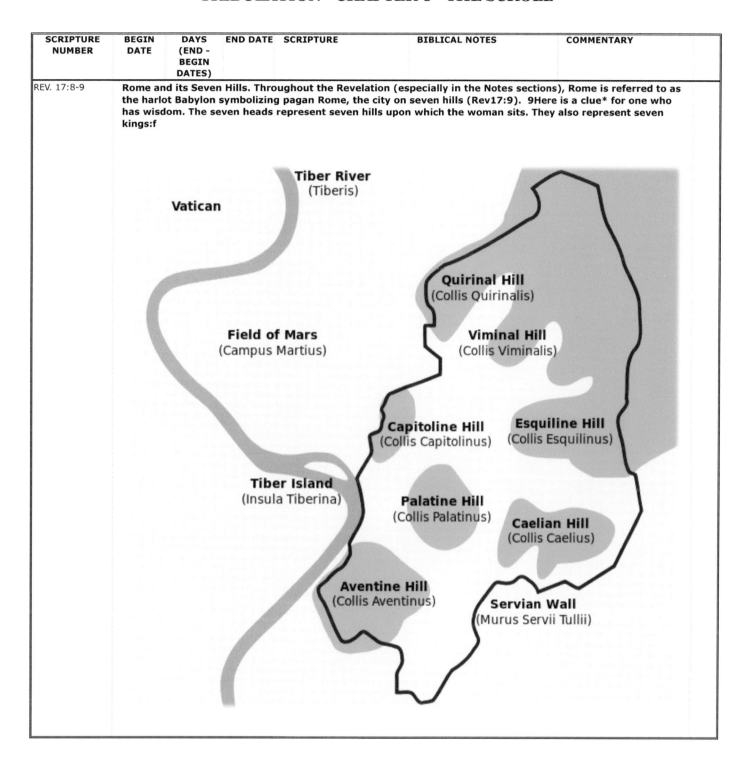

SCRIPTURE NUMBER	BEGIN DATE	DAYS (END - BEGIN DATES)	END DATE	SCRIPTURE	BIBLICAL NOTES	COMMENTARY
				Rome is a near the sea with the Tiber River dividing the city. Houston, TX was built next to Buffalo Bayou, which divides Harris County. Harris County is near the Gulf of Mexico. The seven hills and seven kings, respectively represent the 7 Congressional Districts in Harris County, TX and the 7 Representatives for the districts. This should in no way reflect that Rome is the New Babylon.		

THE ORIGINAL PLAN OF HOUSTON

SCRIPTURE NUMBER	BEGIN DATE	DAYS (END - BEGIN DATES)	END DATE	SCRIPTURE	BIBLICAL NOTES	COMMENTARY
REV. 17:10-12				10five have already fallen, one still lives, and the last has not yet come,* and when he comes he must remain only a short while. 11The beast* that existed once but exists no longer is an eighth king, but really belongs to the seven and is headed for destruction. 12The ten horns that you saw represent ten kings who have not yet been crowned;* they will receive royal authority along with the beast for one hour.g	* [17:10] There is little agreement as to the identity of the Roman emperors alluded to here. The number seven (Rev 17:9) suggests that all the emperors are meant; see note on Rev 1:4. * [17:11] The beast: Nero; see note on Rev 17:8.	It is difficult to determine the identity of six of the kings (oil companies in this case). BP (British Petroleum) will be "The beast* that existed once but exists no longer." BP Capital is the eighth king, but really belongs to the seven and is headed for destruction. "Headed for destruction" means utilizing natural gas to bridge a move to renewable energy and after that move, relying minimally on fossil fuels.
DAN.7:24				24The ten horns shall be ten kings rising out of that kingdom; another shall rise up after them, Different from those before him, who shall lay low three kings		See commentary Rev.13:11-14

SCRIPTURE NUMBER	BEGIN DATE	DAYS (END - BEGIN DATES)	END DATE	SCRIPTURE	BIBLICAL NOTES	COMMENTARY
REV. 17:13-16				13They are of one mind and will give their power and authority to the beast. 14They will fight with the Lamb, but the Lamb will conquer them, for he is Lord of lords and king of kings, and those with him are called, chosen, and faithful."h 15Then he said to me, "The waters that you saw where the harlot lives represent large numbers of peoples, nations, and tongues. 16The ten horns* that you saw and the beast will hate the harlot; they will leave her desolate and naked; they will eat her flesh and consume her with fire.i	* [17:12–13] Ten kings who have not yet been The ten horns: the ten pagan kings (Rev 17:12) who unwittingly fulfill God's will against harlot Rome, the great city; cf. Ez 16:37. * [17:16–18] The ten horns: the ten pagan kings (Rev 17:12) who unwittingly fulfill God's will against harlot Rome, the great city; cf. Ez 16:37.	12 HORNS / KINGS OPEC: 1. SAUDI ARABIA 2. VENEZUELA 3. IRAN 4. IRAQ 5. KUWAIT 6. UAE 7. LIBYA 8. QATAR 9. ALGERIA 10. NIGERIA 11. ECUADOR 12. ANGOLA "They are of one mind and will give their power and authority to the beast." means they will give their power and authority to the oil companies.
2MC13:4				4But the King of kingsb aroused the anger of Antiochus against the scoundrel. When the king was shown by Lysias that Menelaus was to blame for all the trouble, he ordered him to be taken to Beroea* and executed there in the customary local method.	* [13:4] Beroea: the Greek name of Aleppo in Syria.	
1TIM6:15				15that the blessed and only ruler will make manifest at the proper time, the King of kings and Lord of lords,I	* [6:11–16] Timothy's position demands total dedication to God and faultless witness to Christ (1 Tm 6:11–14) operating from an awareness, through faith, of the coming revelation in Jesus of the invisible God (1 Tm 6:15–16).	
ROM.1:6				6among whom are you also, who are called to belong to Jesus Christ;f		
1PT 2-9				9then the Lord knows how to rescue the devout from trial and to keep the unrighteous under punishment for the day of judgment,g	* [2:5–10a] Although God did not spare the sinful, he kept and saved the righteous, such as Noah (2 Pt 2:5) and Lot (2 Pt 2:7), and he knows how to rescue the devout (2 Pt 2:9), who are contrasted with the false teachers of the author's day. On Noah, cf. Gn 5:32–9:29, especially 7:1. On Lot, cf. Gn 13 and 19.	
JUDE1				1* Jude, a slave of Jesus Christ and brother of James,* to those who are called, beloved in God the Father and kept safe for Jesus Christ:a	* [1] Jude…brother of James: for the identity of the author of this letter, see Introduction. * [1] To those who are called: the vocation to the Christian faith is God's free gift to those whom he loves and whom he safely protects in Christ until the Lord's second coming.	

SCRIPTURE NUMBER	BEGIN DATE	DAYS (END - BEGIN DATES)	END DATE	SCRIPTURE	BIBLICAL NOTES	COMMENTARY
EZ.16:37-41				37u therefore, I will now gather together all your lovers with whom you found pleasure, both those you loved and those you hated; I will gather them against you from all sides and expose you naked for them to see. 38* I will inflict on you the sentence of adultery and murder; I will bring on you bloody wrath and jealous anger.v 39I will hand you over to them to tear down your platform and demolish your high place, to strip you of your garments and take away your splendid ornaments, leaving you stark naked.w 40They shall lead an assembly against you to stone you and hack you to pieces with their swords.x 41y They shall set fire to your homes and inflict punishments on you while many women watch. Thus I will put an end to your prostitution, and you shall never again offer payment.	* [16:38] As a jealous husband, Yhwh severely punishes Jerusalem for her adultery: i.e., her worship of idols. Adultery was considered a capital crime in ancient Israel; cf. Lv 20:10–14; Nm 5:11–28; Dt 22:22.	
EZ.23:25-29				25I will direct my jealousy against you, so that they deal with you in fury, cutting off your nose and ears; what is left of you shall fall by the sword. They shall take away your sons and daughters, and what is left of you shall be devoured by fire. 26They shall strip off your clothes and seize your splendid jewelry. 27I will put an end to your depravity and to your prostitution from the land of Egypt; you shall no longer look to them, nor even remember Egypt again. 28For thus says the Lord GOD: I am now handing you over to those whom you hate, to those from whom you recoil. 29They shall treat you with hatred, seizing all that you worked for and leaving you stark naked, so that your indecent nakedness is exposed.l Your depravity and prostitution	* [23:23] Pekod, Shoa and Koa: nations along the Tigris River, part of "greater Babylonia."	

SCRIPTURE NUMBER	BEGIN DATE	DAYS (END - BEGIN DATES)	END DATE	SCRIPTURE	BIBLICAL NOTES	COMMENTARY
REV. 17:17-18				17For God has put it into their minds to carry out his purpose and to make them come to an agreement to give their kingdom to the beast until the words of God are accomplished. 18The woman whom you saw represents the great city that has sovereignty over the kings of the earth."		Commentary Rev.17:13-18. The OPEC members will give their authority to the "beast" (oil companies). The "beast", including their lobbyists, acting for the 10 horns, will first attack the Lamb for publishing this book and those who have faith in this book. With the failed attempt of destroying or discrediting the Lamb, the "beast" will then probably relocate their operations, which service the oil exploration and production for the "ten horns" and U.S. domestic exploration and production. They will relocate their base in Harris County, TX. to a new location; thereby moving thousands of jobs, leaving Houston, TX ("the Harlot") "desolate and naked". The Catch 22 in this case is that if "the beast" chooses to do nothing, it and "the Harlot" will probably face the calamitous events described earlier in this Book. The symbolic beast in this case would be a consortium of major Oil E & P companies. See http://bottomline.msnbc.msn.com/_news/2012/06/28/12460198-exxonmobil-ceo-assailed-for-claims-on-climate-change?lite regarding remarks from Exxon-Mobil's CEO Rex Tillerson about climate change. "This is an industry that made $137 billion (Rev. 13:7) in profits in 2011. They're asking the rest of the world to adapt to the hardship they're imposing on other people," said Bob Deans, spokesman for the National Resource Defense Council Action Fund."

SCRIPTURE NUMBER	BEGIN DATE	DAYS (END - BEGIN DATES)	END DATE	SCRIPTURE	BIBLICAL NOTES	COMMENTARY
REV. 18:1-3				The Fall of Babylon.* 1After this I saw another angel coming down from heaven, having great authority, and the earth became illumined by his splendor.a 2* He cried out in a mighty voice: "Fallen, fallen is Babylon the great.b She has become a haunt for demons. She is a cage for every unclean spirit, a cage for every unclean bird, [a cage for every unclean] and disgusting [beast]. 3For all the nations have drunk* the wine of her licentious passion. The kings of the earth had intercourse with her, and the merchants of the earth grew rich from her drive for luxury."c 4Then I heard another voice from heaven say: "Depart from her,* my people, so as not to take part in her sins and receive a share in her plagues,d	* [18:1–19:4] A stirring dirge over the fall of Babylon-Rome. The perspective is prophetic, as if the fall of Rome had already taken place. The imagery here, as elsewhere in this book, is not to be taken literally. The vindictiveness of some of the language, borrowed from the scathing Old Testament prophecies against Babylon, Tyre, and Nineveh (Is 23; 24; 27; Jer 50–51; Ez 26–27), is meant to portray symbolically the inexorable demands of God's holiness and justice; cf. Introduction. The section concludes with a joyous canticle on the future glory of heaven. * [18:2] Many Greek manuscripts and versions omit a cage for every unclean…beast. * [18:3–24] Rome is condemned for her immorality, symbol of idolatry (see note on Rev 14:4), and for persecuting the church; cf. Rev 19:2.	3For all the nations have drunk* the wine of her licentious passion. The kings of the earth had intercourse with her, and the merchants of the earth grew rich from her drive for luxury."c Idolatry from oil money.
EZ.43:2				2and there was the glory of the God of Israel coming from the east! His voice was like the roar of many waters, and the earth shone with his glory.		
IS.21:9				9Here he comes— a single chariot, a pair of horses— He calls out and says, 'Fallen, fallen is Babylon! All the images of her gods are smashed to the ground!'"h		
JER.50:2-3				2Proclaim this among the nations, announce it! Announce it, do not hide it, but say: Babylon is captured, Bel* put to shame, Marduk terrified; its images are put to shame, its idols shattered. 3A nation from the north advances against it, making the land desolate So that no one can live there; human beings and animals have fled.b	* [50:2] Bel: originally the title of the god of Nippur in Mesopotamia, later associated with Merodach (Marduk), chief god of Babylon (cf. Is 46:1).	
JER.51:7-8				7who pays out her due.d Babylon was a golden cup in the hand of the LORD making the whole earth drunk; The nations drank its wine, thus they have gone mad.e 8Babylon suddenly falls and is broken: wail over her! Bring balm for her wounds, in case she can be healed.f		

SCRIPTURE NUMBER	BEGIN DATE	DAYS (END - BEGIN DATES)	END DATE	SCRIPTURE	BIBLICAL NOTES	COMMENTARY
REV. 18:4-7				4Then I heard another voice from heaven say: "Depart from her,* my people, so as not to take part in her sins and receive a share in her plagues,d 5for her sins are piled up to the sky, and God remembers her crimes.e 6Pay her back as she has paid others. Pay her back double for her deeds. Into her cup pour double what she poured.f 7To the measure of her boasting and wantonness repay her in torment and grief; for she said to herself, 'I sit enthroned as queen; I am no widow, and I will never know grief.'g	* [18:4] Depart from her: not evacuation of the city but separation from sinners, as always in apocalyptic literature.	I partially agree with the Biblical Note on Scripture Rev. 18:4 for 2 reasons: 1) Pope Benedict XIV made a statement regarding New York City in mid-February of 2012, calling it today's Sodom and Gomorra. The remark was quickly refuted by then-Archbishop, and now-Cardinal Timothy Dolan ... and me. 2)The voice from Heaven (Word of God) could very well be this book and would be 2 messages: To not only separate yourself from sin but to also depart the city. God was willing to spare the righteous in Sodom and Gomorrah at the pleading of Abraham, who's nephew Lot was the only righteous person. This was just prior to God's destruction of Sodom, Gomorrah, Admah, Zeboim and Bela. God turned the cities to ashes and they have become synonymous with impenitent sin, and their fall with a proverbial manifestation of God's wrath. See Gen.18:20-33, 19:1-29. The message here is don't take anything for granted for God will come like a thief in the night (See Rev.3:3). Jeff Lynne, formerly of ELO and a member of the Traveling Wilbury's, sings it best in the song "End Of The Line": "Every Day is Judgment Day"... so live your life like God wants you to. "Her sins are piled up to the sky" which is describing idolatry. See Rom.1:16-32. "I am no widow, and I will never know grief.'g" is the arrogance of the harlot to think that people would never abandon her because of her idolatrous hold on them. The issue here is how the Holy See views apocalyptic literature, starting with the story of Sodom and Gomorra in the Book of Genesis (the first Book of the Bible), through the Old Testament Prophetic Books, The Gospels, the Epistles, the Catholic Letters and finishing with the Apocalypse, or Revelation to John, the last book of the

SCRIPTURE NUMBER	BEGIN DATE	DAYS (END - BEGIN DATES)	END DATE	SCRIPTURE	BIBLICAL NOTES	COMMENTARY
REV. 18:4-7						Bible, which is one of the most difficult to understand because it abounds in unfamiliar and extravagant symbolism. Somewhere, in all of that "apocalyptic literature", are real stories written to "literally scare the Hell out of you".
GEN.14:10				10Now the Valley of Siddim was full of bitumen pits; and as the king of Sodom and the king of Gomorrah fled, they fell into these, while the rest fled to the mountains.		Symbolism is the Canadian "tar sand trap" and the Keystone XL Pipeline. http://www.washingtonpost.com/business/economy/keystone-xl-pipeline-expansion-driven-by-oil-rich-tar-sands-in-alberta/2012/06/30/gJQAVe4ZEW_story_3.html Don't look for ways to lessen the exploration and production costs of oil, look for opportunities to replace oil with natural gas and renewables. This a great article from Scientific American about the detrimental environmental effects of Tar Sand exploration and refining: http://www.scientificamerican.com/article.cfm?id=tar-sands-and-keystone-xl-pipeline-impact-on-global-warming&WT.mc_id=SA_sharetool_Twitter
IS.48:20				20Go forth from Babylon, flee from Chaldea! With shouts of joy declare this, announce it; Make it known to the ends of the earth, Say: "The LORD has redeemed his servant Jacob.		
JER.50:8				8Shout against her round about: she hath given her hand: her foundations are fallen, her walls are thrown down: for it is the vengeance of the LORD: take vengeance upon her; as she hath done, do unto her.	8Flee from the midst of Babylon, leave the land of the Chaldeans, be like rams at the head of the flock.g	
JER.51:9				9"We have tried to heal Babylon, but she cannot be healed. Leave her, each of us must go to our own land." The judgment against her reaches the heavens, it touches the clouds.g		Mushroom cloud from explosion. Smoke of fires reaching the clouds overhead.

SCRIPTURE NUMBER	BEGIN DATE	DAYS (END - BEGIN DATES)	END DATE	SCRIPTURE	BIBLICAL NOTES	COMMENTARY
JER.50:15				15raise the war cry against it on every side. It surrenders, its bastions fall, its walls are torn down:* This is retribution from the LORD! Take retribution on her, as she has done, do to her; for she sinned against the LORD.l	* [50:15] Its walls are torn down: the prophet describes the downfall of Babylon in conventional language. Babylon surrendered peacefully to the Persians in 539 B.C.	**Impenitent Sin**: **Isaiah 24:5-6** 5 The earth is polluted because of its inhabitants, for they have transgressed laws, violated statutes, broken the ancient covenant.* d 6Therefore a curse devours the earth, and its inhabitants pay for their guilt; **Rev.1:7-8** 7Behold, he is coming amid the clouds, and every eye will see him, even those who pierced him. All the peoples of the earth will lament him. Yes. Amen.f 8"I am the Alpha and the Omega,"* says the Lord God, "the one who is and who was and who is to come, the almighty."g **Rev.1:18** 18the one who lives. Once I was dead, but now I am alive forever and ever. I hold the keys to death and the netherworld.* **Rev.11:18** 18The nations raged, but your wrath has come, and the time for the dead to be judged, and to recompense your servants, the prophets, and the holy ones and those who fear your name, the small and the great alike, and **to destroy those who destroy the earth.**"g
JER.16:18				18I will at once repay them double for their crime and their sin because they profaned my land with the corpses of their detestable idols, and filled my heritage with their abominations.m		
IS.47:8-9				8Now hear this, voluptuous one, enthroned securely, Saying in your heart, "I, and no one else!* I shall never be a widow, bereft of my children"—9Both these things shall come to you suddenly, in a single day: Complete bereavement and widowhood shall come upon you Despite your many sorceries and the full power of your spells;*	* [47:8, 10] I, and no one else: Babylon is mockingly presented as making the same claim as the Lord (cf. 45:6, 14, 22; 46:9), a claim that events will soon prove to be false and foolish (v. 11). * [47:9-13, 15] Babylon was known for its sorcery and astrology.	

SCRIPTURE NUMBER	BEGIN DATE	DAYS (END - BEGIN DATES)	END DATE	SCRIPTURE	BIBLICAL NOTES	COMMENTARY
REV. 18:8-11				8Therefore, her plagues will come in one day, pestilence, grief, and famine; she will be consumed by fire. For mighty is the Lord God who judges her." 9The kings of the earth who had intercourse with her in their wantonness will weep and mourn over her when they see the smoke of her pyre. 10They will keep their distance for fear of the torment inflicted on her, and they will say: "Alas, alas, great city, Babylon, mighty city. In one hour your judgment has come." 11The merchants of the earth will weep and mourn for her, because there will be no more markets* for their cargo:	* [18:11] Ironically, the merchants weep not so much for Babylon-Rome, but for their lost markets; cf. Ez 27:36.	10They will keep their distance for fear of the torment inflicted on her, and they will say: "Alas, alas, great city, Babylon, mighty city. In one hour your judgment has come." A double entendre. Both figurative and literal meanings: Keeping their distance meaning "no association". Keeping their distance due to proximate harm. (heat, radiation, flooding, etc.)
REV. 18:12-15				12their cargo of gold, silver, precious stones, and pearls; fine linen, purple silk, and scarlet cloth; fragrant wood of every kind, all articles of ivory and all articles of the most expensive wood, bronze, iron, and marble; 13cinnamon, spice,* incense, myrrh, and frankincense; wine, olive oil, fine flour, and wheat; cattle and sheep, horses and chariots, and slaves, that is, human beings. 14"The fruit you craved has left you. All your luxury and splendor are gone, never again will one find them."h 15The merchants who deal in these goods, who grew rich from her, will keep their distance for fear of the torment inflicted on her. Weeping and mourning,	* [18:13] Spice: an unidentified spice plant called in Greek amōmon.	
HOS.10:5				5The inhabitants of Samaria are afraid for the calf of Beth aven;* Its people mourn for it and its idolatrous priests wail over it, —over its glory which has departed from it.bEdition.	* [10:5] The calf of Beth-aven: see note on 4:15.	
AM:6-7				"7Therefore, now they shall be the first to go into exile, and the carousing of those who lounged shall cease.		

SCRIPTURE NUMBER	BEGIN DATE	DAYS (END - BEGIN DATES)	END DATE	SCRIPTURE	BIBLICAL NOTES	COMMENTARY
REV. 18:16-19				16they cry out: "Alas, alas, great city, wearing fine linen, purple and scarlet, adorned [in] gold, precious stones, and pearls.i 17In one hour this great wealth has been ruined." Every captain of a ship, every traveler at sea, sailors, and seafaring merchants stood at a distance 18and cried out when they saw the smoke of her pyre, "What city could compare with the great city?" 19j They threw dust on their heads and cried out, weeping and mourning: "Alas, alas, great city, in which all who had ships at sea grew rich from her wealth. In one hour she has been ruined.		
EZ.27:27-32				27Your wealth, your goods, your wares, your sailors, your crew, The caulkers of your seams, those who traded for your goods, All the warriors with you, the whole crowd with you Sank into the heart of the sea on the day of your downfall.k 28At the sound of your sailors' shouts the waves shudder,l 29Down from their ships come all who ply the oars; Sailors, all the seafaring crew, stand on the shore. 30They raise their voices over you and shout their bitter cries; They pour dust on their heads and cover themselves with ashes. 31For you they shave their heads bald and put on sackcloth; For you they weep bitterly, in anguished lament.m 32They raise a lament for you; they wail over you: "Who was ever destroyed like Tyre in the midst of the sea?"n		

SCRIPTURE NUMBER	BEGIN DATE	DAYS (END - BEGIN DATES)	END DATE	SCRIPTURE	BIBLICAL NOTES	COMMENTARY
REV.18:20-22				20Rejoice over her, heaven, you holy ones, apostles, and prophets. For God has judged your case against her."k 21A mighty angel picked up a stone like a huge millstone and threw it into the sea and said: "With such force will Babylon the great city be thrown down, and will never be found again.l 22No melodies of harpists and musicians, flutists and trumpeters, will ever be heard in you again. No craftsmen in any trade will ever be found in you again. No sound of the millstone will ever be heard in you again.m		
DT.32:43				43Exult with him, you heavens, bow to him, all you divine beings! For he will avenge the blood of his servants, take vengeance on his foes; He will requite those who hate him, and purge his people's land.c		
JER.51:63				63When you have finished reading this scroll, tie a stone to it and throw it into the Euphrates,d 64and say: Thus Babylon shall sink. It will never rise, because of the disaster I am bringing upon it." Thus far the words of Jeremiah.		
EZ.26:21				21I will make you a horror, and you shall be no more; You shall be sought for, but never found again— oracle of the Lord GOD.		
IS.24:8				8Stilled are the cheerful timbrels, ended the shouts of the jubilant, stilled the cheerful harp.g		
EZ.26:13				13I will bring an end to the noise of your songs; the music of your lyres will be heard no more.		
REV.18:23-24				23No light from a lamp will ever be seen in you again. No voices of bride and groom will ever be heard in you again. Because your merchants were the great ones of the world, all nations were led astray by your magic potion.n 24In her was found the blood of prophets and holy ones and all who have been slain on the earth."o		"Magic Potion" is oil and its derivatives.

SCRIPTURE NUMBER	BEGIN DATE	DAYS (END - BEGIN DATES)	END DATE	SCRIPTURE	BIBLICAL NOTES	COMMENTARY
JER.7:34				34I will silence the cry of joy, the cry of gladness, the voice of the bridegroom and the voice of the bride, in the cities of Judah and in the streets of Jerusalem; for the land will be turned to rubble.w		
JER.16:9				9For thus says the LORD of hosts, the God of Israel: Before your eyes and in your lifetime, I will silence in this place the song of joy and the song of gladness, the song of the bridegroom and the song of the bride.e		
JER.25:10				10Among them I will put to an end the song of joy and the song of gladness, the voice of the bridegroom and the voice of the bride, the sound of the millstone and the light of the lamp.	* [25:1–14] The fourth year of Jehoiakim: 605 B.C. Officially, the first year of Nebuchadnezzar began the following year; but as early as his victory over Egypt at Carchemish in 605, Nebuchadnezzar wielded dominant power in the Near East. Jeremiah saw in him the fulfillment of his prophecy of the enemy to come from the north (cf. 1:13; 6:22–24). In vv. 11–12 the prophecy of the seventy years' exile occurs for the first time; cf. 29:10. This number signifies that the present generation must die out; cf. forty in the exodus tradition (Nm 14:20–23).	
REV. 19:1-4				1After this I heard what sounded like the loud voice of a great multitude in heaven, saying: "Alleluia!* Salvation, glory, and might belong to our God, 2for true and just are his judgments. He has condemned the great harlot who corrupted the earth with her harlotry. He has avenged on her the blood of his servants."a 3They said a second time: "Alleluia! Smoke will rise from her forever and ever."b 4The twenty-four elders and the four living creatures fell down and worshiped God who sat on the throne, saying, "Amen. Alleluia."	* [19:1, 3, 4, 6] Alleluia: found only here in the New Testament, this frequent exclamation of praise in the Hebrew psalms was important in Jewish liturgy.	

SCRIPTURE NUMBER	BEGIN DATE	DAYS (END - BEGIN DATES)	END DATE	SCRIPTURE	BIBLICAL NOTES	COMMENTARY
DN.3:27				27For you are just in all you have done; all your deeds are faultless, all your ways right, and all your judgments proper. .	* [3:24–90] These verses are additions to the Aramaic text of Daniel, translated from the Greek form of the book. They were probably first composed in Hebrew or Aramaic, but are no longer extant in the original language. The Roman Catholic Church has always regarded them as part of the canonical Scriptures..	
JER.51:48:49				Jeremiah 51:48 Then the heaven and the earth, and all that is therein, shall sing for Babylon: for the spoilers shall come unto her from the north, saith the LORD. Jeremiah 51:49 As Babylon hath caused the slain of Israel to fall, so at Babylon shall fall the slain of all the earth.	48Then heaven and earth and everything in them shall shout over Babylon with joy, when the destroyers come against her from the north—oracle of the LORD.x 49Babylon, too, must fall, you slain of Israel, because by the hand of Babylon the slain of all the earth have fallen.	
IS.34:10				10It shall not be quenched night nor day; the smoke thereof shall go up for ever: from generation to generation it shall lie waste; none shall pass through it for ever and ever.	* [34:1–35:10] These two chapters form a small collection which looks forward to the vindication of Zion, first by defeat of its enemies (chap. 34), then by its restoration (chap. 35). They are generally judged to be later than the time of Isaiah (eighth century), perhaps during the Babylonian exile or thereafter; they are strongly influenced by Deutero-Isaiah (sixth century). In places they reflect themes from other parts of the Isaian collection.	
REV. 19:5-8				The Victory Song.* 5A voice coming from the throne said: "Praise our God, all you his servants, [and] you who revere him, small and great."c 6Then I heard something like the sound of a great multitude or the sound of rushing water or mighty peals of thunder, as they said: "Alleluia! The Lord has established his reign, [our] God, the almighty. 7Let us rejoice and be glad and give him glory. For the wedding day of the Lamb* has come, his bride has made herself ready.d 8She was allowed to wear a bright, clean linen garment."e (The linen represents the righteous deeds of the holy ones.)*	* [19:5–10] A victory song follows, sung by the entire church, celebrating the marriage of the Lamb, the union of the Messiah with the community of the elect. * [19:7] The wedding day of the Lamb: symbol of God's reign about to begin (Rev 21:1–22:5); see note on Rev 10:7. His bride: the church; cf. 2 Cor 11:2; Eph 5:22–27. Marriage is one of the biblical metaphors used to describe the covenant relationship between God and his people; cf. Hos 2:16–22; Is 54:5–6; 62:5; Ez 16:6–14. Hence, idolatry and apostasy are viewed as adultery and harlotry (Hos 2:4–13; Ez 16:15–63); see note on Rev 14:4.	"The entire church" are the 7 churches as one. "The elect" are those who God selects for divine mercy or favor, especially for salvation. "Marriage is one of the biblical metaphors used to describe the covenant relationship between God and His People." Uniting the Covenants would be the Covenants of the Old Testament and The New Covenant in Christianity as described in Jer.31:31-34 and Heb.10:11-18 and with acceptance of the Messiah, as such.
PS.115:13				13Will bless those who fear the LORD, small and great alike.		

SCRIPTURE NUMBER	BEGIN DATE	DAYS (END - BEGIN DATES)	END DATE	SCRIPTURE	BIBLICAL NOTES	COMMENTARY
MT.22:11-12				11* But when the king came in to meet the guests he saw a man there not dressed in a wedding garment. 12He said to him, 'My friend, how is it that you came in here without a wedding garment?' But he was reduced to silence.	* [22:11] A wedding garment: the repentance, change of heart and mind, that is the condition for entrance into the kingdom (Mt 3:2; 4:17) must be continued in a life of good deeds (Mt 7:21–23).	
REV. 19:9-10				9Then the angel said to me, "Write this: Blessed* are those who have been called to the wedding feast of the Lamb." And he said to me, "These words are true; they come from God."f 10I fell at his feet to worship him. But he said to me, "Don't! I am a fellow servant of yours and of your brothers who bear witness to Jesus. Worship God.g Witness to Jesus is the spirit of prophecy."*	* [19:9] Blessed: see note on Rev 1:3. * [19:10] The spirit of prophecy: as the prophets were inspired to proclaim God's word, so the Christian is called to give witness to the Word of God (Rev 19:13) made flesh; cf. Rev 1:2; 6:9; 12:17.	
MT.8:11				11d I say to you,* many will come from the east and the west, and will recline with Abraham, Isaac, and Jacob at the banquet in the kingdom of heaven,	* [8:11–12] Matthew inserts into the story a Q saying (see Lk 13:28–29) about the entrance of Gentiles into the kingdom and the exclusion of those Israelites who, though descended from the patriarchs and members of the chosen nation (the children of the kingdom), refused to believe in Jesus. There will be wailing and grinding of teeth: the first occurrence of a phrase used frequently in this gospel to describe final condemnation (Mt 13:42, 50; 22:13; 24:51; 25:30). It is found elsewhere in the New Testament only in Lk 13:28.	
LK.14:15				15One of his fellow guests on hearing this said to him, "Blessed is the one who will dine in the kingdom of God."	* [14:15–24] The parable of the great dinner is a further illustration by Luke of the rejection by Israel, God's chosen people, of Jesus' invitation to share in the banquet in the kingdom and the extension of the invitation to other Jews whose identification as the poor, crippled, blind, and lame (Lk 14:21) classifies them among those who recognize their need for salvation, and to Gentiles (Lk 14:23). A similar parable is found in Mt 22:1–10.	

SCRIPTURE NUMBER	BEGIN DATE	DAYS (END - BEGIN DATES)	END DATE	SCRIPTURE	BIBLICAL NOTES	COMMENTARY
REV.19:11-14				The King of Kings. 11* Then I saw the heavens opened, and there was a white horse; its rider was [called] "Faithful and True." He judges and wages war in righteousness.h 12His eyes were [like] a fiery flame, and on his head were many diadems. He had a name* inscribed that no one knows except himself.i 13He wore a cloak that had been dipped in* blood, and his name was called the Word of God.j 14The armies of heaven followed him, mounted on white horses and wearing clean white linen.k	* [19:11–16] Symbolic description of the exalted Christ (cf. Rev 1:13–16) who together with the armies of heaven overcomes the beast and its followers; cf. Rev 17:14. * [19:12] A name: in Semitic thought, the name conveyed the reality of the person; cf. Mt 11:27; Lk 10:22. * [19:13] Had been dipped in: other Greek manuscripts and versions read "had been sprinkled with"; cf. Rev 19:15. The Word of God: Christ is the revelation of the Father; cf. Jn 1:1, 14; 1 Jn 2:14.	The "White Horse" is the Sikorsky VH-60N "WhiteHawk" Marine One Helicopter. The motto of the U.S. Marine Corp is "Semper Fidelis" which means "Always Faithful". See commentary from Rev.9:5-8 for the comparison of horses to helicopters from the history of the U.S. Army 7th Calvary. Dictionary.com defines "Fidelity" as 1.strict observance of promises, duties, etc. 2.loyalty: 3.conjugal faithfulness. 4.adherence to fact or detail. 5.accuracy; exactness.
IS.11:4				4But he shall judge the poor with justice, and decide fairly for the land's afflicted.c He shall strike the ruthless with the rod of his mouth, and with the breath of his lips he shall slay the wicked.d	* [11:1–16] Isaiah 11 contains a prophecy of the rise of a new Davidic king who will embody the ancient ideal of Davidic kingship (vv. 1–9), an elaboration of that prophecy in a further description of that king's rule (v. 10), and a prophecy of God's deliverance of the chosen people from exile and cessation of enmities (vv. 11–16). * [11:1–9 (10)] Here Isaiah looks forward to a new Davidide who will realize the ancient ideals (see Ps 72). The oracle does not seem to have a particular historical person in mind.	This scripture describes my relentless attacks against the Tea Party, using the Word of God.
LK.10:22				22All things have been handed over to me by my Father. No one knows who the Son is except the Father, and who the Father is except the Son and anyone to whom the Son wishes to reveal him."u		
IS.63:1				1Who is this that comes from Edom, in crimsoned garments, from Bozrah? Who is this, glorious in his apparel, striding in the greatness of his strength? "It is I, I who announce vindication, mighty to save."a	* [63:1–6] Two questions are raised at the approach of a majestic figure coming from Edom. It is the Lord, his garments red with the blood from the judgment battle. Edom (its capital Bozrah) plundered Judah after the fall of Jerusalem; cf. 34:5–17. Wine press: here a symbol of a bloody judgment; cf. Lam 1:15; Jl 4:13.	

SCRIPTURE NUMBER	BEGIN DATE	DAYS (END - BEGIN DATES)	END DATE	SCRIPTURE	BIBLICAL NOTES	COMMENTARY
JN.1:1				1In the beginning* was the Word, and the Word was with God, and the Word was God.a	* [1:1] In the beginning: also the first words of the Old Testament (Gn 1:1). Was: this verb is used three times with different meanings in this verse: existence, relationship, and predication. The Word (Greek logos): this term combines God's dynamic, creative word (Genesis), personified preexistent Wisdom as the instrument of God's creative activity (Proverbs), and the ultimate intelligibility of reality (Hellenistic philosophy). With God. the Greek preposition here connotes communication with another. Was God: lack of a definite article with "God" in Greek signifies predication rather than identification.	
REV. 19:15-18				15Out of his mouth came a sharp sword to strike the nations. He will rule them with an iron rod, and he himself will tread out in the wine press* the wine of the fury and wrath of God the almighty.l 16He has a name written on his cloak and on his thigh, "King of kings and Lord of lords."m 17* Then I saw an angel standing on the sun. He cried out [in] a loud voice to all the birds flying high overhead, "Come here. Gather for God's great feast, 18to eat the flesh of kings, the flesh of military officers, and the flesh of warriors, the flesh of horses and of their riders, and the flesh of all, free and slave, small and great."n	* [19:17–21] The certainty of Christ's victory is proclaimed by an angel, followed by a reference to the mustering of enemy forces and a fearsome description of their annihilation. The gruesome imagery is borrowed from Ez 39:4, 17–20.	
IS.63:3				3"The wine press I have trodden alone, and from the peoples no one was with me. I trod them in my anger, and trampled them down in my wrath; Their blood spurted on my garments, all my apparel I stained.	* [63:1–6] Two questions are raised at the approach of a majestic figure coming from Edom. It is the Lord, his garments red with the blood from the judgment battle. Edom (its capital Bozrah) plundered Judah after the fall of Jerusalem; cf. 34:5–17. Wine press: here a symbol of a bloody judgment; cf. Lam 1:15; Jl 4:13.	
2MAC.13:4				4But the King of kingsb aroused the anger of Antiochus against the scoundrel. When the king was shown by Lysias that Menelaus was to blame for all the trouble, he ordered him to be taken to Beroea* and executed there in the customary local method.	* [13:4] Beroea: the Greek name of Aleppo in Syria.	

SCRIPTURE NUMBER	BEGIN DATE	DAYS (END - BEGIN DATES)	END DATE	SCRIPTURE	BIBLICAL NOTES	COMMENTARY
EZ.39:17-20				17As for you, son of man, thus says the Lord GOD: Say to birds of every kind and to every wild beast: "Assemble! Come from all sides for the sacrifice I am making for you, a great slaughter on the mountains of Israel. You shall eat flesh and drink blood! 18You shall eat the flesh of warriors and drink the blood of the princes of the earth: rams, lambs, and goats, bulls and fatlings from Bashan, all of them.g 19From the sacrifice I slaughtered for you, you shall eat fat until you are sated and drink blood until you are drunk. 20At my table you shall be sated with horse and rider, with warrior and soldier of every kind—oracle of the Lord GOD.		
REV. 19:19-21				19Then I saw the beast and the kings of the earth and their armies gathered to fight against the one riding the horse and against his army. 20The beast was caught and with it the false prophet* who had performed in its sight the signs by which he led astray those who had accepted the mark of the beast and those who had worshiped its image. The two were thrown alive into the fiery pool burning with sulfur.o 21The rest were killed by the sword that came out of the mouth of the one riding the horse, and all the birds gorged themselves on their flesh.	* [19:20] Beast…false prophet: see notes on Rev 13. The fiery pool…sulfur: symbol of God's punishment (Rev 14:10; 20:10, 14–15), different from the abyss; see note on Rev 9:1.	

SCRIPTURE NUMBER	BEGIN DATE	DAYS (END - BEGIN DATES)	END DATE	SCRIPTURE	BIBLICAL NOTES	COMMENTARY
REV.20:1-4				The Thousand-year Reign. 1* Then I saw an angel come down from heaven, holding in his hand the key to the abyss* and a heavy chain.a 2He seized the dragon, the ancient serpent, which is the Devil or Satan,* and tied it up for a thousand yearsb 3and threw it into the abyss, which he locked over it and sealed, so that it could no longer lead the nations astray until the thousand years are completed. After this, it is to be released for a short time. 4Then I saw thrones; those who sat on them were entrusted with judgment. I also saw the souls of those who had been beheaded for their witness to Jesus and for the word of God, and who had not worshiped the beast or its image nor had accepted its mark* on their foreheads or hands. They came to life and they reigned with Christ for a thousand years.c	* [20:1–6] Like the other numerical values in this book, the thousand years are not to be taken literally; they symbolize the long period of time between the chaining up of Satan (a symbol for Christ's resurrection-victory over death and the forces of evil) and the end of the world. During this time God's people share in the glorious reign of God that is present to them by virtue of their baptismal victory over death and sin; cf. Rom 6:1–8; Jn 5:24–25; 16:33; 1 Jn 3:14, Eph 2:1. * [20:1] Abyss: see note on Rev 9:1. * [20:2] Dragon...serpent...Satan: see notes on Rev 12:3, 9, 10, 15. * [20:4] Beast...mark: see Rev 13 and its notes.	From a symbolic standpoint, I agree that 1,000 represents immensity and the long period from the time between the chaining up of Satan (from the 2nd Coming of Christ-victory over death and the forces of evil) and the 2nd Judgement. From a literal and symbolic standpoint, the 1,000 years can represent the time that the Dragon is confined to the abyss: The oil wells are all capped in the next few decades. The coal mines are sealed. Eventually, most of the gas wells are capped when energy is completely renewable. All of this for 1,000 years. It may very well take 1,000 years to get our environment back to where it was in pre-1900 times. See Notes Rev. 9:1 for a description of the abyss and See Rev. 22-18,19 regarding content of the Book of Revelation.
GN.3:1				1Now the snake was the most cunning* of all the wild animals that the LORD God had made. He asked the woman, "Did God really say, 'You shall not eat from any of the trees in the garden'?"	* [3:1] Cunning: there is a play on the words for "naked" (2:25) and "cunning/wise" (Heb. 'arum). The couple seek to be "wise" but end up knowing that they are "naked."	

SCRIPTURE NUMBER	BEGIN DATE	DAYS (END - BEGIN DATES)	END DATE	SCRIPTURE	BIBLICAL NOTES	COMMENTARY
MT.19:28				28* n Jesus said to them, "Amen, I say to you that you who have followed me, in the new age, when the Son of Man is seated on his throne of glory, will yourselves sit on twelve thrones, judging the twelve tribes of Israel.	* [19:28] This saying, directed to the Twelve, is from Q; see Lk 22:29–30. The new age: the Greek word here translated "new age" occurs in the New Testament only here and in Ti 3:5. Literally, it means "rebirth" or "regeneration," and is used in Titus of spiritual rebirth through baptism. Here it means the "rebirth" effected by the coming of the kingdom. Since that coming has various stages (see notes on Mt 3:2; 4:17), the new age could be taken as referring to the time after the resurrection when the Twelve will govern the true Israel, i.e., the church of Jesus. (For "judge" in the sense of "govern," cf. Jgs 12:8, 9, 11; 15:20; 16:31; Ps 2:10). But since it is connected here with the time when the Son of Man will be seated on his throne of glory, language that Matthew uses in Mt 25:31 for the time of final judgment, it is more likely that what the Twelve are promised is that they will be joined with Jesus then in judging the people of Israel.	
REV. 20:5-8				5The rest of the dead did not come to life until the thousand years were over. This is the first resurrection. 6Blessed* and holy is the one who shares in the first resurrection. The second death has no power over these; they will be priests of God and of Christ, and they will reign with him for [the] thousand years. 7* When the thousand years are completed, Satan will be released from his prison. 8He will go out to deceive the nations at the four corners of the earth, Gog and Magog,* to gather them for battle; their number is like the sand of the sea.d	* [20:6] Blessed: see note on Rev 1:3. Second death: see note on Rev 2:11. Priests: as in Rev 1:6; 5:10; cf. 1 Pt 2:9. * [20:7-10] A description of the symbolic battle to take place when Satan is released at the end of time, when the thousand years are over; see note on Rev 20:1–6.	With all of our discussion and definition of the dragon, the release of satan can be literally uncapping the oil and gas wells and opening the coal mines, by the forces of evil, to pollute the earth (similar to what Saddam Hussein did in Desert Storm) or for the purpose of idolatry (money and greed) or the deception that fossil fuels are a better (more efficient) source of energy.

SCRIPTURE NUMBER	BEGIN DATE	DAYS (END - BEGIN DATES)	END DATE	SCRIPTURE	BIBLICAL NOTES	COMMENTARY
EZ.38:2,9,16				2Son of man, turn your face against Gog* of the land of Magog, the chief prince of Meshech and Tubal, and prophesy against him.a 9You shall come up like a sudden storm, covering the land like a cloud, you and all your troops and the many nations with you.d 16You shall rise up over my people Israel like a cloud covering the land. In those last days, I will let you invade my land so that the nations acknowledge me, when in their sight I show my holiness through you, Gog.	* [38:2] Gog: the name is symbolic, probably derived from Gyges, king of Lydia. The gloss Magog may be an Akkadian expression, mat-Gog, "the land of Gog." Meshech and Tubal, as well as Gomer and Beth-togarmah (v. 6), were countries around the Black Sea, the northernmost countries known to the Israelites. The north was the traditional direction from which invasion was expected; cf. Jer 1:13–15.	
REV. 20:9-11				9They invaded the breadth of the earth* and surrounded the camp of the holy ones and the beloved city. But fire came down from heaven and consumed them.e 10The Devil who had led them astray was thrown into the pool of fire and sulfur, where the beast and the false prophet were. There they will be tormented day and night forever and ever. The Large White Throne.* 11Next I saw a large white throne and the one who was sitting on it. The earth and the sky fled from his presence and there was no place for them.f	* [20:8] Gog and Magog: symbols of all pagan nations; the names are taken from Ez 38:1–39:20. * [20:9] The breadth of the earth: Palestine. The beloved city: Jerusalem; see note on Rev 14:1. * [20:11-15] A description of the final judgment. After the intermediate reign of Christ, all the dead are raised and judged, thus inaugurating the new age.	"10The Devil who had led them astray was thrown into the pool of fire and sulfur, where the beast and the false prophet were." If the goal of satan is to pollute the earth by igniting the oil and gas wells, his demise would be in the same hell as the beast and the false prophet. The beloved city, then Jerusalem and now: "I Love New York"
EZ.38:22				22I will execute judgment on him: disease and bloodshed; flooding rain and hailstones, fire and brimstone, I will rain down on him, on his troops and on the many nations with him.k	* [38:1–39:20] These three oracles against Gog (38:2-13; 14-23; 39:1-20) describe a mythic attack of God against a final enemy of his people sometime in the future. Like the oracles against the nations, their purpose is to strengthen Israel's hope in God, since they end with God's triumph on behalf of the people.	

SCRIPTURE NUMBER	BEGIN DATE	DAYS (END - BEGIN DATES)	END DATE	SCRIPTURE	BIBLICAL NOTES	COMMENTARY
2PTR.3:7,10,12				7The present heavens and earth have been reserved by the same word for fire, kept for the day of judgment and of destruction of the godless.f 10But the day of the Lord will come like a thief,* and then the heavens will pass away with a mighty roar and the elements will be dissolved by fire, and the earth and everything done on it will be found out.i 12* waiting for and hastening the coming of the day of God,k because of which the heavens will be dissolved in flames and the elements melted by fire. 13But according to his promise we await new heavens and a new earth* in which righteousness dwells.l	* [3:8–10] The scoffers' objection (2 Pt 3:4) is refuted also by showing that delay of the Lord's second coming is not a failure to fulfill his word but rather a sign of his patience: God is giving time for repentance before the final judgment (cf. Wis 11:23–26; Ez 18:23; 33:11). * [3:10] Like a thief: Mt 24:43; 1 Thes 5:2; Rev 3:3. Will be found out: cf. 1 Cor 3:13–15. Some few versions read, as the sense may demand, "will not be found out"; many manuscripts read "will be burned up"; there are further variants in other manuscripts, versions, and Fathers. Total destruction is assumed (2 Pt 3:11). * [3:11–16] The second coming of Christ and the judgment of the world are the doctrinal bases for the moral exhortation to readiness through vigilance and a virtuous life; cf. Mt 24:42, 50–51; Lk 12:40; 1 Thes 5:1–11; Jude 20–21. * [3:12] Flames…fire: although this is the only New Testament passage about a final conflagration, the idea was common in apocalyptic and Greco-Roman thought. Hastening: eschatology is here used to motivate ethics (2 Pt 3:11), as elsewhere in the New Testament. Jewish sources and Acts 3:19–20 assume that proper ethical conduct can help bring the promised day of the Lord; cf. 2 Pt 3:9. Some render the phrase, however, "desiring it earnestly."	
REV. 20:12-15				12I saw the dead, the great and the lowly, standing before the throne, and scrolls were opened. Then another scroll was opened, the book of life.* The dead were judged according to their deeds, by what was written in the scrolls.g 13The sea gave up its dead; then Death and Hades* gave up their dead. All the dead were judged according to their deeds. 14h Then Death and Hades were thrown into the pool of fire. (This pool of fire is the second death.*) 15Anyone whose name was not found written in the book of life was thrown into the pool of fire.	* [20:12] The book of life: see note on Rev 3:5. Judged…scrolls: see note on Rev 14:12. * [20:13] Hades: the netherworld; see note on Rev 1:18. * [20:14] Second death: see note on Rev 2:11.	"14h Then Death and Hades were thrown into the pool of fire. (This pool of fire is the second death.*) " with the assumption that "Death and Hades" are the ones described in Rev.6:7-8, the pale green horse.

SCRIPTURE NUMBER	BEGIN DATE	DAYS (END - BEGIN DATES)	END DATE	SCRIPTURE	BIBLICAL NOTES	COMMENTARY
ROM.2:6				6e who will repay everyone according to his works:*	* [2:6] Will repay everyone according to his works: Paul reproduces the Septuagint text of Ps 62:12 and Prv 24:12.	
1COR15:26,54,55				26* The last enemym to be destroyed is death, 54* And when this which is corruptible clothes itself with incorruptibility and this which is mortal clothes itself with immortality, then the word that is written shall come about:c "Death is swallowed up in victory. 55Where, O death, is your victory? Where, O death, is your sting?"d	* [15:54–55] Death is swallowed up in victory: scripture itself predicts death's overthrow. O death: in his prophetic vision Paul may be making Hosea's words his own, or imagining this cry of triumph on the lips of the risen church.	
REV. 21:1-4				The New Heaven and the New Earth. 1a Then I saw a new heaven and a new earth. The former heaven and the former earth had passed away, and the sea was no more.* 2I also saw the holy city, a new Jerusalem,* coming down out of heaven from God, prepared as a bride adorned for her husband.b 3I heard a loud voice from the throne saying, "Behold, God's dwelling is with the human race.c He will dwell with them and they will be his people* and God himself will always be with them [as their God].* 4He will wipe every tear from their eyes, and there shall be no more death or mourning, wailing or pain, [for] the old order has passed away."d	* [21:1] Sea…no more: because as home of the dragon it was doomed to disappear; cf. Jb 7:12. * [21:2] New Jerusalem…bride: symbol of the church (Gal 4:26); see note on Rev 19:7. * [21:3–4] Language taken from Ez 37:27; Is 25:8; 35:10; cf. Rev 7:17. * [21:3] People: other ancient manuscripts read a plural, "peoples."	
IS.65:17				17* See, I am creating new heavens and a new earth; The former things shall not be remembered nor come to mind.e	* [65:17–18] The new creation (cf. 66:22) is described with apocalyptic exuberance: long life, material prosperity, and so forth. As the former events in 43:18 are to be forgotten, so also the new creation wipes out memory of the first creation.	
IS.66:22				22Just as the new heavens and the new earth which I am making Shall endure before me—oracle of the LORD— so shall your descendants and your name endure.k		

SCRIPTURE NUMBER	BEGIN DATE	DAYS (END - BEGIN DATES)	END DATE	SCRIPTURE	BIBLICAL NOTES	COMMENTARY
ROM.8:19-23				19For creation awaits with eager expectation the revelation of the children of God; 20for creation was made subject to futility, not of its own accord but because of the one who subjected it,o in hope 21that creation itself would be set free from slavery to corruption and share in the glorious freedom of the children of God.p 22We know that all creation is groaning in labor pains even until now;q 23and not only that, but we ourselves, who have the firstfruits of the Spirit, we also groan within ourselves as we wait for adoption, the redemption of our bodies.r	* [8:18–27] The glory that believers are destined to share with Christ far exceeds the sufferings of the present life. Paul considers the destiny of the created world to be linked with the future that belongs to the believers. As it shares in the penalty of corruption brought about by sin, so also will it share in the benefits of redemption and future glory that comprise the ultimate liberation of God's people (Rom 8:19–22). After patient endurance in steadfast expectation, the full harvest of the Spirit's presence will be realized. On earth believers enjoy the firstfruits, i.e., the Spirit, as a guarantee of the total liberation of their bodies from the influence of the rebellious old self (Rom 8:23).	
2PT.3:13				2PT.3:13 13But according to his promise we await new heavens and a new earth* in which righteousness dwells.l	* [3:13] New heavens and a new earth: cf. Is 65:17; 66:22. The divine promises will be fulfilled after the day of judgment will have passed. The universe will be transformed by the reign of God's righteousness or justice; cf. Is 65:17–18; Acts 3:21; Rom 8:18–25; Rev 21:1.	
EZ.37:27				27My dwelling shall be with them; I will be their God, and they will be my people.k		
IS.25:8				8He will destroy death forever. The Lord GOD will wipe away the tears from all faces; The reproach of his people he will remove from the whole earth; for the LORD has spoken.d	* [25:1–9] These verses praise God for carrying out his plan to destroy the enemy and to save the poor of his people in Zion (14:32), and they announce the victory banquet to be celebrated in the Lord's city.	
IS.35:10				10And the ransomed of the LORD shall return, and enter Zion singing, crowned with everlasting joy; They meet with joy and gladness, sorrow and mourning flee away.i	* [35:1–10] This chapter contains a number of themes similar to those in Deutero-Isaiah (chaps. 40–55), for example, the blossoming of the wilderness (vv. 1–2; cf. 41:18–19), which is now well-irrigated (v. 7; cf. 43:19–20); sight to the blind (vv. 5–6; cf. 42:7, 16); a highway in the wilderness (v. 8; cf. 41:3); and the return of the redeemed/ransomed to Zion (vv. 9–10; cf. 51:11). Nevertheless, it forms a unit with chap. 34 (see note on 34:1–35:10) and reflects, along with that chapter, themes found in chaps. 1–33.	

SCRIPTURE NUMBER	BEGIN DATE	DAYS (END - BEGIN DATES)	END DATE	SCRIPTURE	BIBLICAL NOTES	COMMENTARY
REV. 21:5-8				5The one who sat on the throne* said, "Behold, I make all things new." Then he said, "Write these words down, for they are trustworthy and true."e 6He said to me, "They are accomplished.* I [am] the Alpha and the Omega, the beginning and the end. To the thirsty I will give a gift from the spring of life-giving water.f 7The victor* will inherit these gifts, and I shall be his God, and he will be my son.g 8But as for cowards,* the unfaithful, the depraved, murderers, the unchaste, sorcerers, idol-worshipers, and deceivers of every sort, their lot is in the burning pool of fire and sulfur, which is the second death."h	* [21:5] The one...on the throne: God himself; cf. Rev 4:1–11. * [21:6] They are accomplished: God's reign has already begun; see note on Rev 20:1–6. Alpha...Omega: see note on Rev 1:8. Life-giving water: see note on Rev 7:17. * [21:7] The victor: over the forces of evil; see the conclusions of the seven letters (Rev 2:7, 11, 17, 26; 3:5, 12, 21). He will be my son: the victorious Christian enjoys divine affiliation by adoption (Gal 4:4–7; Rom 8:14–17); see note on Rev 2:26–28.	
IS.43:19				19See, I am doing something new! Now it springs forth, do you not perceive it? In the wilderness I make a way, in the wasteland, rivers.		
2COR.5:17				17k So whoever is in Christ is a new creation: the old things have passed away; behold, new things have come.	* [5:16–17] Consequently: the death of Christ described in 2 Cor 5:14–15 produces a whole new order (2 Cor 5:17) and a new mode of perception (2 Cor 5:16). According to the flesh: the natural mode of perception, characterized as "fleshly," is replaced by a mode of perception proper to the Spirit. Elsewhere Paul contrasts what Christ looks like according to the old criteria (weakness, powerlessness, folly, death) and according to the new (wisdom, power, life); cf. 2 Cor 5:15, 21; 1 Cor 1:17–3:3. Similarly, he describes the paradoxical nature of Christian existence, e.g., in 2 Cor 4:10–11, 14. A new creation: rabbis used this expression to describe the effect of the entrance of a proselyte or convert into Judaism or of the remission of sins on the Day of Atonement. The new order created in Christ is the new covenant (2 Cor 3:6).	
PS.36:8-9				8How precious is your mercy, O God! The children of Adam take refuge in the shadow of your wings.*d 9They feast on the rich food of your house; from your delightful streame you give them drink.	* [36:8] The shadow of your wings: metaphor for divine protection. It probably refers to the winged cherubim in the holy of holies in the Temple, cf. 1 Kgs 6:23–28, 32; 2 Chr 3:10–13; Ez 1:4–9.	

SCRIPTURE NUMBER	BEGIN DATE	DAYS (END - BEGIN DATES)	END DATE	SCRIPTURE	BIBLICAL NOTES	COMMENTARY
IS.55:1				1All you who are thirsty,* come to the water! You who have no money, come, buy grain and eat; Come, buy grain without money, wine and milk without cost!a	* [55:1–3] The prophet invites all to return, under the figure of a banquet; cf. the covenant banquet in Ex 24:9–11 and wisdom's banquet in Prv 9:1–6. The Lord's covenant with David (2 Sm 7) is now to be extended beyond his dynasty.	
2SAM.7:14				14I will be a father to him, and he shall be a son to me. If he does wrong, I will reprove him with a human rod and with human punishments;j		
ROM.1:29-32				29y They are filled with every form of wickedness, evil, greed, and malice; full of envy, murder, rivalry, treachery, and spite. They are gossips 30and scandalmongers and they hate God. They are insolent, haughty, boastful, ingenious in their wickedness, and rebellious toward their parents. 31They are senseless, faithless, heartless, ruthless. 32Although they know the just decree of God that all who practice such things deserve death, they not only do them but give approval to those who practice them.z		
REV. 21:9-13				The New Jerusalem.* 9One of the seven angels who held the seven bowls filled with the seven last plagues came and said to me, "Come here. I will show you the bride, the wife of the Lamb."* 10He took me in spirit to a great, high mountain and showed me the holy city Jerusalem coming down out of heaven from God.i 11It gleamed with the splendor of God. Its radiance was like that of a precious stone, like jasper, clear as crystal.j 12It had a massive, high wall, with twelve gates where twelve angels were stationed and on which names were inscribed, [the names] of the twelve tribes of the Israelites. 13There were three gates facing east, three north, three south, and three west.k	* [21:8] Cowards: their conviction is so weak that they deny Christ in time of trial and become traitors. Second death: see note on Rev 2:11. * [21:9–22:5] Symbolic descriptions of the new Jerusalem, the church. Most of the images are borrowed from Ez 40–48. * [21:9] The bride, the wife of the Lamb: the church (Rev 21:2), the new Jerusalem (Rev 21:10); cf. 2 Cor 11:2.	"11It gleamed with the splendor of God. Its radiance was like that of a precious stone, like jasper, clear as crystal.j" New York City at night, particularly Times Square.

SCRIPTURE NUMBER	BEGIN DATE	DAYS (END - BEGIN DATES)	END DATE	SCRIPTURE	BIBLICAL NOTES	COMMENTARY
EZ.40:2				2In a divine vision he brought me to the land of Israel, where he set me down on a very high mountain. In front of me, there was something like a city built on it.b	* [40:1–48:35] This lengthy vision of a new Temple and a restored Israel is dated in v. 1 to April 28, 573 B.C. The literary form of the vision is sometimes compared to a mandala, a sacred model through which one can move symbolically to reach the world of the divine. Ezekiel describes the Temple through its boundaries, entrances, and exits in chaps. 40–43; by its sacred and profane use and space in 44–46; and by its central place within the land itself in 47–48. The prophet could not have expected a literal fulfillment of much of what he described. The passage doubtless went through several editorial stages, both from the prophet and from later writers.	
HEB.11:10				10for he was looking forward to the city with foundations, whose architect and maker is God.i		
EZ.48:31-35				31the gates are named after the tribes of Israel—on the north, three gates: the gate of Reuben, one; the gate of Judah, one; and the gate of Levi, one. 32On the east side, measuring forty-five hundred cubits, three gates: the gate of Joseph, one; the gate of Benjamin, one; and the gate of Dan, one. 33On the south side, measuring forty-five hundred cubits, three gates: the gate of Simeon, one; the gate of Issachar, one; and the gate of Zebulun, one. 34On the west side, measuring forty-five hundred cubits, three gates: the gate of Gad, one; the gate of Asher, one; and the gate of Naphtali, one.m 35The circuit of the city shall be eighteen thousand cubits. From now on the name of the city is "The LORD is there."thousand cubits.		

SCRIPTURE NUMBER	BEGIN DATE	DAYS (END - BEGIN DATES)	END DATE	SCRIPTURE	BIBLICAL NOTES	COMMENTARY
REV. 21:14-17				14The wall of the city had twelve courses of stones as its foundation, on which were inscribed the twelve names of the twelve apostles* of the Lamb.l 15* The one who spoke to me held a gold measuring rod to measure the city, its gates, and its wall. 16The city was square, its length the same as [also] its width. He measured the city with the rod and found it fifteen hundred miles* in length and width and height. 17He also measured its wall: one hundred and forty-four cubits* according to the standard unit of measurement the angel used.	* [21:14] Courses of stones...apostles: literally, "twelve foundations"; cf. Eph 2:19–20. * [21:15–17] The city is shaped like a gigantic cube, a symbol of perfection (cf. 1 Kgs 6:19–20). The measurements of the city and its wall are multiples of the symbolic number twelve; see note on Rev 7:4–9. * [21:16] Fifteen hundred miles: literally, twelve thousand stades, about 12,000 furlongs (see note on Rev 14:20); the number is symbolic: twelve (the apostles as leaders of the new Israel) multiplied by 1,000 (the immensity of Christians); cf. Introduction. In length and width and height: literally, "its length and width and height are the same." * [21:17] One hundred and forty-four cubits: the cubit was about eighteen inches in length. Standard unit of measurement the angel used: literally, "by a human measure, i.e., an angel's."	Fifteen hundred miles* in length and width and height could be a sphere.
EPH.2:20				20built upon the foundation of the apostles and prophets,r with Christ Jesus himself as the capstone.*	* [2:20] Capstone: the Greek can also mean cornerstone or keystone.	
REV. 21:18-21				18* The wall was constructed of jasper, while the city was pure gold, clear as glass. 19The foundations of the city wall were decorated with every precious stone; the first course of stones was jasper, the second sapphire, the third chalcedony, the fourth emerald,m 20the fifth sardonyx, the sixth carnelian, the seventh chrysolite, the eighth beryl, the ninth topaz, the tenth chrysoprase, the eleventh hyacinth, and the twelfth amethyst. 21The twelve gates were twelve pearls, each of the gates made from a single pearl; and the street of the city was of pure gold, transparent as glass.	* [21:18–21] The gold and precious gems symbolize the beauty and excellence of the church; cf. Ex 28:15–21; Tb 13:16–17; Is 54:11–12.	Think about the electronic video screens / billboards in Times Square. That could very well be the vision.

SCRIPTURE NUMBER	BEGIN DATE	DAYS (END - BEGIN DATES)	END DATE	SCRIPTURE	BIBLICAL NOTES	COMMENTARY
IS.54:11-12				11O afflicted one,* storm-battered and unconsoled, I lay your pavements in carnelians, your foundations in sapphires;f 12I will make your battlements of rubies, your gates of jewels, and all your walls of precious stones.	* [54:11] Afflicted one: Jerusalem. .	
REV. 21:22-27				22* n I saw no temple in the city, for its temple is the Lord God almighty and the Lamb. 23* The city had no need of sun or moon to shine on it,o for the glory of God gave it light, and its lamp was the Lamb. 24The nations will walk by its light,* and to it the kings of the earth will bring their treasure.p 25During the day its gates will never be shut, and there will be no night there. 26The treasure and wealth of the nations will be brought there, 27but nothing unclean will enter it, nor any[one] who does abominable things or tells lies. Only those will enter whose names are written in the Lamb's book of life.q	* [21:22] Christ is present throughout the church; hence, no temple is needed as an earthly dwelling for God; cf. Mt 18:20; 28:20; Jn 4:21. * [21:23] Lamp...Lamb: cf. Jn 8:12. * [21:24–27] All men and women of good will are welcome in the church; cf. Is 60:1, 3, 5, 11. The...book of life: see note on Rev 3:5.	
JN.2:19-20				19Jesus answered and said to them,* k "Destroy this temple and in three days I will raise it up." 20The Jews said, "This temple has been under construction for forty-six years,* and you will raise it up in three days?"	* [2:19] This saying about the destruction of the temple occurs in various forms (Mt 24:2; 27:40; Mk 13:2; 15:29; Lk 21:6; cf. Acts 6:14). Mt 26:61 has: "I can destroy the temple of God..."; see note there. In Mk 14:58, there is a metaphorical contrast with a new temple: "I will destroy this temple made with hands and within three days I will build another not made with hands." Here it is symbolic of Jesus' resurrection and the resulting community (see Jn 2:21 and Rev 21:2). In three days: an Old Testament expression for a short, indefinite period of time; cf. Hos 6:2. * [2:20] Forty-six years: based on references in Josephus (Jewish Wars 1, 21, 1 #401; Antiquities 15, 11, 1 #380), possibly the spring of A.D. 28. Cf. note on Lk 3:1.	

SCRIPTURE NUMBER	BEGIN DATE	DAYS (END - BEGIN DATES)	END DATE	SCRIPTURE	BIBLICAL NOTES	COMMENTARY
IS.60:1-2				1* Arise! Shine, for your light has come, the glory of the LORD has dawned upon you.a 2Though darkness covers the earth, and thick clouds, the peoples, Upon you the LORD will dawn, and over you his glory will be seen.	* [60:1–9] The light the prophet proclaims to Zion symbolizes the blessing to come to her: the glory of the Lord, the return of her children, the wealth of nations who themselves will walk by her light. The passage is famous from its use in the Latin liturgy for the feast of Epiphany.	
IS.60:19-20				19* No longer shall the sun be your light by day, Nor shall the brightness of the moon give you light by night; Rather, the LORD will be your light forever, your God will be your glory.i 20No longer will your sun set,	* [60:19–20] The theme of light is taken up again, but in an apocalyptic vein: the Lord's radiant presence replaces physical light.	
IS.60:11				11Your gates shall stand open constantly; day and night they shall not be closed So that they may bring you the wealth of nations, with their kings in the vanguard.e		
IS.35:8				8A highway will be there, called the holy way; No one unclean may pass over it, but it will be for his people; no traveler, not even fools, shall go astray on it.g	* [35:1–10] This chapter contains a number of themes similar to those in Deutero-Isaiah (chaps. 40–55), for example, the blossoming of the wilderness (vv. 1–2; cf. 41:18–19), which is now well-irrigated (v. 7; cf. 43:19–20); sight to the blind (vv. 5–6; cf. 42:7, 16); a highway in the wilderness (v. 8; cf. 41:3); and the return of the redeemed/ransomed to Zion (vv. 9–10; cf. 51:11). Nevertheless, it forms a unit with chap. 34 (see note on 34:1–35:10) and reflects, along with that chapter, themes found in chaps. 1–33.	
IS.52:1				1Awake, awake! Put on your strength, Zion; Put on your glorious garments, Jerusalem, holy city. Never again shall the uncircumcised or the unclean enter you.		

SCRIPTURE NUMBER	BEGIN DATE	DAYS (END - BEGIN DATES)	END DATE	SCRIPTURE	BIBLICAL NOTES	COMMENTARY
ZEC.13:2				2On that day—oracle of the LORD of hosts—I will destroy the names of the idols from the land, so that they will be mentioned no more; I will also remove the prophets and the spirit of uncleanness from the land.	* [13:1–6] False prophecy is a major theme of Second Zechariah (chaps. 9–14) and figures in many other passages (10:1–2; 11; 12:10). Problems of idolatry and false prophecy occurred in postexilic Judah as they had in preexilic times. The understanding of the role of the prophet as an intermediary was challenged because (1) there was no king in Jerusalem, and (2) the texts of earlier prophets were beginning to be accorded the authority of prophetic tradition.	
Is.56:6-7				6And foreigners who join themselves to the LORD, to minister to him, To love the name of the LORD, to become his servants— All who keep the sabbath without profaning it and hold fast to my covenant, 7* Them I will bring to my holy mountain and make them joyful in my house of prayer; Their burnt offerings and their sacrifices will be acceptable on my altar, For my house shall be called a house of prayer for all peoples.e	* [56:7] This verse continues the theme of universalism found in Is 49:6. As Israel was to be "a light to the nations" so that God's "salvation may reach to the ends of the earth," so now does that come to pass as foreigners, faithful to the divine commands, are brought to the Temple by God and joined to the covenant community of Israel.	The Mormon Church uses Ez.44:4-9 to justify their discrimination of their own followers, along with people of other faiths, with regard to entry into the Mormon Temple and entry into the highest level of their Heavens (plural). There will be no children-of-a-lesser-god in Christianity. If the Mormon argument is that Ezekiel came after Isaiah, then my retort is: Jesus ratified Isaiah's scripture when he cleansed the temple in Mk.11:17 - "Then he taught them saying, "Is it not written: 'My house shall be called a house of prayer for all peoples'? But you have made it a den of thieves." The Book of Mormon contains 19 chapters of Isaiah in their entirety, along with parts of a few other chapters. Specifically, chapters 2-14, 48-51, 53, and 54 of Isaiah are contained in the Book of Mormon. (source Wikipedia) Coincidentally, Isaiah 24 and 56 are omitted. I have serious concerns that this policy of discrimination with "Temple Recommends" (perceived haves and have not's of faith) goes to the core of Mitt Romney's convictions and is now carrying over to U.S. social policies. We've already seen examples in Romney statements about the poor and the 47%

SCRIPTURE NUMBER	BEGIN DATE	DAYS (END - BEGIN DATES)	END DATE	SCRIPTURE	BIBLICAL NOTES	COMMENTARY	
Is.56:6-7						of the electorate who do not pay taxes. RELIGION SHOULD NEVER PROMOTE NOR ACCEPT THE SUBJECTIVE AND UNJUST SEGREGATION OF THE PERCEIVED "HAVES" AND "HAVE-NOTS", REGARDING ANYONE WHO SEEKS REPENTANCE, SALVATION AND THE ETERNAL LIFE IN THE ONE KINGDOM OF GOD.	
REV.22:1-5				1Then the angel showed me the river of life-giving water,* sparkling like crystal, flowing from the throne of God and of the Lamba 2down the middle of its street. On either side of the river grew the tree of life* that produces fruit twelve times a year, once each month; the leaves of the trees serve as medicine for the nations. 3Nothing accursed will be found there anymore. The throne of God and of the Lamb will be in it, and his servants will worship him. 5Night will be no more, nor will they need light from lamp or sun, for the Lord God shall give them light, and they shall reign forever and ever.b	* [22:1, 17] Life-giving water: see note on Rev 7:17. * [22:2] The tree of life: cf. Rev 22:14; see note on Rev 2:7. Fruit…medicine: cf. Ez 47:12. * [22:4] Look upon his face: cf. Mt 5:8; 1 Cor 13:12; 1 Jn 3:2.		

SCRIPTURE NUMBER	BEGIN DATE	DAYS (END - BEGIN DATES)	END DATE	SCRIPTURE	BIBLICAL NOTES	COMMENTARY
EZ.47:1-12				The Wonderful Stream.* 1Then he brought me back to the entrance of the temple, and there! I saw water flowing out from under the threshold of the temple toward the east, for the front of the temple faced east. The water flowed out toward the right side of the temple to the south of the altar.a 2He brought me by way of the north gate and around the outside to the outer gate facing east; there I saw water trickling from the southern side. 3When he continued eastward with a measuring cord in his hand, he measured off a thousand cubits and had me wade through the water; it was ankle-deep. 4He measured off another thousand cubits and once more had me wade through the water; it was up to the knees. He measured another thousand cubits and had me wade through the water; it was up to my waist. 5Once more he measured off a thousand cubits. Now it was a river I could not wade across. The water had risen so high, I would have to swim—a river that was impassable. 6Then he asked me, "Do you see this, son of man?" He brought me to the bank of the river and had me sit down. 7As I was returning, I saw along the bank of the river a great many trees on each side.b 8He said to me, "This water flows out into the eastern district, runs down into the Arabah and empties into the polluted waters of the sea* to freshen them.c 9Wherever it flows, the river teems with every kind of living creature; fish will abound. Where these waters flow they	* [47:1–12] The life and refreshment produced wherever the Temple stream flows evoke the order and abundance of paradise (cf. Gn 1:20–22; 2:10–14; Ps 46:5) and represent the coming transformation Ezekiel envisions for the exiles and their land. Water signifies great blessings and evidence of the Lord's presence (cf. Jl 2:14). * [47:8] The sea: the Dead Sea, in which nothing can live. This vision of the Temple stream which transforms places of death into places of life is similar in purpose to the oracle of dry bones in 37:1–14: it offers the exiles hope for the future. * [47:10] From En-gedi to En-eglaim: En-gedi is about halfway down the western shore of the Dead Sea; En-eglaim may have been at its northern end.	

SCRIPTURE NUMBER	BEGIN DATE	DAYS (END - BEGIN DATES)	END DATE	SCRIPTURE	BIBLICAL NOTES	COMMENTARY
EZ.47:1-12				refresh; everything lives where the river goes. 10Fishermen will stand along its shore from En-gedi to En-eglaim;* it will become a place for drying nets, and it will abound with as many kinds of fish as the Great Sea.d 11Its marshes and swamps shall not be made fresh, but will be left for salt. 12Along each bank of the river every kind of fruit tree will grow; their leaves will not wither, nor will their fruit fail. Every month they will bear fresh fruit because the waters of the river flow out from the sanctuary. Their fruit is used for food, and their leaves for healing."e The New Israel		
IS.60:20				20No longer will your sun set, or your moon wane; For the LORD will be your light forever, and the days of your grieving will be over.	* [60:19–20] The theme of light is taken up again, but in an apocalyptic vein: the Lord's radiant presence replaces physical light.	
REV.22:6-9				6And he said to me, "These words are trustworthy and true, and the Lord, the God of prophetic spirits, sent his angel to show his servants what must happen soon."c 7* "Behold, I am coming soon."* Blessed is the one who keeps the prophetic message of this book.d 8It is I, John, who heard and saw these things, and when I heard and saw them I fell down to worship at the feet of the angel who showed them to me. 9But he said to me, "Don't! I am a fellow servant of yours and of your brothers the prophets and of those who keep the message of this book. Worship God."e	* [22:6–21] The book ends with an epilogue consisting of a series of warnings and exhortations and forming an inclusion with the prologue by resuming its themes and expressions; see note on Rev 1:1–3. * [22:7, 12, 20] I am coming soon: Christ is the speaker; see note on Rev 1:3. * [22:7, 14] Blessed: see note on Rev 1:3.	

SCRIPTURE NUMBER	BEGIN DATE	DAYS (END - BEGIN DATES)	END DATE	SCRIPTURE	BIBLICAL NOTES	COMMENTARY
REV.22:10-14				10Then he said to me, "Do not seal up the prophetic words of this book, for the appointed time* is near. 11Let the wicked still act wickedly, and the filthy still be filthy. The righteous must still do right, and the holy still be holy." 12"Behold, I am coming soon. I bring with me the recompense I will give to each according to his deeds.f 13I am the Alpha and the Omega,g the first and the last, the beginning and the end."*14Blessed are they who wash their robes so as to have the right to the tree of life and enter the city* through its gates.h	* [22:10] The appointed time: see note on Rev 1:3. * [22:13] Christ applies to himself words used by God in Rev 1:8. * [22:14] The city: heavenly Jerusalem; see note on Rev 21:2.	
PS.62:12				12*One thing God has said; two things I have heard:f Strength belongs to God;	* [62:12] One thing...two things: parallelism of numbers for the sake of variation, a common device in Semitic poetry. One should not literally add up the numbers, cf. Am 1:3; Prv 6:16–19; 30:15, 18, 21.	
2TIM.4:14				14Alexander* the coppersmith did me a great deal of harm; the Lord will repay him according to his deeds.l	* [4:14–18] Alexander: an opponent of Paul's preaching (2 Tm 4:14–15), perhaps the one who is mentioned in 1 Tm 1:20. Despite Paul's abandonment by his friends in the province of Asia (cf. 2 Tm 1:15–16), the divine assistance brought this first trial to a successful issue, even to the point of making the gospel message known to those who participated in or witnessed the trial (2 Tm 4:16–17).	
IS.41:4				4Who has performed these deeds? Who has called forth the generations from the beginning?a I, the LORD, am the first, and at the last* I am he.	* [41:1–4] Earlier prophets had spoken of the Assyrians and Babylonians as the Lord's instruments for the punishment of Israel's sins; here the Lord is described as raising up and giving victory to a foreign ruler in order to deliver Israel from the Babylonian exile. The ruler is Cyrus (44:28; 45:1), king of Anshan in Persia, a vassal of the Babylonians. He rebelled against the Babylonian overlords in 556 B.C., and after a series of victories, entered Babylon as victor in 539; the following year he issued a decree which allowed the Jewish captives to return to their homeland (2 Chr 36:22–23;	

SCRIPTURE NUMBER	BEGIN DATE	DAYS (END - BEGIN DATES)	END DATE	SCRIPTURE	BIBLICAL NOTES	COMMENTARY
IS.41:4					Ezr 1:1–4). For Second Isaiah, the meteoric success of Cyrus was the work of the Lord to accomplish the deliverance promised by earlier prophets. * [41:4] The first...the last: God as the beginning and end encompasses all reality. The same designation is used in 44:6 and 48:12.	
IS.44:6				6* Thus says the LORD, Israel's king, its redeemer, the LORD of hosts: I am the first, I am the last; there is no God but me.* c	* [44:6–8] Prediction and fulfillment are here seen as the hallmarks of true divinity. See note on 43:9.	
REV.22:15-18				15Outside are the dogs, the sorcerers, the unchaste, the murderers, the idol-worshipers, and all who love and practice deceit.i 16"I, Jesus, sent my angel to give you this testimony for the churches. I am the root and offspring of David,* the bright morning star."j 17The Spirit and the bride* say, "Come." Let the hearer say, "Come." Let the one who thirsts come forward, and the one who wants it receive the gift of life-giving water.k 18I warn everyone who hears the prophetic words in this book: if anyone adds to them, God will add to him the plagues described in this book,	* [22:16] The root...of David: see note on Rev 5:5. Morning star: see note on Rev 2:26–28. * [22:17] Bride: the church; see note on Rev 21:2.	

SCRIPTURE NUMBER	BEGIN DATE	DAYS (END - BEGIN DATES)	END DATE	SCRIPTURE	BIBLICAL NOTES	COMMENTARY
ROM.1:29-32				29y They are filled with every form of wickedness, evil, greed, and malice; full of envy, murder, rivalry, treachery, and spite. They are gossips 30and scandalmongers and they hate God. They are insolent, haughty, boastful, ingenious in their wickedness, and rebellious toward their parents. 31They are senseless, faithless, heartless, ruthless. 32Although they know the just decree of God that all who practice such things deserve death, they not only do them but give approval to those who practice them.z		
IS.55:1				1All you who are thirsty,* come to the water! You who have no money, come, buy grain and eat; Come, buy grain without money, wine and milk without cost!a	* [55:1-3] The prophet invites all to return, under the figure of a banquet; cf. the covenant banquet in Ex 24:9-11 and wisdom's banquet in Prv 9:1-6. The Lord's covenant with David (2 Sm 7) is now to be extended beyond his dynasty.	
REV.22:19-21				19and if anyone takes away from the words in this prophetic book, God will take away his share in the tree of life and in the holy city described in this book.l 20* m The one who gives this testimony says, "Yes, I am coming soon." Amen! Come, Lord Jesus! 21The grace of the Lord Jesus be with all.	* [22:20] Come, Lord Jesus: a liturgical refrain, similar to the Aramaic expression Marana tha—"Our Lord, come!"—in 1 Cor 16:22; cf. note there. It was a prayer for the coming of Christ in glory at the parousia; see note on Rev 1:3.	
DT.4:2				2In your observance of the commandments of the LORD, your God,b which I am commanding you, you shall not add to what I command you nor subtract from it.		

SCRIPTURE NUMBER	BEGIN DATE	DAYS (END - BEGIN DATES)	END DATE	SCRIPTURE	BIBLICAL NOTES	COMMENTARY
ACTS3:20-21				20and that the Lord may grant you times of refreshment and send you the Messiah already appointed for you, Jesus,* 21whom heaven must receive until the times of universal restoration* of which God spoke through the mouth of his holy prophets from of old.	* [3:20] The Lord...and send you the Messiah already appointed for you, Jesus: an allusion to the parousia or second coming of Christ, judged to be imminent in the apostolic age. This reference to its nearness is the only explicit one in Acts. Some scholars believe that this verse preserves a very early christology, in which the title "Messiah" (Greek "Christ") is applied to him as of his parousia, his second coming (contrast Acts 2:36). This view of a future messiahship of Jesus is not found elsewhere in the New Testament. * [3:21] The times of universal restoration: like "the times of refreshment" (Acts 3:20), an apocalyptic designation of the messianic age, fitting in with the christology of Acts 3:20 that associates the messiahship of Jesus with his future coming.	
1COR16:21-24				21I, Paul, write you this greeting in my own hand.l 22If anyone does not love the Lord, let him be accursed.* Marana tha.m 23The grace of the Lord Jesus be with you.n 24My love to all of you in Christ Jesus.	The greetings of the Asian churches are probably to be read, along with the letter, in the liturgy at Corinth, and the union of the church is to be expressed by a holy kiss (1 Cor 16:19-20). Paul adds to this his own greeting (1 Cor 16:21) and blessings (1 Cor 16:23-24). * [16:22] Accursed: literally, "anathema." This expression (cf. 1 Cor 12:3) is a formula for exclusion from the community; it may imply here a call to self-examination before celebration of the Eucharist, in preparation for the Lord's coming and judgment (cf. 1 Cor 11:17-34). Marana tha: an Aramaic expression, probably used in the early Christian liturgy. As understood here ("O Lord, come!"), it is a prayer for the early return of Christ. If the Aramaic words are divided differently (Maran atha, "Our Lord has come"), it becomes a credal declaration. The former interpretation is supported by what appears to be a Greek equivalent of this acclamation in Rev 22:20 "Amen. Come, Lord Jesus!"	

SCRIPTURE NUMBER	BEGIN DATE	DAYS (END - BEGIN DATES)	END DATE	SCRIPTURE	BIBLICAL NOTES	COMMENTARY
1COR.15:23				23but each one in proper order: Christ the firstfruits; then, at his coming, those who belong to Christ;j .	* [15:30–34] A life of sacrifice, such as Paul describes in 1 Cor 4:9–13 and 2 Corinthians, would be pointless without the prospect of resurrection; a life of pleasure, such as that expressed in the Epicurean slogan of 1 Cor 15:32, would be far more consistent. I fought with beasts: since Paul does not elsewhere mention a combat with beasts at Ephesus, he may be speaking figuratively about struggles with adversaries.	
1COR.16:22				22If anyone does not love the Lord, let him be accursed.* Marana tha.m	* [16:22] Accursed: literally, "anathema." This expression (cf. 1 Cor 12:3) is a formula for exclusion from the community; it may imply here a call to self-examination before celebration of the Eucharist, in preparation for the Lord's coming and judgment (cf. 1 Cor 11:17–34). Marana tha: an Aramaic expression, probably used in the early Christian liturgy. As understood here ("O Lord, come!"), it is a prayer for the early return of Christ. If the Aramaic words are divided differently (Maran atha, "Our Lord has come"), it becomes a credal declaration. The former interpretation is supported by what appears to be a Greek equivalent of this acclamation in Rev 22:20 "Amen. Come, Lord Jesus!"	

SCRIPTURE NUMBER	BEGIN DATE	DAYS (END - BEGIN DATES)	END DATE	SCRIPTURE	BIBLICAL NOTES	COMMENTARY
2TIM.3:1-9				**The Dangers of the Last Days**.* 1But understand this: there will be terrifying times in the last days.a 2People will be self-centered and lovers of money, proud, haughty, abusive, disobedient to their parents, ungrateful, irreligious,b 3callous, implacable, slanderous, licentious, brutal, hating what is good, 4traitors, reckless, conceited, lovers of pleasure rather than lovers of God, 5as they make a pretense of religion but deny its power. Reject them.c 6For some of these slip into homes and make captives of women weighed down by sins, led by various desires,d 7always trying to learn but never able to reach a knowledge of the truth.e 8Just as Jannes and Jambres opposed Moses, so they also oppose the truth—people of depraved mind, unqualified in the faith.f 9But they will not make further progress, for their foolishness will be plain to all, as it was with those two.	* [3:1–9] The moral depravity and false teaching that will be rampant in the last days are already at work (2 Tm 3:1–5). The frivolous and superficial, too, devoid of the true spirit of religion, will be easy victims of those who pervert them by falsifying the truth (2 Tm 3:6–8), just as Jannes and Jambres, Pharaoh's magicians of Egypt (Ex 7:11–12, 22), discredited the truth in Moses' time. Exodus does not name the magicians, but the two names are widely found in much later Jewish, Christian, and even pagan writings. Their origins are legendary.	The biggest issues are greed, abortion, divorce and the promotion and acceptance (by individuals, governments, and some of the clergy) of same-sex marriage. Christ focused on helping the poor and the weak, not the rich. His underlying message was the repentance of sin and salvation (Mt.21:28-32 and Mt.9:12-13). But He did so with the expectation that the sinners would seek repentance (Jn.8:7-11, Mt.18:6-9, 2Pt.3:8-10). Christ defined marriage between a man and a woman (Mt.19:1-12).
LK.21:25	11-Mar-11	7	18-Mar-11	**The Coming of the Son of Man**. "There will be signs in the sun, the moon, and the stars, and on earth nations will be in dismay, perplexed by the roaring of the sea and the waves.t		The Fukushimi earthquake and tsunami occured on Mar. 11, 2011. Supermoon rises on Mar. 18, 2011: which was the biggest full moon in 18 Years. On Mar. 13, 2011, I depart for New York City. On Mar.19, 2011, I left New York City after signing an apartment lease and making a commitment to move here and finish writing this book..."my reward".

Epilogue

If a really good trial lawyer has ever deposed you, you know that they have the ability to herd cats, paint you in a corner, and build a jail around you with your own words. I don't intend to let skeptics do that to me with this book.

For the next several pages, I'll measure my words.

2 Timothy 3:16–17

16[208] All scripture[209] is inspired by God and is useful for teaching, for refutation, for correction, and for training in righteousness,[210] 17so that one who belongs to God may be competent, equipped for every good work.[211]

On Religion and Politics

When did the word "conservative" become synonymous with the word "religion," or synonymous with the actions of God-fearing or God-loving people? "Conservative" and its variants are found twice in the New American Bible.

Some may confuse the word "conservative" with the word "orthodox," which is defined as follows (courtesy of Dictionary.com):

---

[208] [3:16–17] Useful for teaching…every good work: because as God's word the scriptures share his divine authority. It is exercised through those who are ministers of the word.

[209] [3:16] Rom 15:4; 2 Pt 1:19–21.

[210] [3:16] All scripture is inspired by God: this could possibly also be translated, "All scripture inspired by God is useful for…." In this classic reference to inspiration, God is its principal author, with the writer as the human collaborator. Thus the scriptures are the word of God in human language. See also 2 Pt 1:20–21.

[211] [3:17] 2:21.

or·tho·dox

1. of, pertaining to, or conforming to the approved form of any doctrine, philosophy, ideology, etc.

2. of, pertaining to, or conforming to beliefs, attitudes, or modes of conduct that are generally approved.

3. customary or conventional, as a means or method; established.

4. sound or correct in opinion or doctrine, especially theological or religious doctrine.

5. conforming to the Christian faith as represented in the creeds of the early church.

I'm tired of seeing and hearing of people who want wave the supposed flag of conservatism (a Gadsden flag . . . with a snake on it?) and think that it somehow ties to goodness or godliness. It does not. This is the way of the Tea Party, which was recently evidenced by the rebuke received by Rep. Paul Ryan (R–WI) from the United States Conference of Catholic Bishops for his liberal use of the word "Catholicism" to support his budget.

If you want to continue to make "conservative" synonymous with the Republican Party, that's the business of politicians, but God never gave anyone the authority to the brand the word "conservative" to His love or

His holiness. However, using the word search in the Kindle New American Bible, I found the word "moderate", or a variant, seven times.

On the Tea Party and Mitt Romney

Be very cognizant of the following scripture and the fourth seal.

Revelation 6:7–8

7When he broke open the fourth seal, I heard the voice of the fourth living creature cry out, "Come forward." 8I looked, and there was a pale green[212] horse. Its rider was named Death, and Hades accompanied him. They were given authority over a quarter of the earth, to kill with sword, famine, and plague, and by means of the beasts of the earth.[213]

In May 2009, I predicted that Mitt Romney would be the next Republican presidential candidate. In December 2009, I predicted from Revelation 6:7–8 that the pale green horse would be the Tea Party. Make no mistake: Mormonism is not Christianity, and the Tea Party does not walk the path of Jesus Christ. Several Scripture passages support this view:

2 Corinthians 11:3–4

3But I am afraid that, as the serpent deceived Eve[214] by his cunning, your thoughts may be corrupted from a sincere [and pure] commitment to

---

[212] [6:8] Pale green: symbol of death and decay; cf. Ez 14:21.
[213] [6:8] Ez 14:21.
[214] [11:3] As the serpent deceived Eve: before Christ can return for the community Paul fears a repetition of the primal drama of seduction. Corruption of minds is satanic activity (see 2 Cor 2:11; 4:4). Satanic imagery recurs in 2 Cor 11:13–15, 20; 12:7b, 16–17; see notes on these passages.

Christor.[215] 4For if someone comes and preaches another Jesus[216] than the one we preached,[217] or if you receive a different spirit from the one you received or a different gospel from the one you accepted, you put up with it well enough.

1 Timothy 1:1–7

Greeting [218] 1Paul, an apostle of Christ Jesus by command of God our savior and of Christ Jesus our hope,[219] 2to Timothy, my true child in faith: grace, mercy, and peace from God the Father and Christ Jesus our Lord.[220]

II. SOUND TEACHING

Warning against False Doctrine. 3[221] I repeat the request I made of you when I was on my way to Macedonia,[222] that you stay in Ephesus to instruct certain people not to teach false doctrines 4[223] or to concern themselves with myths and endless genealogies, which promote speculations rather than the plan of God that is to be received by faith.[224]

---

215 [11:3] Gn 3:1–6.

216 [11:4] *Preaches another Jesus:* the danger is specified, and Paul's opponents are identified with the cunning serpent. The battle for minds has to do with the understanding of Jesus, the Spirit, the gospel; the Corinthians have flirted with another understanding than the one that Paul handed on to them as traditional and normative.

217 [11:4] Gal 1:6–9.

218 [1:1–2] For the Pauline use of the conventional epistolary form, see note on Rom 1:1–7.

219 [1:1] 2:3; Lk 1:47; Ti 1:3; 2:10 / Col 1:27.

220 [1:2] 2 Tm 1:2; Ti 1:4.

221 [1:3–7] Here Timothy's initial task in Ephesus (cf. Acts 20:17–35) is outlined: to suppress the idle religious speculations, probably about Old Testament figures (1 Tm 1:3–4, but see note on 1 Tm 6:20–21), which do not contribute to the development of love within the community (1 Tm 1:5) but rather encourage similar useless conjectures (1 Tm 1:6–7).

222 [1:3] Acts 20:1.

223 [1:4] *The plan of God that is to be received by faith:* the Greek may also possibly mean "God's trustworthy plan" or "the training in faith that God requires."

224 [1:4] 4:7; Ti 1:14; 3:9; 2 Pt 1:16.

5The aim of this instruction is love from a pure heart, a good conscience, and a sincere faith.[225] 6Some people have deviated from these and turned to meaningless talk,[226] 7wanting to be teachers of the law, but without understanding either what they are saying or what they assert with such assurance.

2 John 7–11

7[227] Many deceivers have gone out into the world, those who do not acknowledge Jesus Christ as coming in the flesh; such is the deceitful one and the antichrist.[228] 8Look to yourselves that you[229] do not lose what we worked for but may receive a full recompense. 9[230] Anyone who is so "progressive"[231] as not to remain in the teaching of the Christ does not have God; whoever remains in the teaching has the Father and the Son. 10[232] If anyone comes to you and does not bring this doctrine, do not receive him in your house or even greet him;[233] 11for whoever greets him shares in his evil works.

---

[225] [1:5] Rom 13:10.

[226] [1:6] 6:4, 20; Ti 1:10.

[227] [7] 1 Jn 2:22; 4:2.

[228] [7] The antichrist: see 1 Jn 2:18–19, 22; 4:3.

[229] [8] You (plural): it is not certain whether this means the Christians addressed or includes the Presbyter, since some of the ancient Greek manuscripts and Greek Fathers have "we."

[230] [9] Jn 8:31; 1 Jn 2:23; 4:15.

[231] [9] Anyone who is so "progressive": literally, "Anyone who goes ahead." Some gnostic groups held the doctrine of the Christ come in the flesh to be a first step in belief, which the more advanced and spiritual believer surpassed and abandoned in his knowledge of the spiritual Christ. The author affirms that fellowship with God may be gained only by holding to the complete doctrine of Jesus Christ (1 Jn 2:22–23; 4:2; 5:5–6).

[232] [10–11] At this time false teachers were considered so dangerous and divisive as to be shunned completely. From this description they seem to be wandering preachers. We see here a natural suspicion of early Christians concerning such itinerants and can envisage the problems faced by missionaries such as those mentioned in 3 Jn 10.

[233] [10] Rom 16:17; 2 Thes 3:6.

Them I will bring to my holy

    mountain

        and make them joyful in my house

    of prayer;

Their burnt offerings and their

    sacrifices

        will be acceptable on my altar,

For my house shall be called

    a house of prayer for all peoples.[234]

Some in the Mormon Church use Ezekiel 44:4–9 to justify their discrimination against their own followers, along with people of other faiths, with regard to entry into the Mormon temple and entry into the highest level of their heavens (plural). My statement is this: there will be no children of a lesser god in Christianity. If the Mormon argument is that Ezekiel came after Isaiah, then my retort is that Jesus ratified Isaiah's scripture when he cleansed the temple in Mark 11:17: "Then he taught them saying, 'Is it not written: "My house shall be called a house of prayer for all peoples"? But you have made it a den of thieves.'" The Book of Mormon contains nineteen chapters of Isaiah in their entirety, along with parts of a few other chapters. Specifically, chapters 2–14, 48–51, 53, and 54 of Isaiah are contained in the Book of Mormon. Coincidentally, Isaiah 24 and 56 are omitted.

---

[234] [56:7] This verse continues the theme of universalism found in Is 49:6. As Israel was to be "a light to the nations" so that God's "salvation may reach to the ends of the earth," so now does that come to pass as foreigners, faithful to the divine commands, are brought to the Temple by God and joined to the covenant community of Israel.

I have serious concerns that this policy of discrimination with "Temple Recommends" (perceived haves and have-nots of faith) goes to the core of Mitt Romney's convictions and would have carried over to U.S. social policies. We saw examples in Romney statements about not caring for the poor and not caring for the 47% of the U.S. population not paying federal income taxes.

I say that religion should never promote nor accept the subjective and unjust segregation of the perceived "haves" and "have-nots," regarding anyone who seeks repentance, salvation, and the eternal life in the one kingdom of God.

The more that I research the Mormon Faith, it appears that Joseph Smith cherry-picked the King James Version of the Holy Bible for his personal benefit in writing the Book of Mormon. Because he was obviously an isolationist, he chose to write the Book of Mormon and develop a faith that would ensure further covert isolation and satisfy some sort of vision of religious purity, to the point of segregating some within his own faith. His methods seem similar to those of Judge Roy Bean, as portrayed by Paul Newman, ripping a page out of his law book if he didn't like a specific law.

The Holy Bible and the Torah, through Abraham, Isaac, Jacob, Moses, the prophets, and Jesus Christ, are the Word of God and God's law. God plainly states in Revelation 22:18–19, "I warn everyone who hears the prophetic words in this book: if anyone adds to them, God will add to him the plagues described in this book, and if anyone takes away from the words in this prophetic book, God will take away his share in the tree of life and in the holy city described in this book."

I lived in Delta, Utah, from November 1985 to September 1986. Most of the people in the town were known as "Jack Mormons" and were very good people. "Jack Mormon" is the term used to refer to an individual deemed by adherents of the Church of Jesus Christ of Latter-day Saints (LDS Church) to be an inactive or lapsed member who, despite his personal religious viewpoint, maintains good relations with and positive feelings toward the LDS Church. (Source: http://en.wikipedia.org/wiki/Jack_Mormon). Despite their positive feelings, they are still unwelcome in the Mormon temple. As Christ said in Mt. 9:13; "I did not come to call the righteous but sinners." Later in life, I'm happy knowing I may have had a more positive affect on the lives of the "sinners" than the lives of the "saints".

Matthew 9:9–13

The Call of Matthew.[235] 9As Jesus passed on from there,[236] he saw a man named Matthew[237] sitting at the customs post. He said to him, "Follow me." And he got up and followed him. 10While he was at table in his house,[238] many tax collectors and sinners came and sat with Jesus and his disciples.[239] 11The Pharisees saw this and said to his disciples, "Why does your teacher[240] eat with tax collectors and sinners?" 12He heard this and

---

[235] [9:9–17] In this section the order is the same as that of Mk 2:13–22.

[236] [9:9–13] Mk 2:14–17; Lk 5:27–32.

[237] [9:9] A man named Matthew: Mark names this tax collector Levi (Mk 2:14). No such name appears in the four lists of the twelve who were the closest companions of Jesus (Mt 10:2–4; Mk 3:16–19; Lk 6:14–16; Acts 1:13 [eleven, because of the defection of Judas Iscariot]), whereas all four list a Matthew, designated in Mt 10:3 as "the tax collector." The evangelist may have changed the "Levi" of his source to Matthew so that this man, whose call is given special notice, like that of the first four disciples (Mt 4:18–22), might be included among the twelve. Another reason for the change may be that the disciple Matthew was the source of traditions peculiar to the church for which the evangelist was writing.

[238] [9:10] His house: it is not clear whether his refers to Jesus or Matthew. Tax collectors: see note on Mt 5:46. Table association with such persons would cause ritual impurity.

[239] [9:10] 11:19; Lk 15:1–2.

[240] [9:11] Teacher: see note on Mt 8:19.

said, "Those who are well do not need a physician, but the sick do.[241] 13Go and learn the meaning of the words,[242] 'I desire mercy, not sacrifice.'[243] I did not come to call the righteous but sinners."

On Same-Sex Unions

In 2 John 1:7–11, the term "progressive" can relate to any teaching which deviates from the teachings of Jesus Christ, including the liberalism and subsequent decline in some Protestant churches and their acceptance of same sex unions.

On July 16, 2012, Time.com published an article by Jon Meacham titled "God and Gays." I offered this on Facebook:

> *Jon is a great writer who I hope to meet one day. I disagree with Jon on acceptance of the increased liberalism of the Churches in granting same-sex unions. In The Revelation, the Church of Philadelphia is commended for keeping to God's Word, yet the Church of Ephesus is reprimanded for losing its love it had at first. Think about it: Ephesus started losing it's love in the 16th Century with the Protestant Reformation and has continued to lose its love with its increasing liberal beliefs concerning homosexuality and abortion. In the Gospels, the Love of Christ truly shines as The Light of the World. Jesus had no fear of challenging Mosaic*

---

[241] [9:12] See note on Mk 2:17.
[242] [9:13] 12:7; Hos 6:6.
[243] [9:13] Go and learn…not sacrifice: Matthew adds the prophetic statement of Hos 6:6 to the Marcan account (see also Mt 12:7). If mercy is superior to the temple sacrifices, how much more to the laws of ritual impurity.

Law for the benefit of Christianity. He had no hesitation of sharing time with prostitutes, tax collectors, and other sinners while granting His mercy and working for their repentance and salvation (Mt. 9:12–13 and Mt. 21:28–32). However, he preached the Temptation of Sin (Mt. 18:6–9), the Definition of Marriage (Mt. 19:1–12) and the Power of Saving a Sinner (Jn. 8:1-11). He did all of these things with the expectation that sinners would accept God's Love and Mercy and repent of their sins. God wants us all to be Holy, so as Christians, our job is "that all should come to repentance" (2Ptr. 3:8–10) and fill our lives with the Greatest Commandment (Mk. 12:28–34).

Colossians 3:5—10

Renunciation of Vice.[244] 5Put to death, then, the parts of you that are earthly:[245] immorality, impurity, passion, evil desire, and the greed that is idolatry.[246] 6Because of these the wrath of God[247] is coming [upon the disobedient].[248] 7By these you too once conducted yourselves, when you lived in that way. 8But now you must put them all away:[249] anger, fury, malice, slander, and obscene language out of your mouths.[250] 9Stop lying to one another, since you have taken off the old self with its practices

---

[244] [3:5–17] In lieu of false asceticism and superstitious festivals, the apostle reminds the Colossians of the moral life that is to characterize their response to God through Christ. He urges their participation in the liturgical hymns and prayers that center upon God's plan of salvation in Christ (Col 3:16).

[245] [3:5] Mt 15:19; Rom 1:29–30; Gal 5:19–21; Eph 5:3, 5.

[246] [3:5, 8] The two lists of five vices each are similar to enumerations at Rom 1:29–31 and Gal 5:19–21.

[247] [3:6] The wrath of God: see note on Rom 1:18. Many manuscripts add, as at Eph 5:6, "upon the disobedient."

[248] [3:6] Rom 1:18.

[249] [3:8–10] Put...away; have taken off; have put on: the terms may reflect baptismal practice, taking off garments and putting on new ones after being united with Christ, here translated into ethical terms.

[250] [3:8] Eph 4:22, 25, 31.

[251] 10[252]and have put on the new self, which is being renewed, for knowledge, in the image of its creator.[253]

Hebrews 13:8

Jesus Christ is the same yesterday, today, and forever.

Luke 21:33

Heaven and earth will pass away, but my words will not pass away.[254]

On Abortion

Exodus 20:13. You shall not kill.[255] [256] *Life begins at conception. I ask for divine guidance on the following: asking a woman to carry a child which is a product of rape or incest is akin to condemnation of that woman. Neither should a woman be required to carry a child when her (the mother) life is in jeopardy.*

On the Role of Women in the World

The day of the requirement of women to be submissive is over and should have officially ended with suffrage, yet the issue of inequality still exists. The resolution to inequality is one of admiration and mutual respect. If women

---

[251] [3:9] Rom 6:4, 6; Eph 4:22–25; Heb 12:1; 1 Pt 2:1; 4:2.
[252] [3:10] Image: see note on Col 1:15.
[253] [3:10] Gn 1:26–27.
[254] [21:33] 16:17.
[255] [20:13] Kill: as frequent instances of killing in the context of war or certain crimes (see vv. 12–18) demonstrate in the Old Testament, not all killing comes within the scope of the commandment. For this reason, the Hebrew verb translated here as "kill" is often understood as "murder," although it is in fact used in the Old Testament at times for unintentional acts of killing (e.g., Dt 4:41; Jos 20:3) and for legally sanctioned killing (Nm 35:30). The term may originally have designated any killing of another Israelite, including acts of manslaughter, for which the victim's kin could exact vengeance. In the present context, it denotes the killing of one Israelite by another, motivated by hatred or the like (Nm 35:20; cf. Hos 6:9).
[256] [20:13] Mt 5:21.

can raise our kids and have a career (two jobs at the same time), serve in the armed forces and vote, to me, that's a minimum for complete equality with men, and women should be treated and compensated as such. Angela Merkel was recently anointed as the most powerful woman in the world, and if it were not for her and her prudent governance as Germany's chancellor, the prosperity of Europe would probably have been significantly diminished.

Jesus never demanded submissiveness of a woman, as was demanded in the Old Testament and by St. Paul, in the Epistles. Mary of Magdala is an example of one of the most important disciples discussed in the Gospels. She was at the base of the cross when Jesus died, along with Mary, the mother of Jesus, Mary of Clopas, and St. John, the beloved apostle: one man and three women.

John 19:25–27

25[257] [258] Standing by the cross of Jesus were his mother and his mother's sister, Mary the wife of Clopas, and Mary of Magdala. 26When Jesus saw his mother[259] and the disciple there whom he loved, he said to his mother, "Woman, behold, your son."[260] 27Then he said to the disciple, "Behold, your mother." And from that hour the disciple took her into his home.

---

[257] [19:25] It is not clear whether four women are meant, or three (i.e., Mary the wife of Cl[e]opas [cf. Lk 24:18] is in apposition with his mother's sister) or two (his mother and his mother's sister, i.e., Mary of Cl[e]opas and Mary of Magdala). Only John mentions the mother of Jesus here. The synoptics have a group of women looking on from a distance at the cross (Mk 15:40).

[258] [19:25] Mt 27:55; Mk 15:40–41; Lk 8:2; 23:49.

[259] [19:26–27] This scene has been interpreted literally, of Jesus' concern for his mother; and symbolically, e.g., in the light of the Cana story in Jn 2 (the presence of the mother of Jesus, the address woman, and the mention of the hour) and of the upper room in Jn 13 (the presence of the beloved disciple; the hour). Now that the hour has come (Jn 19:28), Mary (a symbol of the church?) is given a role as the mother of Christians (personified by the beloved disciple); or, as a representative of those seeking salvation, she is supported by the disciple who interprets Jesus' revelation; or Jewish and Gentile Christianity (or Israel and the Christian community) are reconciled.

[260] [19:26] 13:23.

To me, this is one of the most beautiful passages in Scripture. It shows the mutually reverent love that should be between a mother and her son.

Luke 8:1–3

Galilean Women Follow Jesus.[261] 1Afterward he journeyed from one town and village to another, preaching and proclaiming the good news of the kingdom of God.[262] Accompanying him were the Twelve[263] and some women who had been cured of evil spirits and infirmities, Mary, called Magdalene, from whom seven demons had gone out, 3Joanna, the wife of Herod's steward Chuza, Susanna, and many others who provided for them out of their resources.

Mary of Magdala was the first to enter the tomb after Jesus had been resurrected, the first person that Jesus approached after his resurrection, and the person He sent to the apostles to tell them, "I am going to my Father and your Father, to my God and your God." (Jn. 20-17). Contrary what a few think, Mary of Magdala was not an adulteress; rather, she was a woman who had been possessed by seven demons, which were exorcised from her by Jesus.

Looking at the shining examples of the current German chancellor, Angela Merkel, the former British Prime Minister Margaret Thatcher, and the current

---

[261] [8:1–3] Luke presents Jesus as an itinerant preacher traveling in the company of the Twelve and of the Galilean women who are sustaining them out of their means. These Galilean women will later accompany Jesus on his journey to Jerusalem and become witnesses to his death (Lk 23:49) and resurrection (Lk 24:9–11, where Mary Magdalene and Joanna are specifically mentioned; cf. also Acts 1:14). The association of women with the ministry of Jesus is most unusual in the light of the attitude of first-century Palestinian Judaism toward women. The more common attitude is expressed in Jn 4:27, and early rabbinic documents caution against speaking with women in public.
[262] [8:1] 4:43.
[263] [8:2–3] 23:49; 24:10; Mt 27:55–56; Mk 15:40–41; Jn 19:5.

US secretary of state Hillary Rodham Clinton, there will never be a reason that a woman can't govern as well as a man. Further, I think it's a tragedy that the Republicans will not afford women the opportunity to represent their party as president of the United States.

On the Environment

Isaiah 24:5–6

5The earth is polluted because of its

    inhabitants,

        for they have transgressed laws,

    violated statutes,

        broken the ancient covenant.[264] [265]

6Therefore a curse devours the earth,

        and its inhabitants pay for their

    guilt;

Therefore they who dwell on earth have

    dwindled,

        and only a few are left.[266]

"Stay-in-business" projects extend the useful lives of existing production assets. This includes replacement of vehicles, plant, and machinery, and capital expenditures related to safety, health, and the environment (migrating primary energy sources to natural gas and the phase-out of oil and coal as the primary sources).

---

[264] [24:5] Ancient covenant: God's commandments to all humankind (cf. Gn 9:4–6).

[265] [24:5] Nm 35:33; Hos 4:2–3.

[266] [24:6] Lv 26:15–16.

If oil and coal companies won't do something to start reducing climate change, because their management and shareholders can't get a return on investment, God will do it for them (see the chapter –"The Scroll"). On energy, the GOP: 1) wants to increase coal production; 2) wants to cut federal permitting hurdles for oil and gas development; 3) wants to give states major authority over energy development; 4) thinks federal hydraulic fracturing regulations are onerous; 5) would not extend the production tax credit and investment tax credit for wind energy.

Mitt Romney said, "You can't drive a car with a windmill on it." (Source: http:// www.forbes.com/fdc/welcome_mjx.shtml) Well, you can drive a Chevy Volt, with a substantially diminished carbon footprint.

The GOP also 6) will roll back tax credits for the solar and wind industries, but will not seek to cut tax breaks for oil companies, which are estimated at $40 billion over ten years; and 7) has an energy plan that does not mention energy conservation or efficiency, nor climate change or global warming. (Source: Items 1-7: Christian Science Monitor http://www.csmonitor.com/USA/ DC-Decoder/2012/0831/Obama-vs.-Romney-101-7-ways-they-differ-on-energy-issues/Coal-power)

On All of The Above

The Supreme Court is made up of six men and three women, including six Catholics and three Jews. Of those, four men are considered to be conservative, and one man and three women (sound familiar?) are considered to be liberal.

As we recently experienced with the Affordable Care Act decision, the chief justice was fair and impartial, as he should be.

So how does one arrive at the conclusion that being a certain sex, a certain religion, or aligned with a certain political philosophy are in any way related? Leave religion and politics separate; however, each should respect the rights of the other, with the impetus being a respect for religious liberty.

The fact that there are only three women on the court means that, biologically, it only takes three women to do the same number of jobs as six men, even with all that testosterone.

With this country being torn apart at the seams on environmental issues, the court needs to get ready to start deciding environmental lawsuits, state by state.

Finally, as I said earlier in the book, I am a messenger. I've given you a lot of Scripture, intertwined with life's events, good and bad. As the words go in the song "Amazing Grace":

> *Amazing Grace, how sweet the sound,*
> *That saved a wretch like me.*
> *I once was lost but now am found,*
> *Was blind, but now, I see.*

I was truly a wretch. I went through all kinds of hell, I literally laughed at the Devil, and I received the grace of God. I hope my story has inspired you to get through tough times, when they arise. Regardless of the mistakes you make, regardless of how bad things may seem, the Almighty God will always be there for your repentance and salvation with His ever-present Love.

May The Almighty God Bless You All!

Matthew 4:19

He said to them, "Come after me, and I will make you fishers of men."

About the Author

Gary Miller started working in the energy sector (oil, gas, coal, and petrochemicals) at age seventeen. After college, he started his professional career in 1984 and was laid off for the last time in 2009. In December 2009, God, giving him more clarity about His Word, dramatically changed his life. After living for fifty years in the greater Houston Texas area, he now lives in New Canaan, Connecticut with his son John, but calls New York City, home.

About the Book

This book covers my life through the aftermath of a failed suicide attempt, through two tribulations from February 2003 to March 2011 and the period after that, through present day. The book's purpose is to convey divine messages to everyone.

CPSIA information can be obtained
at www.ICGtesting.com
Printed in the USA
LVIC06n0800221113
362324LV00003B/3